"I FELT REAL FEAR FOR THE FIRST TIME IN MY LIFE!"

Jeffrey Dahmer had seemed like a nice guy, a guy who appeared easy to talk to about anything. When Tracy Edwards, thirty-two, met him on July 22, 1991 in Milwaukee's Grand Avenue Mall, the tall, blond, handsome man had been so genuine and friendly that Edwards agreed to follow him back to his apartment for a few drinks.

But once there, Dahmer changed. His facial structure and body posture became tense, aggressive; his muscles tight, his expression almost possessed. He turned on Edwards, handcuffing his wrist and pushing a long knife sharply against his ribs.

The nightmare went on for four hours.

At one terrifying stage, Dahmer forced Edwards down on the floor, then lay on top of him, sliding the knife slowly down to the frightened young man's groin area. Resting his head firmly on Edwards's chest, the deranged man listened intently to his heart beat for a few moments.

Then, pressing the knife harder against his genitals, Dahmer whispered, "I'm going to eat your heart out of your chest."

JEFFREY DAHMER

DR. JOEL NORRIS

PINNACLE BOOKS
WINDSOR PUBLISHING CORP.

*To the memory of the victims of
Jeffrey Dahmer and their survivors.
To Marguerite Jones McKinney and
the memory of Melvin David Maurer
for their loving support of my work.
This book is written in the hope that
we learn from this tragedy.*

PINNACLE BOOKS

are published by

Windsor Publishing Corp.
475 Park Avenue South
New York, NY 10016

First printing: July, 1992

Printed in the United States of America

ACKNOWLEDGMENTS

Doris Tate, Ron and Scott Snyder; Dr. Bill Walsh; Rosealyce Thayer; Carolyn and Theresa Smith; Greg Burndrige; Brother John Paul Ranieri; E.O.C; Civia Tamarkin; Bob Springer; Goldie Adams; Robert Walstrom; the staff at the Knickerbocker-on-the-Lake Hotel; Paul Dinas, senior editor; Ron Geiman; Terry Belcher; Steve Daniels; Mike Newton and all the people that spent endless hours talking to try to reach some conclusions about the case of Jeffrey Dahmer; and Glenda Cleveland, one of the heroes of this book.

Faye Snyder, Director of Center for Professional Parenting, Sherman Oaks, California, for her expertise in early childhood and parenting.

Special recognition to master photojournalist Cheryl L. Franklin of Soujourner Illustration of Milwaukee, for most of the photographs in the book and for her keen insight into the racial, homophobic and moral issues surrounding the Dahmer case and its aftermath in Milwaukee.

Prologue

Judge Laurence C. Gram, Jr., turned to face the jury. He'd already read their verdicts to himself on the fifteen pages in front of him, and now it was time to announce the decisions to the court and the television cameras. The Jeffrey Dahmer trial had ended. It had been an historic event, the first major serial killer trial carried live on television. Now an entire nation was waiting to hear the verdicts that only the jury and the judge had seen. The pages in the judge's hand were the results of jury deliberations that followed weeks of complicated and conflicting testimony about homicide, violent aberrant sex, torture, and necrophilia. In the end, only one question would hang over the court as the judge turned to the jury: Had they found Jeffrey Dahmer sane?

The stories about the stone-faced defendant Jeffrey L. Dahmer had gripped the nation's imagination since the summer night he was arrested in his Milwaukee apartment and subsequently confessed to seventeen homicides, mutilations, cannibalism, and necrophilia.

Now he sat there before the judge and the families of the victims he'd killed and dismembered. He seemed without emotion; almost as if the sobbing and bellowing, the wolflike howling, the almost demonic screams he emitted during his arrest while being pinned facedown by the police on the floor of his apartment in the early hours of July 23, 1991, were the last bits of his life leaving his body. Now it looked as if he was only a brain-dead shell of flesh being piloted through the motions of this trial.

To the public and the victims' families, all that was left of the killer was the impassive figure who was shuffled in and out of the court. Perhaps behind the expressionless eyes there was a hint of the cruelty that drove him to seek out, murder, and then devour parts of his victims' bodies. Maybe the lack of emotion and his unresponsiveness was just a thin veneer over the primal hate that had been so active during his seventeen-year killing spree which had the notorious distinction of being one of the longest in history. That was what the hearing was supposed to determine: Was this defendant sane? Judge Gram faced the jury and asked the questions required by law.

"Did Jeffrey Dahmer suffer from mental illness? And if he did, did he have the capacity to appreciate the 'wrongfulness' of his conduct or the 'ability to conform to the law'?"

The requisite ten of the twelve jurors responded that he did not suffer from a mental illness. They disregarded all expert testimony they had heard from both defense and prosecution experts over the previous three weeks. He was legally sane and he would have to go to jail. Still nobody knew why he did what he did. The mystery that Jeffrey Dahmer embodied when he was arrested the previous year would still remain a mystery as Dahmer was escorted out of the courtroom by the officers. Nobody really asked why a serial killer like him kills, how he gets created, what propels him from crime to crime, and what long-term denial shields his soft psyche from the repeated trauma of the violence he is perpetrating. No one asked because these weren't the question before the court. Nor did anyone ask the most telling questions of all: Was Jeffrey Dahmer spiritually still alive or had he died somewhere deep in his soul a long, long time ago? And if he were a walking dead man, the mystery remained: What killed Jeffrey Dahmer?

Both the defense and the prosecution agreed that Dahmer exhibited abnormal behavior. The question they debated was whether that behavior was abnormal enough to be considered the result of a mental disease; one which diminished Dahmer's capacity to form judgments so that he was unable to conform his actions to the law. Prosecutor Michael McCann marched his experts to the stand to testify that even though Dahmer might have had a mental disease, the disease had not incapacitated him. McCann seemed to have conceded the issue of mental illness and focused his case on Dahmer's capacity to mediate his behavior. He tried to prove that the decisions Dahmer made about hiding his crimes, cruising for victims, selecting his victims, duping them into going back to his apartment, and springing the trap meant that he knew exactly what he was doing. He was sane, albeit disturbed. One of his star prosecution witnesses was California psychiatrist and FBI consultant Park Dietz, who summed it up most clearly when he pointed to Dahmer's capacity to exert control as an indicator of his sanity and premeditation.

Look at how he covered up the evidence of his crimes, McCann's experts argued. They pointed to Dahmer's deliberateness and intensity in filleting the flesh from the bones of his victims once they were dead. They pointed to the efficiency of the acid bath that Dahmer used to render or melt down the flesh, the bone locker in his apartment where he stored the remains, and the extra freezer he brought in to preserve the dismembered corpses until he could dispose of them. The prosecution experts argued that all of this pointed to premeditation, and premeditation was an indicator of Dahmer's fear of discovery. They reasoned, not only did he know right from wrong, but was taking pains to conceal the wrongness of his actions from the authorities so that he would not be punished. All of this argued strongly for sanity under the second definition posed by the court: Was the severity of Dahmer's mental illness sufficient to prevent him from controlling his actions so that he would not commit a crime?

Defense counsel Gerald Boyle's platoon of experts argued that the symptoms that Dahmer exhibited were so bizarre, so out of the range of normal behavior, that they indicated a mental condition that prevented Dahmer's ability to form correct judgments. Boyle's experts focused on Dahmer's paraphilia, a dysfunctional sexual aberration based upon forbidden or taboo stimuli as an example of a debilitating mental illness. Dahmer, they said, had to drug and bind his victims in order to have sex with them. Sex for Dahmer was premised on his establishing rigid territoriality, obtaining and exercising physical control of his partner, and was consummated by his inflicting pain and ultimately death. The experts also pointed to Dahmer's necrophilia, his need to have sex repeatedly with the corpses of his victims. Defense experts said that he kept the victims as trophiss, for the purposes of sexual gratification and proof that he still wielded control over their bodies. These conditions were examples of a severe and crippling mental illness which rendered him incapable of conforming to the law.

It was straightforward logic, the defense's expert witnesses testified. If Dahmer were addicted to a sexual condition that required his performing illegal acts to satisfy his addiction, then his mental illness rendered him unable to conform to the law even though he might have been aware that what he was doing was illegal. That's why he went to such lengths to camouflage his behavior. He knew it was illegal, but he simply couldn't control his actions. He was therefore insane under the definition of insanity posed by the second question.

The news media was fascinated by Dahmer's appearances in court. Even stranger to commentators than the defendant was his plea of guilty to the charges. He'd already confessed to the murders and the attendant violence. What else was he trying to prove? Gerald Boyle said that he was pleading his client as insane because he believed him to be insane. He wanted his client sentenced to a mental health facility where his condition could be studied and documented. Legal commentators saw a simple defense strategy at work. If he were found guilty and sentenced, he would likely never be set free again. If he were found insane and sentenced to a mental institution, he would have been able to petition the court for his release when hie doctors judged him recovered from his mental illness. It was one way, for Dahmer to avoid serving time in prison for the rest of his life.

The jury seemed to have rejected the testimony of the experts when they ruled that Dahmer did not have a mental illness. The jury found that whatever governed Dahmer's behavior sprang from criminal intent and not from a psychological or medical condition. They were not prepared to write his actions off to a mental illness and then rule on the degree to which that mental illness affected his judgment. In the minds of millions of people who had been following this case from the morning of July 23, 1991, when it first broke on the national news, a central question still remained unanswered. If Dahmer's behavior wasn't the result of insanity, just what was it?

Chapter One

The Verdict

The Jeffrey Dahmer story crashed into public awareness during the final hours of July 22, 1991, when the Squad 31 police officers Robert Rauth and Rolf Mueller spotted Tracy Edwards through the windshield of their patrol car running toward them down North Twenty-fifth Street as if he were in terror. It was almost 11:30 P.M. The officers noticed that the young black man had a pair of handcuffs hanging from his left wrist. When he saw the police, he began waving frantically for their attention. He was panicked; he had been running and was breathing hard. When they rolled the driver's side window down to listen to the man's story, they heard him ask if they could take the handcuffs off his wrist. How did the handcuffs get on there in the first place? they asked the young man. He told them about a blond, good-looking young man who had just put him through a four-hour ordeal of terror. The man had invited Edwards to his apartment for a few drinks, when he suddenly turned crazy, pulled out a pair of handcuffs, and snapped them on Edwards's wrist. He held him prisoner at knife point and threatened to eat his heart out while they watched *Exorcist III*. Edwards seized an opportunity to escape and managed to run out the door into the street where he saw the patrol car.

The following day, the story of Jeffrey Dahmer began to unfold in the press. However, the real story of Jeffrey Dahmer, a story so dark and tragic that it would threaten to tear apart the social fabric of Milwaukee, lay beyond the comprehension of most people who tried to figure it out. Maybe Tracy Edwards, Dahmer's last victim and one of the precious few individuals to leave that apartment alive, would figure it out in time. But in the final moments of July 22, as he flagged down the patrol car, Edwards was simply thankful to be alive, thankful that he had the brains and determination to stay until he saw his chance to escape.

When Tracy Edwards first met Jeffrey Dahmer earlier that evening, he had no idea that the tall, blond man was the person responsible for the disappearances of young men in Milwaukee's gay community. Edwards was not gay, nor did he frequent the gay bars in downtown Milwaukee, but he remembered seeing Dahmer once or twice in the neighborhood.

The afternoon of Monday, July 22, Tracy Edwards and his friends, one white and one black, were hanging out at the Grand Avenue Mall, having a few beers, and watching people come and go. One of the people they watched approaching them through the crowd was Jeffrey Dahmer, who struck up a conversation when he saw them.

Dahmer told Edwards and his friends that he was from Chicago and had relocated to Milwaukee to take care of a sick grandmother over in the West Allis section of town. He claimed to be a photographer, always scouting for good-looking models whom he paid for their services. Suddenly, he asked if any of them wanted to pose for pictures. These would be nude pictures, but he would pay them to pose. Was anybody interested?

Tracy Edwards and his friends talked about the offer. In Edwards's words, "We wanted to see what was going on." What did this guy really want, and did any of the men want to pose nude for this stranger? Dahmer kept the conversation going at the mall. He told the group that he wanted to buy them all drinks and maybe they could have a party up at his place and talk over his proposal some more. He had an apartment over on North Twenty-fifth, but first took the group over to a liquor store on Wisconsin and Seventh where he bought some rum and some cigarettes.

Tracy Edwards waited outside the store with his two companions. The three of them talked about Dahmer's offer and decided that two of them would go home, change clothing, and meet up with Tracy at Dahmer's place later for drinks. By then, Tracy would have "checked out" Dahmer's story and decided what he was going to do about the photographs and the one hundred dollars Dahmer was offering.

Nobody suspected anything dangerous about Dahmer. He seemed like an outgoing, interesting, friendly guy who was looking for some other people to join him in some drinks. In hindsight, Dahmer didn't come onto them and act as if he were gay. Tracy wasn't even put off by the fact that Dahmer was a white guy striking up a conversation with black strangers because Tracy's best friend was white. It was a just a pleasant summer evening in Milwaukee, and Tracy had decided to go along with the flow of the evening.

The four men walked over to the bus depot on Wisconsin Avenue where Dahmer ordered a cab to take Tracy and him back to his apartment. He turned to Edwards's companions, gave them an address, and told them to meet him at the apartment later. What Tracy Edwards didn't know until later, and what his friends wouldn't find out until they tried to get to the apartment, was that Dahmer had deliberately given them the wrong address. He wanted Tracy Edwards all to himself. Like any practiced serial killer who had rehearsed his method of winning his victim's confidence, cutting him out of a crowd, isolating him, and then springing the trap, Dahmer knew exactly what he was doing. He had used the photography ruse on at least ten other young men and was confident that he would have Tracy Edwards completely in his power.

Dahmer figured that by the time Edwards's two friends managed to locate him again, he would say that Tracy got drunk, left the apartment to look for them, and he never saw him again. That, too, had worked very successfully before. Edwards would simply be another young man who had been seen in Dahmer's presence shortly before he disappeared. Sure, there were rumors brewing about Dahmer and the disappearing young men. Of course, people had seen Dahmer try to drug a victim in one of the bathhouses he frequented. And there was even a local minister in downtown Milwaukee warning gay men to stay away from Jeffrey Dahmer because he was dangerous. But no one was actively pursuing Dahmer, least of all the police whom he'd already tricked once, and he felt he could continue picking up victims at will.

As Dahmer and Tracy Edwards rode to his apartment in the back of the cab, they engaged in small talk. Dahmer seemed interested in whatever Edwards had to say, especially his memories of growing up on Air Force bases with his family. Dahmer told Tracy Edwards these were memories he could share, because he, too, had been in the military and had been stationed at different bases far from home. Tracy felt so comfortable that he didn't even become concerned when the cab stopped about a block away from where Dahmer said his apartment was and the two men had to walk the final block through some back alleys.

"It's safer this way," Jeffrey told him as they wandered around the backs of buildings on their way to the apartment.

Tracy didn't get concerned when they stood before Dahmer's apartment door and he watched the stranger fiddle with at least five police locks and a burglar alarm system. This was a rough area, Dahmer told him as he unlocked the deadbolts. He had been robbed in the building at least once and just wanted to be safe inside his apartment. Once they got inside, though, Tracy Edwards was almost overwhelmed by a foul odor that seemed to seep right out of the walls. But the apartment itself seemed normal, "decent," Edwards would tell police, and Dahmer seemed to have answers to all of Edwards's questions. He asked him about the burglar alarms and Dahmer told him to look around at the TV, VCR, cameras, and a bunch of other expensive items.

"This is a bad neighborhood," Dahmer said. He said he needed the burglar alarms to protect his stuff.

And the foul odor? Edwards asked.

"Sewer pipes," Dahmer said. He told Edwards that some of the sewer pipes had burst behind the wall and under the floor and the odor was wafting out of them. This was something else that Tracy Edwards said he "accepted" because he used to work in a construction company and had been around ruptured sewer pipes. He knew that they emitted a foul odor of rotting organic matter that would hang heavy in the air until the pipes were repaired or capped and the interior spaces vented.

Tracy Edwards also asked Dahmer about the boxes sitting in his living room, and Dahmer explained that was acid. He used to acid to clean bricks, but because the apartment was really quite small, he didn't have any other place to store it except in front. Edwards looked around, and judged the place to be normal. He surveyed the blacklight lamp in one corner, the fish tank in the other corner, and noted the refrigerator through the living room door. Edwards told himself that he didn't have any misgivings about Dahmer's apartment at all. If he had any questions, Jeffrey seemed to be able to answer them without any hesitation.

They sat on the couch and Dahmer mixed up a pair of rum and cokes with glasses of beer on the side as chasers. Dahmer's plan was to ply Edwards with a concoction of liquor laced with drugs until Edwards became too weak to defend himself or, better still, passed out. This, too, was part of Dahmer's script which he had reenacted over and over again with other men he'd picked up downtown.

Once Dahmer's victims were asleep or unconscious, he would handcuff them, undress them, and have sex with them. Next he would murder, mutilate, dismember, and cannibalize them while he snapped Polaroids of every stage. The Polaroids of his previous victims were only a few feet away from where Tracy Edwards was sitting, and Edwards didn't have a clue about what was in store for him.

Dahmer turned their conversation toward photography as he waited for the drugs in Tracy Edwards's drink to kick in. Edwards was still hesitant about posing. He needed the money, he would tell police later, but taking off his clothes was too much for him. He was anxious for his friends to get there so they could continue their evening after they'd said goodbye to Dahmer for the night. It was only seven o'clock, and the guys had more of an evening planned. Meanwhile Dahmer was getting edgy; his sedative wasn't working because Tracy Edwards wasn't drinking it. Jeffrey kept on sipping at his beer, but Edwards wouldn't do anything more than taste the rum and coke in his hand.

Dahmer hadn't realized that Edwards wasn't a drinker. He hadn't picked him up at a bar or a bathhouse, where he could evaluate his drinking habits. Edwards had no intention of finishing his drink because he didn't especially like the taste of alcohol. At this point, Edwards started to get nervous. The odor was getting to him, he said. And where were his friends anyway? They should have arrived. Also, how could Dahmer live with this odor? Didn't it get to him the way it was getting to Edwards?

Dahmer began talking about his fish tank. He told Edwards that he really ought to check it out because he owned some interesting fish. Edwards said that he still didn't feel any threats coming from Dahmer, but when he turned to look at the fish tank that Jeffrey was bragging about, Dahmer whipped out a set of handcuffs and a long military knife. Edwards saw the handcuffs, but before he could react, Dahmer had snapped them on his left wrist and shoved the knife point up under his rib cage. Dahmer was holding the other half of the handcuffs as he pushed the knife point deeper into Edwards's chest.

Tracy Edwards said that he felt real fear for the first time that night, but he was also confused. This was a nice guy at first, he had told himself, a guy who seemed easy to talk to about anything. The guy came on so genuinely friendly, Edwards wasn't even worried about the solicitation to pose for photos. But this was Dahmer's script, which he had been generally rehearsing since he was a teenager in Ohio and had killed his first victim, hitchhiker Steven Hicks.

"What's going on?" the terrified Tracy Edwards asked Dahmer. "It's not necessary to pull a knife on me." He could feel the knife point pressing between his ribs. It was sharp and painful and Tracy Edwards was becoming more afraid with every passing moment. "Just what is the problem?" Edwards asked him again.

"You just do exactly as I tell you," Dahmer said, emphasizing what he was saying with the knife point, "or I'll kill you."

Edwards now realized for the first time that Dahmer's demeanor had completely changed. He hadn't noticed that before. Jeffrey was no longer the same guy who had approached him with casual conversation at the mall. His facial structure and body posture were all different, and it was as if he'd gone through an actual physical transformation. Dahmer was aggressive and tense, his muscles were tight, and the lines in his face were strained. He was looking at

Edwards very intently as if he were completely fixated on him. Then, just as suddenly, he seemed to calm down and resume his more relaxed posture.

"I have the key to the cuff in the bedroom," Dahmer said. "You're going to have to go in there with me." And he led him by the other handcuff through the living room door and into the bedroom, constantly pressing the knife in between Edwards's ribs and forcing forward with the pressure and pain.

Edwards looked around the bedroom quickly, measuring distances and trying to get an angle on how he could escape. He noticed a big dark stain on the unmade bed, but couldn't figure out what it was. He also noticed a big fifty-seven-gallon drum in the bedroom. It was conspicuous, totally out of place, and very ominous. However, Edwards decided he was better off not asking any questions about the oil drum because there was a knife in his ribs. Edwards tried to maintain the semblance of conversation. He kept trying to reassure Dahmer that he didn't have to push the knife into him anymore. He said that the handcuffs weren't necessary either.

Dahmer motioned for Edwards to sit down on the bed near the stain while he clicked on his television and VCR. Tracy Edwards could see that he had already cued up an *Exorcist III* tape and began watching it intently. Edwards became very analytical. He later testified in court that his first thoughts, as he watched Dahmer focus on the television and hold the other handcuff tight in his hand, were about finding a way he could escape. He didn't realize that Dahmer had expected the drugs to kick in and make him weak and defenseless. Instead, Dahmer was faced with a live, very aware victim whom he had to control. Edwards looked for the path of least resistance at first. He decided that the more he could convince Dahmer that he was really a friend who wouldn't threaten him, the better his chances were of staying alive.

"I was cool," Edwards told the authorities. "I'm contemplating how to get away. I want to let him know that I'm his friend."

Edwards watched while Dahmer seemed to go through a variety of physical transformations. "One minute he's nice and he's saying how he doesn't want people to leave him or abandon him. Other times, it was like he wasn't the same person. It would come and go," Edwards said. He was particularly aware of Dahmer's reactions to the motion picture. He noticed that Dahmer would become very quiet during certain parts of the movie. Then Dahmer would say that he wanted Edwards to watch the movie very carefully. Then it was as if Dahmer would go into a kind of trance.

"He would start rocking back and forth at certain parts of the movie and start chanting," Tracy Edwards said, describing the experience. "It was like a slow 'mmm.' It kept going off and on throughout the ordeal. He would rock back and forth and chant during the movie from time to time. He seemed most interested in the part of the movie about the preacher that got possessed. That got his attention more than anything. It was like he wanted to mimic that part of the movie: the demon parts."

It was during the demonic sections of the movie that Dahmer became the most aggressive. Every time the demon appeared, Dahmer appeared to become possessed by something himself. He turned on Edwards and demanded that he lie facedown on the floor and handcuff his other wrist. Edwards believed that Dahmer was trying to feel more dominant. Dahmer even told him that it would make him feel better if Edwards would slap the cuffs on his right wrist, but Edwards kept resisting. He knew from observing Dahmer that if he just waited, the urge would pass and Dahmer would become almost passive again and engrossed in the movie.

Dahmer's moods shifted every twenty minutes or so, Edwards realized. He had begun counting the intervals. It was about 7:00 P.M. when Dahmer first put the cuffs on him. Then it was about 7:15 P.M. or so when they went into the bedroom. Now it was much later and Dahmer had been in and out of his aggressive moods a few times. Dahmer came at him again, this time pushing the knife into him a bit harder, and demanded that he lie down on his stomach. Edwards knew that if he complied, if he allowed Dahmer to get the cuffs on both wrists, he was a goner. So he shifted to his side and kind of leaned against his free hand. Edwards was pushing Dahmer to the limit as he bore down on him with the knife.

In a terrifying moment, Dahmer climbed on top of Edwards and held the knife straight at him. Then he slid it down to his genitals. "He laid across me," Edwards remembered, "and put his head across my chest. It was like he was listening to my heart beat because at that point he told me that he was going to eat my heart. He still had the knife pointed at me, but now it was at my groin area."

Edwards felt the pressure of the knife point and the pressure of Dahmer's head on his chest. He knew something was about to happen if he did nothing so he suddenly said, "I have to go to the bathroom." And

Dahmer jumped up and off his chest. He pulled Edwards to his feet by the handcuff. Then he guided him to the bathroom by his shoulders and held him over the toilet while Tracy Edwards urinated. Then, Dahmer led him back to the bedroom where he sat down on the bed again.

The break in the movie seemed to dampen his intensity a bit and Dahmer began talking about the misery he was feeling about losing his job at the chocolate factory. Dahmer complained to Tracy Edwards that he was alone and miserable, that he had no one in the world. Then, just as suddenly as he had transformed the first time, Dahmer transformed again and became intense. It was as if something he thought about had triggered a change in his personality. But Tracy Edwards didn't let it frighten him this time. He kept telling Dahmer that there was no reason to be afraid and that he was no threat. Then, Dahmer changed back and began complaining again that he had no one he could turn to.

"You know, no one cares for me," Dahmer said to Edwards.

"I'm your friend," Edwards said. "I'm not going to run away from you. I'm not going to try anything."

This seemed to calm Jeffrey Dahmer down, and he remained silent while they watched the movie for another ten or fifteen minutes. Then, when a possession scene played out, Dahmer became agitated again. And again Edwards tried to calm him down, reassuring him that he wasn't alone and that Edwards was really his friend. That quieted Jeffrey Dahmer down, and his mood shifted back to the sullen individual who said he was trying to keep some companionship going on a lonely evening. The event was settling into a terrifying pattern.

"Every fifteen or twenty minutes," Edwards recalled, "he'd become fixated on the TV screen and then he would turn to me and ask me to put both my hands behind my back. But I would talk him out of it. I would tell him, 'You could trust me. You don't have to handle me like that.' I would try to calm him down a little bit. I would be quiet, and then he would watch the movie and start conversation with me. He would say I'd have to do this and that. Then at one point he said either I would have to kill him or he would have to kill me."

Dahmer seemed like a completely bizarre individual to Edwards; yet Dahmer also seemed very confused as he shifted back and forth between his moods, now threatening Edwards with the knife, now complaining that he was alone and friendless. Edwards discovered that just by talking Dahmer down, he could mediate his moods and navigate him from one personality state to the next. Edwards somehow realized intuitively that his own intervention in Dahmer's mood swings was saving his life; it was keeping Dahmer under a measure of control.

Edwards had discovered that one way certain serial killers can be controlled and defused is to allow them to talk about how they feel and express their fantasies of misery and rage. Because most serial killers are isolated psychologically, any attempt by an outsider to open a channel into the pain of that isolation is likely to be successful. In Tracy Edwards's case, his intelligence and courage in opening that psychological channel might well have saved his life.

When Dahmer started to get aggressive again and

turned on him with the knife, Edwards said he had to go to the bathroom again. This time, he suggested to Dahmer, rather than walking him into the bathroom and holding him in front of the toilet, Dahmer let him go by himself and stay in there by himself for as long as he had to. Surprisingly, Dahmer agreed. For the first time since he got into the cab with Dahmer from the liquor store on Wisconsin Avenue, Tracy Edwards was alone and had a chance to think.

In the confines of the small bathroom, Edwards contemplated how he would make his move. Would he look for the opportunity to jump right out the window as soon as he had the chance, or would he try another tactic? No, he decided, he would try to work himself back into the living room and make his move for the window at the first chance he got. The trick was to keep Dahmer occupied, keep him off balance, keep him from sitting down in front of the *Exorcist III* movie and working himself into another aggressive mood. Psychologically, Tracy Edwards was again doing exactly the right thing by plotting to move his alternately manic and depressed aggressor around the apartment so he wouldn't focus on killing him.

When Edwards left the bathroom, he put his plan right to work. He asked him for another beer straight off to keep him from going into the bedroom right away. As Dahmer guided him over to the kitchen where he reached over to get a beer, Edwards again made a demand.

"I want to sit up here in front because of the air conditioning," he said. "I'm too hot." That way, Edwards decided, he could either jump out the window or go for the door.

Dahmer took him back over to the couch where

26

Edwards tried again to calm him down. Then Edwards noticed that Dahmer had begun withdrawing into himself again. In Tracy's words, "He started going out of himself again. He was like paying me no attention, like he wasn't there." Jeffrey Dahmer started chanting again, humming a mantra-like sound that seemed to help him drift off. He seemed to become unaware of his surroundings. Tracy Edwards thought the time was right.

"I need to go to the bathroom again," Edwards said.

But this time, Dahmer just followed him to the door. He didn't even have the other half of the cuff in his hand. Edwards explained, "It was like he wasn't even there at that point."

As a hyperalert Tracy Edwards and an almost catatonic Jeffrey Dahmer stood up to walk toward the bathroom, Edwards saw his chance. He reached up and around and hit Dahmer as hard as he could, throwing the man off balance. Then he made a leap for the door and ran away as fast as he could. Dahmer recovered quickly and tried to grab Edwards back in the apartment as they reached the door. But Edwards didn't stop and didn't look back. He kept running down the hall and out the door until he was outside. Then he ran down North Twenty-fifth Street until he saw the Milwaukee police car cruising slowly near the corner and began waving frantically to flag them down.

Chapter Two

The Arrest

Officers Robert Rauth and Rolf Mueller, who had been cruising along Kilbourn, listened to Tracy Edwards talk about a tall blond guy he met downtown who had threatened him with a knife and said he wanted to eat his heart after he had put the cuffs on him. When the guy wasn't looking, Edwards said he jumped up, hit him, and ran out of the apartment. It sounded like an assault, and Rauth and Mueller radioed to their District 3 dispatcher that they were investigating a report of a possible assault on North Twenty-fifth Street between State and Kilbourn. The officers let Edwards climb into the car and drove him back to the middle of North Twenty-fifth, where they stopped in front of 924. Then they went to apartment 213 and knocked on the door.

The peephole opened and Dahmer looked at the two officers and Tracy Edwards. He had been expecting this. It had happened a few months earlier when police had picked up a frightened, tearful, and bleeding Konerak Sinthasomphone who had fled Dahmer's apartment to the safety of neighbors in the street. Dahmer had run after him. The police returned the Laotian youngster to apartment 213 where Dahmer cooly managed to convince them Sinthasomphone was his gay lover who was drunk and disoriented. The police believed him, partly because Sinthasomphone was almost incoherent in English after having been drugged, and they left him in the apartment. Sinthasomphone was dead by the next morning. Now, Dahmer probably thought, he would have to do it again.

While standing outside the apartment door, Rauth and Mueller were very aware of the locks and the electronic gadgetry. They announced themselves to the person who answered the door as the police, and the apartment door was quietly opened from the inside. The tall, sullen, disheveled young man who answered the door ushered them through the doorway. Dahmer was tall enough to put the two officers on a heightened sense of alert. The policemen stood just inside the door after they entered and immediately smelled the foul odor that had first bothered Tracy Edwards hours earlier. Rauth and Mueller were alarmed by the odor because it was so out of the ordinary. Along with Tracy Edwards, they stepped into the living room and looked around the apartment. They could see the bedroom door and could look over to the kitchen where terribly dirty, greasy pots and pans were on the stove. They could see that there were dirty dishes in the sink.

Routinely, the officers began by asking Dahmer what his name was and what was going on. "We were just drinking some beer," Dahmer reportedly told the cops. "I lost my job."

He was trying to act as cool as he could. Maybe the cops would go away as they had a few months ago. But this time it was different. The cops had his name and now they were calling it in. They would run a "priors and warrants" check on this guy, standard procedure in most places for anyone being questioned by police about a possible violation of the law. The answer came back: This man Dahmer had a prior felony conviction for sexual assault on a minor and was currently on probation. If Dahmer were playing around with handcuffing someone and that victim had reported to the police that Dahmer had threatened to kill him, the police had probable cause for an arrest. The police were no longer just following up on the wild story of some guy running through the streets with a handcuff on, they had a possible parole violator and a possible sexual assault and attempted homicide. Whatever Jeffrey Dahmer had been doing up to now, it was over and he was caught in the wheels of the process.

It was time to arrest Jeffrey Dahmer. Officers Rauth and Mueller told him to place his hands behind his back so that they could handcuff him, and that was the first time he resisted them. As the two officers put their hands on his arms, Dahmer stiffened and forced his arms forward. Suddenly the three of them began spinning and tumbling into the living room, crashing across the floor, and yelling as they fought for control. The whole building seemed to shake, some of the residents remembered, and there were terrible screams from inside the apartment. One person told the press that he heard someone yell out "Faggot!" The sound echoed through the building halls. Then they heard Dahmer's voice bellowing and a different voice, maybe one of the cops, yelled that he'd been scratched. There were more violent crashes and shaking as Dahmer tried to force himself up against the combined weight of the two detectives.

Then there was a sudden, long, earsplitting scream that seemed to penetrate through the walls and out into the street. It was a scream so profound in its misery that the people who heard it were frightened and saddened at the very same time. This was Dahmer's scream of acquiescence, a primal scream, a death scream. It would not be the last, however. There were more demons inside of him that would soon fly out. For the time being, however, something inside of him seemed to have died as he surrendered himself to his inevitable fate. And then for the moment there was quiet. Dahmer was in custody, heaving, hands cuffed behind his back, lying facedown on the floor, and no longer resisting. Now the two cops were free to investigate the source of that terrible odor and the nature of the apartment they had found themselves in and to interrogate Dahmer.

They began by asking what had been going on there. Edwards began his story. He told the police that he had met Dahmer at the Grand Avenue Mall and Dahmer had invited him back for a beer. The next thing he knew, Dahmer had slapped a pair of cuffs on his wrist and was leaning over him with a knife. Meanwhile, one of the officers had been looking around the apartment, glancing over the mess in the kitchen, and trying to figure out where this smell was coming from. What the hell had rotted in there?

The cops noticed the power tools spread around the couch in the living room. And in the bedroom, where Tracy Edwards told them Dahmer had dragged him, there appeared to be dark bloodstains on the unmade bed. There was a terrible sensation of imminent horror, then they found the Polaroids. The photos were scattered about innocently enough as if they were photos from a casual office party or a summer vacation at the lakefront. But when you looked at them, you were struck immediately by the horror of what they captured. It was as if you were looking into the heart of darkness.

These weren't just ordinary photographs; they were gory, bloody pictures of what looked like the living dead: upright corpses in various stages of surgical dissection. Some of the men in the photos were in shackles, possibly still alive or even freshly killed, but not yet dismembered. Then, to their ultimate shock, the police officers found what people would later refer to as trophy portraits and severed human remains in various states of preservation. These were the human totems, the most prized possessions of a serial killer's war chest, the individual items that proved just how much control he exercised over his victims. To take a photograph of a dead or unconscious victim over whom the killer wields complete control is a sexual stimulation for the control-type killer that Dahmer was. To store a victim's body part, either to cannibalize or to wear as an article of clothing, is another way of preserving the moment of ultimate control. Jeffrey Dahmer was heavily immersed in this control fantasy, but all the police could react to was the horror that must have taken place in that apartment.

In one especially grisly photograph, police noticed that a head had been severed from a body, painted gold, and set atop the victim's two hands, cupped with the palms up. It was as if what was living had become a statue in perpetual submission for Jeffrey Dahmer, reducing what was once a vital living person to a piece of sculpture. It was truly horrific. In other photographs, police viewed the process of mutilation, various stages of bloody dismemberment scattered around like so many postcards. How long had this been taking place? And where were the bodies?

"There's a head in here," a voice rang out from behind the door of apartment 213. "This guy's sick."

One of the police officers, tracking the source of the foul, rotting odor, and maybe hoping to himself that it wasn't what he thought it might be, had opened the refrigerator and saw the not yet preserved skull of Oliver Lacy sitting in a box on the bottom shelf. Next to the head, in an all but futile attempt to absorb the odor of rotting flesh, Jeffrey Dahmer had set an open container of Arm & Hammer baking soda. Baking soda is widely advertised to be a powerful absorbant of odors. The box of baking soda attracted particular attention because its presence might mean that Dahmer was aware of the stench of rotting flesh, possibly aware that it was a giveaway to something being wrong in the apartment, and sought to control the odor.

Officers Rauth and Mueller called in a report to the District 3 station and began the booking process of their suspect. They also sealed off the apartment in expectation of the crime lab personnel that would soon descend upon them, and put the shackles on Dahmer who would soon be led away by the detectives. Around that time, shortly before midnight, residents of the apartment building reported to the press hearing the sound of a penetrating wail from the apartment. People assumed it was Dahmer himself, screeching and bellowing into the air for the final time before platoons of uniformed officers, lab technicians, and detectives swarmed over the now-sealed apartment. Perhaps the last of whatever psychological demons were haunting Jeffrey Dahmer were now venting themselves and leaving him the mostly empty shell most people saw on television during the trial.

Within the next fifteen minutes, as the police sealed off the alley behind the apartments and backed in crime lab vehicles, the whole record book on serial murders was being rewritten. As the shining light bars threw their patterns across the building's facade, residents called newspapers and television stations. Something big was happening on North Twenty-fifth Street, they said, better get your camera crews down here. Soon the mobile units arrived with their satellite dishes, videocams, and production crews. Shortly after midnight, the news that a major serial killer case had broken in Milwaukee was being flashed to the wire services and to newspapers in major cities.

From midnight and into the early morning hours of Tuesday, July 23, the police crime scene crews continued searching for and logging physical evidence and human remains that would later be evaluated by Milwaukee County medical examiner Jeffrey Jentzen. From the one skull that Rauth and Mueller discovered in the refrigerator, the body count began to rise precipitously. Soon there would be more bits and pieces, human puzzles that forensic specialists would, quite literally, have to rearrange into a composite picture of victims and their respective fates.

In the freezer compartment of the same refrigerator, officers found a human heart wrapped up in a package with flesh of unidentified origin. In a nearby floor freezer chest, they found three additional heads. Those heads, too, had been wrapped up for storage and sealed inside plastic bags. But the horror was continuing. From the kitchen, they went to Dahmer's small bedroom where the bloodstains on the bed had been noted by Rauth and Mueller. There, police found Dahmer's computer box that had been packed with two additional skulls and a photo album containing more pictures of Dahmer's depredations on the bodies of his victims. There were photos of victims in all stages of mutilation, logged with an almost diabolical precision. They were looking at the photo album of a man who didn't just kill, but seemed to relish the act of dissecting his victims and preserving their parts. For some reason, and they couldn't even begin to fathom why, Dahmer seemed almost obsessive about capturing the stages of mutilation that he was inflicting on these victims. What was he looking for? What were these photos supposed to represent? Why would he keep such a precise record of some of the most heinous crimes anybody had ever seen? Most of the crime scene investigators had never seen anything like this firsthand. It was a terrifying experience.

What the investigators had yet to find out was that Dahmer wasn't just a violent murderer. He'd gone way beyond the act of homicide. Dahmer had so much hatred for human life itself that he was taking a particular pleasure in commemorating his acts of deconstructing his human victims. In part, Dahmer was taking posed pictures of the bodies to recapture the sexual thrill associated with control over his victims. But Dahmer was also deriving satisfaction from the act of making his victims look less and less human. When they were just skulls, hands, or parts of muscle he would wear them as articles of clothing, or reassemble them into statue-like creations and then photograph them. By reassembling them, he could exercise control by recreating them in the image he chose. He was like a collector adding more and more human specimens to his anatomy kit.

The search of the apartment continued. Beside the bed, police found a two-drawer storage or filing cabinet, the kind found in most home offices. In the top, investigators discovered that Dahmer had stuffed in three separate skulls. In the bottom, they found a collection of human bones. Then they looked inside Dahmer's bedroom closet where they found two kettles. There was clothing and other personal belongings in there as well, but it was the kettles that they pulled out for a closer examination. Sure enough, inside the kettle from the top shelf of the closet, crime scene investigators found two skulls. Inside the kettle on the bottom of the closet, police recoiled when they saw male genitals and various chopped off hands. If this had been a movie, it might have had more reality than the fact that it was an actual crime scene. Also, had it not been for the portable breathing apparatus that the investigators were wearing, the search itself would have been impossible. How could Dahmer have lived in this place without becoming asphyxiated himself?

This was another important medical clue to the mystery of Jeffrey Dahmer that most investigators did not immediately realize and may still not understand. The vast majority of serial killers have sensory impairments that usually affect their sense of smell. Most serial killers seem impervious to foul odors because either their olfactory nerves are damaged or their neurological systems have been damaged by toxic poisoning such as lead. The infamous Texas serial killer Henry Lee Lucas had a sense of smell so badly impaired that he drove around the western part of the United States with a severed head in the back of his car and the windows rolled up. When he stopped at a toll booth in New Mexico, the toll clerk was so overwhelmed by the smell that he had to stick his head inside the car to make sure everything was all right. Lucas laughed about that incident years later and said that the clerk told him "I can't figure how you can stand that smell." Lucas said he told the clerk, "It's just some garbage I got in the back of the car."

In another case, similar to Dahmer's, residents of an inner-city Philadelphia neighborhood had complained to police for months about the smell of rotting flesh coming from Gary Heidnik's apartment. Heidnik told his neighbors that his freezer had broken after he had invested in a large purchase of meat. Now it was all rotting. But in reality, the smell of rot came from decomposing bodies that Heidnik had stored in a pit in his basement. His ability to live in an atmosphere fouled by that stench was similar to the condition of Texas killer Henry Lee Lucas, who confessed to riding around in his car with a decomposed body for days on end.

Dahmer's resistance to foul odors was prototypical of serial killers. His experience working at the Ambrosia chocolate factory amidst whatever cooking fumes there were might have desensitized him and his repeated abuse of alcohol would also have depressed his neurological system.

Members of the crime scene crew were further repelled by what Dahmer had done to some of the skulls they uncovered. It was bad enough that the guy had decapitated his victims and cut off their arms and hands, but it looked as if he was playing some kind of bizarre game with the body parts. The skulls seemed to have been painted as if they were pieces of greenware. Some of the skulls from the closet had a greyish, blueish tint as if Dahmer had been experimenting with tones and hues. These were the kind of plaster-looking skulls that you might buy at a magic shop or a curio shop. These were the kinds of art pieces heavy metal fans might have on their desks or in their bookshelves. Maybe high school students who wanted to look weird would have these sculptures. These weren't supposed to be real. Yet Dahmer had real skulls that he had severed from his victims' bodies and had burned or pulled off the flesh and painted them. He was preserving them. He had photographed them and turned them into sculpture. What was the significance?

If Dahmer were behaving like a prototypical serial killer—and this wouldn't be debated until his trial—he would naturally be preserving personal possessions or body parts of his victims as artifacts or totems. These articles would not only remind the killer of the specific victim, they would help him reexperience the sexual thrill of performing the crime. Long-term serial killers like Jeffrey Dahmer can motivate themselves from murder to murder by collecting and reorganizing what they've taken from their victims' bodies. In a process not unlike the telling of worry beads, serial killers handle the skulls of their victims, exchange skulls with different bodies, pose the arms and legs of their victims, have

38

masturbatory or coital sex with vital organs or genitalia, and dress the victims' decomposing bodies up in different clothing. Some serial killers visit the burial grounds where they dump the corpses while others simply collect the personal belongings. These totems allow them to feel they are still exercising control and reliving the crimes. The collections of artifacts become the most important items in the serial killer's inventory, and he becomes obsessive about storing and preserving them. This accurately describes what Dahmer was doing. Not only was he obsessive about taking photographs of every stage of the murder and mutilation, he owned his victims' lives by preserving their skulls and other vital remains. He had eaten the vital organs of his victims to refortify himself with iron and vitamins that had been depleted through his alcohol. He had retreated to the feral savage state of a serial killer who was living by consuming victims. He was spiritually dead, but had become a vampire, a kind of walking dead who existed only to prey on his next victim. He was the closest thing to a *nosferatu*.

The search through the living room, kitchen, and adjoining bedroom continued. On the stove, they found evidence that Dahmer had been boiling off the flesh of his victims in the pots and pans he had left there. They could see a kind of organic goo that had spilled out over the surface of the boiling water as if it were soup scum left to bubble over. They could see where Dahmer had left bones still uncatalogued or put away, and all around there was evidence of a light but sticky film of blood. The whole place smelled rank, even through the chemical decontamination suits the crime scene processors were forced to wear. For the police, it was like foraging for artifacts through a museum of horrors. How could Dahmer have lived in this environment? No one knew. Still the real horror of what Jeffrey Dahmer was and what he had done to the community was months away.

Above Dahmer's bedroom wall, police noted the posted-up photos of victims he'd killed. More of the same kind of photos Rauth and Mueller had first discovered scattered around the couch in the living room. These were akin to pin-ups of death and mutilation that the forensic report would refer to as nothing short of a slaughter. One of the photos was later identified as fourteen-year-old Konerak Sinthasomphone, an earlier victim. Now he was a trophy just like the rest of them.

The police finally came to the large blue-black fifty-seven-gallon chemical drum that was sitting like an obelisk in the bedroom. Hours earlier, Tracy Edwards had noticed the drum, but it had looked so ominous and obvious even he was afraid to ask about it. It was as if everyone, including Tracy Edwards, knew what was inside though they denied it to themselves. Someone would have to look inside and take the inventory.

It was up to the crime scene processors to break open the top. The smell emanating from that drum was overpowering. It either contained skulls or all sorts of bones. When police broke off the top, even they were shocked at what they found. Crammed inside the vat as if they were still alive and hiding from the world were the headless torsos of three of Dahmer's victims, slowly decomposing in acid into a raw flesh soup. It was a hideous sight, and the smell of rot was so devastating that the police decided to put the top back on the can and transport it to the medical examiner. The county coroner's assistants sealed the drum up tight and strapped it to a dolly which they wheeled out to the waiting van.

Cameras waiting outside the apartment building caught the sight of police officers wheeling out the oil drum and the chest freezer. They captured photographs of the decontamination suited police officers wearing gas masks and oxygen equipment moving back and forth from the apartment with evidence bags. They could hear snippets of conversation about heads, torsos, arms, and acid baths. Soon there would be an official statement, but already the neighbors were telling lurid tales of unearthly smells and screams that emanated from apartment 213. They talked about the stream of young men who would enter the apartment with the tall, blond, good-looking occupant but would never be seen again. Where did they go? What had happened to them? Were the evidence bags, the large drum, and the freezer all that was left of these young men?

The stories told that night also fed the growing media frenzy in the alley and on North Twenty-fifth Street. Who was the person they were all talking about? Then, a sullen, disheveled Jeffrey Dahmer was led out of the building in shackles and leg irons. He looked so emotionless, so harmless, as if he were a robot being led away. Who was this man and was he responsible for all this activity? They said his name was Jeffrey Dahmer. But who was Jeffrey Dahmer and how could he explain all this?

Chapter Three

Who Was Jeffrey Dahmer?

"You think you've seen it all out here, then something like this happens," Officer Mueller said after he made the discovery of the bodies and the Polaroid photos of victims at Dahmer's apartment. His shock at what was going on inside the apartment was echoed by the shock of other police officers and the community at large. Even Dahmer's neighbors, used to the sound of sporadic gunfire in the streets at night and the violence of street crime, were in a collective state of shock. They had smelled the foul odors creeping out of apartment 213 and wafting over the whole street and had heard the strange hacking noises throughout the time Dahmer was a tenant in the Oxford Apartments, but this was something beyond even their worst fears.

As the police hazardous waste removal teams wearing yellow rubber protective suits, head gear, and breathing apparatus pulled the containers of body parts out of the apartment, neighbors commented that they believed strange goings-on were taking place in the apartment but didn't know what. Larry Marion, the building manager, said that residents of the building had complained of the stench, especially just a few months earlier in the spring. "Had we been veterans," Marion was quoted in the newspapers, "we would have known the stench of death." He said that he had told one of the other residents just the day before that if the stench hadn't stopped, he was going to report it to the police to investigate. He said that when the smell was particularly strong the summer before, he went to Dahmer's apartment to inquire about it.

Dahmer told the building manager that he couldn't smell anything. "To be honest," Marion remembered, "when he said he couldn't smell anything, I thought his sense gland was malfunctioning. But other than that, nothing unusual." The building manager said that the smell was so bad, however, that the woman who lived on the floor above Dahmer became ill and had to be moved to a different apartment in the building to get away from the stench.

Gene Mitchell, the building manager for the apartments next door, agreed with Marion. He said that the smell from the Oxford Apartments permeated the air over the neighborhood on hot windless days as if it were a plague. "I thought it was sewage. You'd just open the door and you'd smell it," he said.

Vernell Bass, who lives on Dahmer's floor in the building, told the newspapers that he had even visited the apartment and noticed the awful stench. "I saw the big barrel in his apartment and I asked him how he carried it in on the bus, because he didn't drive. He evaded the question, but you just never think anything like this." He told the newspapers that the Dahmer tragedy was the last straw and that he was moving out of the neighborhood. Other neighbors recounted they sometimes heard the sound of sawing coming from the apartment during all hours of the day and night. Bass said that the sounds were so loud that he had wondered aloud to his wife Pamela about what Dahmer could have been constructing in that apartment. Pamela said she had once knocked on Dahmer's door herself to complain, but he never answered it. Then, she said, she slipped a note under his door complaining about the foul smell. But nothing ever happened. Despite the smells and the noises, Bass never believed anything in that apartment could be as bad as what the police were saying they had found.

Yrana Thomas, who lived on the floor above Dahmer, said that he always seemed to have an excuse, no matter what the manager said to him about the odor. She said that the smells kept on reminding her of Ed Gein, the serial killer who skinned his victims and later became the model for Norman Bates in *Psycho*. Whenever it got hot, the smell became intolerable, but Dahmer always had an excuse for it. "Whenever the manager got on him, the smell would die down. I asked the manager a year ago, 'Do you have another Ed Gein here?' This happened last summer when it got hot. Everybody was cleaning and searching to see where it was coming from," Thomas recalled.

Jeffrey Dahmer was also a loner, a stranger who minded his own business but always remained on the outside. "He just kind of kept to himself," a neighbor observed. Still another neighbor in the Oxford Apartments told the press that Dahmer was quiet, didn't talk much to anybody, but was also dirty and a little strange. "I'd see him walking through the alley at all times," the neighbor said. "I thought that went beyond strange."

Other people saw Dahmer sitting in front of the building with men, some of whom may have wound up becoming his victims. One person said she saw him every afternoon whenever she left for work. Yet Jeffrey's grandmother, Catherine Dahmer, who lived in West Allis, told the press that her grandson was always "a loner," and "very quiet." "He's not well," she said about the man who had killed a number of victims in the basement of her house before getting his own place in the city. "He's very thin and looks sick."

Experts in Milwaukee were quick to categorize Dahmer's crimes as soon as the press reported them. He was characterized as a murderer practicing "homosexual overkill" on his victims by using more force than was necessary to murder them. Medical Examiner Jeffrey Jentzen was quoted as saying that Dahmer reacted out of the fury of repressed homosexual desires because he had deeply repressed homosexual feelings. Another expert from a local university commented that cases of "homosexual overkill" usually involved torture or mutilations of the sexual organs. He pointed to the ritualism aspects of the crimes and drew comparisons between Dahmer's crimes and the fictional crimes of Hannibal Lecter. A second expert, however, said that Dahmer's crimes were less sexual and more hate or rage driven. Rather than a result of repressed sexual feelings, Professor Anthony Fazio proposed that Dahmer's crimes might be the result of hidden anger. He suggested that the acting out of this anger and a display of dominance were the critical factors as opposed to sex.

The gay community in the Milwaukee area reacted quickly to the stories about "homosexual overkill" that appeared in the local papers. Spokesmen argued that Dahmer's crimes weren't any more indicative of the gay community than Ted Bundy's crimes were indicative of the straight community. Terry Boughner, editor of the *Wisconsin Light,* went on the record saying that the term "homosexual overkill" was another term for gay bashing. "Using homosexual as an adjective to describe a hideous act is no more accurate than saying Bundy's was a case of heterosexual overkill," he said. "Simply put, mass murderers are a sick people in a class by themselves."

What was particularly ominous in those first few hours was that the bodies that had been discovered might somehow be linked to the growing numbers of gay men that had disappeared over the previous two years. Families had been searching, reports had been filed with the police, but there had been no trace of at least eleven young men from the area. Many of them had socialized with one another at local clubs and bathhouses and had been a part of the community. Thus, the continuing disappearances, seemingly into thin air, had sent a chill throughout the gay community. Now body parts had been discovered at the apartment of someone who had frequented some of the same clubs and bars where the disappearances had taken place. Was there a connection? It was Tuesday, July 23, just hours after the body parts had been removed from Jeffrey Dahmer's apartment, and already the public and private speculation was under way about the nature of the Jeffrey Dahmer murders.

Within a day of his arrest, the newspapers had identified Dahmer as a defendant in a prior sexual assault offense who had been convicted and sentenced to probation. Chillingly ironic, the papers reported, Dahmer had been arrested in September, 1988, after he had picked up Sounthome Sinthasomphone, a thirteen-year-old child. He had offered him fifty dollars to pose for nude pictures in his apartment, the same story Dahmer had used to pick up Tracy Edwards. During the photo session, Dahmer had given Sounthome a cup of drugged coffee which made the boy very woozy and frightened. He felt paralyzed, as if he were going to pass out, and realized that Dahmer was fondling him. Sounthome panicked and ran away. He told his parents what the tall blond man had done, and his parents reported Dahmer to the police. Ironically, Sounthome Sinthasomphone was Konerak Sinthasomphone's older brother, and Konerak was the child who had escaped from Dahmer's apartment and had been brought to the police. Dahmer had successfully talked his way out of trouble when two police officers brought Konerak back to his apartment.

Dahmer was arrested after Sounthome's complaint and pleaded guilty in 1989 to second degree sexual assault. He was placed on five years' probation including a year in custody at the county workhouse during which he was allowed to keep his job at the Ambrosia chocolate factory. Yet, for some reason, the probation visits and checkups on Dahmer had stopped, and Dahmer seemingly returned to his old pattern of behavior. Neither the newspapers nor the probation department realized that Dahmer had never left his old pattern of behavior. He had been killing before the Sounthome Sinthasomphone case, while he served time in the county workhouse, and while he was on probation. He had successfully camouflaged what he was doing so that he was almost free to kill. According to a report in the *Milwaukee Journal,* his caseworker, Donna Chester, who kept in close contact with Dahmer, had little idea of his lifestyle. Because of her heavy caseload, her supervisor had granted Chester an administrative waiver, freeing her from the state requirement of making regular monthly visits to his home.

Dahmer had been in trouble with the law prior to the Sounthome Sinthasomphone case. In 1982, he had been arrested by State Fair Park police for disorderly conduct.

In 1986 Milwaukee police arrested him for "lewd and lascivious behavior" because, according to reports, he was observed masturbating in public. He later claimed that he was simply urinating, albeit in public, because he'd had so much to drink. The charge was subsequently reduced to a disorderly conduct complaint. Dahmer was sentenced to one year's probation and released.

Dahmer's escalating confrontations with the law in Milwaukee, while he was killing young men, fit easily into the pattern of both long-term and spree-type serial killers. Most people believe that serial killers live completely ordinary lives that never bring them to the attention of the police until they are actually caught. There is a popular belief that serial killers can operate for years without creating a stir and without ever crossing paths with the justice system. That is only a myth, however. Most serial killers have numerous confrontations with the police and are regarded as oddballs or weirdos by people in their community. People who know them are usually aware there's something terribly wrong, but either deny the reality or choose not to get involved. Most serial killers also commit crimes of escalating violence that bring them into contact with the police while they are killing.

Some serial killers have even gone to jail on lesser charges in between their sprees. Many times these lesser crimes act as emotional safety valves which blow off the building tension and fear. The confrontations with the courts or the police are sometimes like litmus tests. If the killer is not identified as the serial killer, he knows it's safe to return to the community. More often than not, killers who choose not to confess are not identified as serial killers. They resume their sprees after they are released by the police or serve out their short sentences. Dahmer fit into this pattern. He was cited twice for misdemeanor charges and then charged with a felony sexual assault. He was eventually released after each conviction, only to return to his pattern of killing. With Dahmer's arrest that pattern and the mystery surrounding it would come to an end.

The mystery of Jeffrey Dahmer that confronted Milwaukee police officers Robert Rauth and Rolf Mueller began to unravel when detectives Patrick Kennedy and Michael Dubis arrived at the apartment shortly after midnight on Tuesday, July 23. Rauth and Mueller reported to the detectives that they had called in an arrest of Jeffrey Dahmer for the attempted homicide of Tracy Edwards and that they had discovered evidence of other possible homicides or assaults on men. They told the detectives about the human skull they had found in the refrigerator and the Polaroids of mutilations of human bodies and human heads.

The photos were readily visible around the couch and in the dresser, the officers said. They also alerted the detectives to the heavy-duty security alarm system Dahmer had installed, the deadbolt locks on the apartment door and on his bedroom door, and the video cameras he had positioned to scan the living room. Already the hazardous waste disposal teams were pulling up outside and the apartment had been sealed off. Now the detectives would take over.

As Jeffrey Dahmer was led out of the building in shackles, he could see the array of police vehicles and news vans lining the alley. He could see the people milling outside around the apartment. The police had found the evidence of his murders, mutilations, and bizarre sexual activities, and they had the photographs to prove it. The police had even found the genitals he had removed from his victims and was preserving in formaldehyde. They had a living witness who had already complained to the police and put it on the public record. Was there any doubt that Tracy Edwards would soon tell his story to the world? It was obvious that in just a few short hours, the secret life of Jeffrey Dahmer, his humiliation and his shame, his deepest and most protected secrets, would be the stuff of tabloid headlines.

The charade of normalcy that Dahmer had tried to maintain since the time he was eighteen and committed his first homicide had now been ripped away. He would soon be exposed as the very sick homicidal person he knew himself to be. Maybe for all these years he had tried denying what he was to himself just as he'd done to his probation officer and to the court when he was arrested for taking Polaroid pictures of a minor. He was even committing homicides while he was on a work-release probation at a local Milwaukee correctional facility. That story, too, would eventually have to come out. Like other serial killers before him, such as Florida's Bobby Joe Long and New York's Arthur Shawcross, both of whom were confronted with the evidence, obviousness, and the enormity of their crimes, Dahmer's denial was broken. As he would later tell the interrogating detectives, he just wanted to "sit and talk about his offenses."

Dahmer's first reaction once in custody was to play back the tape of his crimes and relieve himself of as much of the burden of hiding the truth as possible. He was ready to talk. When detectives Patrick Kennedy and Michael Dubis took Jeffrey Dahmer into custody and transported him to the Criminal Investigation Bureau (CIB), they found a suspect willing to talk to them. Dahmer was anxious to release himself from the secrets he had been carrying since his first homicide back in Ohio in 1978 just after he'd graduated Revere High School. The Milwaukee detectives who took him to the station reported that they gave him his Miranda warnings and asked him if he understood what his constitutional rights were. At that point, Detective Kennedy wrote that Dahmer said he wished to "freely make a statement regarding the incident."

If the sight of the decomposing bodies and disembodied heads filling up the shelves of Dahmer's apartment was shocking to the police, perhaps even more shocking was the tale Jeffrey Dahmer began to unfold once he was in the interrogation room of the Criminal Investigation Bureau. He began, according to Detective Patrick Kennedy's report, by admitting that he was still on probation for having taken Polaroid pictures of a minor. Then he began talking about his first homicide in Ohio when he was only eighteen, the beginning of his thirteen-year killing spree.

He told the detectives that he was living in Richfield, Ohio, and had just graduated from high school when he picked up a nineteen-year-old hitchhiker named Steven Hicks whom he took back to his house. They were drinking beer, got drunk, and were having homosexual relations when the hitchhiker got up to leave. They got into a "physical fight," Dahmer told the cops, during which he hit Hicks over the head with a barbell that killed him. He buried the body outside, let it decompose for a couple of weeks, dug it up, and smashed the bones into small pieces with a sledgehammer. He scattered these in the woods surrounding his father's house.

Dahmer told the cops that he served a three-year tour in the Army and spent a year in Florida during which, "nothing of this nature happened," before he returned to Milwaukee to live at his grandmother's house in West Allis. It was during his stay there, he said, in the summer of 1984, that he committed his second homicide. He met a twenty-five-year-old white male whom he later identified as Steven Tuomi at the 219 Tavern and brought him over to the Ambassador Hotel where they got a room, got to drinking, and passed out from intoxication. According to Dahmer, when he woke up, the guy had blood streaming out of his mouth and was dead. Dahmer went over to the shopping mall, bought a suitcase large enough to hold the man's body, and returned to the Ambassador Hotel where he stuffed the corpse into the case. He brought the trunk back to his grandmother's house where, in the basement over the floor drain, he systematically filleted the man's flesh from the bone and then dismembered the corpse. He disposed of the body parts by stuffing them into plastic bags and putting them out with the trash.

In a manner typical of many serial killers, Dahmer felt it important to stress to the police that this was only one incident of homicide among many incidents of sexual relationships with other men during which no violence occurred. Dahmer also professed to having no memory of actually killing the man, only dismembering him. Like the Stephen Hicks homicide, which took place because Hicks and Dahmer had gotten into a physical struggle, Dahmer seemed to take only a reduced responsibility for killing the man. He woke up; the man was dead; he had to dispose of the body. It was as if Dahmer were a part of the killing without actually having been the killer. This, too, is part of what a serial murderer does as he builds up his levels of denial to protect himself from the reality of what he has done. By the time he has come to the end of his spree, he will have become so distanced from most of the murders that he will be able to describe them in quasi legalese as if they were historical events that happened in and of themselves. When self-professed Texas serial killer Henry Lee Lucas confessed to the Georgia Bureau of Investigation, he described his victims as "that was a woman who had been shot" or "a man who had been stabbed." He described his own murder of a Jane Doe hitchhiker nicknamed "Orange Socks" as "that would have been a strangle."

Dahmer told the police at the Milwaukee CIB that about two months after the first homicide in Milwaukee, he met another young man at the 219 Tavern. He took him directly back to his grandmother's house, had sex with him, drugged him with sleeping pills that he slipped into his drink, and then strangled him after he fell asleep. As he did the first time, he took this body down to the floor drain in the basement, dismembered him with a knife, broke up the bones with a sledgehammer as he had done with Stephen Hicks's body, and threw out the body parts in plastic trash bags.

A month later, he met another partner at a local tavern called Lacage, took him back to his grandmother's house where he had sex with him, drugged him, strangled and dismembered him, and disposed of him in the same way he had disposed of his two previous victims. Dahmer didn't kill again for almost a year, he told police. Then he met a young man at the 219 Tavern and repeated the same pattern he had used in the three previous homicides.

Dahmer told the police about his conviction for taking Polaroid pictures of Sounthome Sinthasomphone and the year of work release at the House of Correction. He didn't tell them initially that he had committed at least one homicide while he was on work release and that he had left the body in his locker at the Ambrosia chocolate factory. Upon his release from the House of Correction, Dahmer returned to live with his grandmother for the next six months. After that, he rented the apartment at 924 North Twenty-fifth Street, where he had been arrested on July 22, and began his final killing spree. He repeated the same pattern, he told the police, time after time. He would pick up a young man at the Grand Avenue Mall, or at one of the bars or bathhouses he frequented, even at a local store. He would take the man back to his apartment, have sex with him, drug him, strangle him, dismember him and dissolve his body in acid, and dispose of the remains.

It was a grisly tale that he unfolded, more grisly in the relentlessness of his patterns than in the actual crimes themselves. Once a listener accepted that someone like Dahmer could actually fillet flesh from bone and process human remains as if they were waste, the subsequent crimes themselves seemed to decrease in their shock value. However, the continuously repeating pattern of homicidal behavior and the aggressiveness of Dahmer's commitment to it were startling. It seemed that once Dahmer had established a successful method of luring men to his apartment and murdering them, that became his singular pattern of sexual behavior.

This was also typical of serial killers who are setting up for the long term. Once they establish themselves successfully as fixtures in the community from which they select their victims, they become part of the environment, a component of the social ecosystem, feeding on the victims they can lure into their trap. Killers like Dahmer find the routines themselves as exciting as the actual lures and control. Just thinking about trolling, spotting likely victims, and engaging them in a conversation that will lead to a deadly assignation is the beginning of the thrill. The carrying out of the murder and the body disposal process become secondary to the thrill of the hunt. In this, serial killers like Dahmer display many of the same reactions that long-term drug addicts do. For the addict, simply thinking about the rush of drugs prior to inhaling or injecting them is enough to stimulate all of the brain's pleasure receptors and make the addict that much more fixated on administering the drug.

On the morning he was arrested, Dahmer described eleven or so different homicides to the detectives. His only problem seemed to be, he explained, that the disposal of the body parts was taking too much time and space. He said that he was able to explain away the odor of disintegrating flesh to the satisfaction of anyone who questioned him, so that was no longer a problem. But physical storage of the human remains in that apartment seemed to be an issue. Dahmer explained, therefore, that he obtained a fifty-seven-gallon oil drum and used it to store some of the torsos of victims prior to their disposal. Dahmer signed his confessions after having been advised again of his rights against making self-incriminating statements and was taken from the interrogation room of the CIB to the county lockup.

This wasn't the end of the interrogation process, however. Like many serial killers, Dahmer had only chosen to talk about those aspects of his crimes which he believed were the most apparent or about which he harbored the least feelings. He was still holding information back from the detectives. Maybe these were crimes in which he had some attachment to the victim. Maybe these were crimes which were especially embarrassing to him. It was still too early in the case to tell. Nevertheless, a few hours after his first interrogation ended, Dahmer asked that the detectives come to the jail so that he could talk to them some more about his crimes. "I've told you everything already," he said to the detectives. "I have nothing to hide so I might as well tell you about these ones I forgot."

Dahmer told the police about a young man he met in Chicago who went back to Milwaukee with him and stayed at his place for two days. They had oral sex, and seemed to be getting along until on the second day the man said that he had to leave. Dahmer followed his typical pattern; he invited the man to have a final cup of coffee into which he had already slipped some sleeping pills. The man passed out, Dahmer strangled him, dismembered him, and put the head in his refrigerator. Dahmer stated this was a murder he'd forgotten to mention earlier in the day when he gave his first confessions.

Jeffrey Dahmer also revealed that he would "cut off the penis and body parts, and put them in formaldehyde to preserve them and then look at them and masturbate for gratification." In this behavior, Dahmer's patterns are typical of other serial killers who find a sexual thrill in preserving specific body parts of their victims. In some cases, the body parts give specific pleasure because they are genital organs, in other cases they are identified with specific victims. Genesee River killer Arthur Shawcross, for example, told police how he cut out the vagina of a victim he particularly liked. Killer Edmund Kemper preserved the head of a victim whose death he relished. Texas killer Henry Lee Lucas said he liked to have sex with the remains of his victims.

In a final set of statements, Dahmer said that he had skinned one of his victims and later submersed the skin in acid. Then, he flushed it and rest of the body parts down the toilet when it became a slushy substance that wouldn't clog the pipes. He kept a set of biceps from one of his victims, he told the police, because they were big and he wanted to consume the flesh. That admission seemed to upset Dahmer because he said that he didn't want to talk about this any more. Again, typical of most serial killers, Dahmer kept on talking, trying to reveal as much as possible until he felt he had done something that was painful to him. Admitting to eating the flesh from one of his victims seemed too hurtful for him to contemplate, so he simply shut down after revealing that he masturbated in front of his victims' body parts because it brought back memories. That thought seemed to please him.

It was now the afternoon of July 23, 1991, and the detectives had the start of a composite of the man who had committed so many crimes. But there were much larger missing pieces to the puzzle of Jeffrey Dahmer that needed fitting together. Detectives had the "who, how, where and when." They just didn't have the "why." That was something not even the most prominent forensic psychiatrists in the state could answer with absolute certainty.

Chapter Four

Dahmer's Early Childhood

"He loved skulls," a grade school friend of Jeffrey Dahmer's recalled to an Ohio newspaper reporter looking for childhood information about Dahmer. The person remembered that even as a child in elementary school Jeffrey would collect animals, dismember them, "separate them by body parts and put them in jars."

Ted Lehr, another friend, said that Dahmer was "a fun kid to be around," even though he did go through occasional bouts of sadness. Sue Lehr, Ted's mother, described him as an attractive, little kid you'd want to hug. He was a thin and blond schoolboy who didn't want to do anything wrong. He seemed to want to please adults and "anticipated what you wanted of him." In fact, she said, she probably hugged him herself once or twice as he was growing up and playing around her house. Yet, there was a disquieting aspect about Jeffrey Dahmer, Sue Lehr recalls. She said that she knew "he was a frightened child."

Jeffrey's father, Lionel Dahmer, told the *Milwaukee Sentinel* just after his son's arrest that "Jeff's never been socially adaptive. He's always been out of the social mainstream." In his father's words, Jeffrey always seemed "different." Lionel said that he didn't realize how sick his son was. After the revelations of his son's murders, Lionel said he realized his son was mentally ill. "I did not know the extent," he explained. "He was a person who was basically kind, but deeply, deeply troubled by something, and he has been for a long time. How could anyone be polite and kind and pretty normal otherwise and yet do these horrible things unless they are extremely troubled and insane?" Dahmer told an Akron, Ohio, newspaper.

Wherever and whenever Jeffrey Dahmer's troubles began, people who knew him seem to agree that they started a long time before he arrived in Milwaukee to live with his grandmother. His troubles may have begun even before he was born. According to an interview with Lionel and Shari Dahmer, Jeffrey's father and step-mother, on the television magazine program "Inside Edition" aired shortly after Jeffrey was found guilty, Jeffrey's birth mother, Joyce Flint, was taking a prescription medication for her bouts of anxiety depression during the first trimester when she was pregnant with Jeffrey. Like alcohol, which operates directly on the developing neurological system of a fetus, prescription sedatives taken during pregnancy can also have an adverse effect on the nervous system or the brain of an unborn child. These effects are similar to the damage observed in a condition known as Fetal Alcohol Syndrome (FAS). Neurologists have now identified the symptoms of FAS which can range from a mild impairment to severe degrees of mental retardation. FAS is a physiological condition that results when alcohol consumed by the mother during the critical stages of her pregnancy can impair the brain of the fetus to such an extent that the resulting child never fully develops into a competent adult. In many cases, adult FAS victims have dramatically poor impulse control or may be subject to the violent urges and fantasies of a troubled six- or seven-year-old child. Many adult FAS victims are often in trouble with the law throughout their lives because they cannot adjust to a rule-governed society. Some even repeatedly commit violent crimes because they never learn to mediate their behavior.

If Shari Dahmer is correct in her statement that Jeffrey's biological mother was taking strong prescription medication for her depression during the early weeks of her pregnancy, Jeffrey may well have a condition similar to Fetal Alcohol Syndrome which may have impaired his ability to control his most violent urges. This might have become an issue at Dahmer's trial had it been introduced into evidence regarding the Dahmer family medical history.

Joyce Flint Dahmer, Jeffrey's mother, hailed from Chippewa Falls, Wisconsin. On August 22, 1959, she married a Marquette University undergraduate chemistry student named Lionel Dahmer in West Allis. On May 21 of the following year, while Lionel was still an undergraduate, the couple's first son, Jeffrey, was born. Lionel Dahmer finished his bachelor's degree in 1961, stayed at Marquette to complete his masters the following year, and then moved the family to Ames, Iowa, where he would stay for the next four years to pursue his doctorate in chemistry at Iowa State.

In 1966, after receiving his Ph.D. in chemistry, Lionel Dahmer got a job at PPG Industries in Barberton, Ohio, and moved the family to Doylestown, which was near Akron, Ohio. Jeffrey had just turned six and was enrolled in the first grade at Hazel Harvey Elementary School. It was here that the first formal notations were made in a file of what would eventually turn out to be one of the most carefully scrutinized developmental histories of a serial killer ever assembled.

Joyce was already expecting the family's second child by the time the Dahmers moved to Doylestown. According to friends who spoke to the *Akron Beacon Journal* as anonymous sources, she was having a difficult time with the pregnancy. She was already depressed, sources told the newspapers, and had become worried about the delivery. Jeffrey, according to school sources, was also having a difficult time with his mother's pregnancy and was showing early signs of feeling abandoned. Sources said that he was harboring feelings of ill will toward his new brother even before he was born on December 18.

Whatever the precise nature of Joyce Dahmer's troubles during her pregnancy, it was apparent that the birth of David Dahmer did not end them. Jeffrey's first grade teacher made a cryptic notation on Jeffrey's report card that during his mother's "illness," the six-year-old schoolboy seemed to feel "neglected." By the time David was born, Jeffrey seemed to have developed deep feelings of resentment toward him.

Most child development experts agree that it's perfectly natural for a young elementary-school-aged child to experience feelings of abandonment when his mother has a second baby. Suddenly all the attention that the mother showered on the first child is withdrawn because she's involved with a second baby who, by its very nature, is more demanding of attention than the older child. Older siblings between the ages of three and six are particularly vulnerable to these feelings because they haven't developed a solid structure of friendships and relationships outside the home. They're still very dependent on the goings-on in the home even though they might be in first or second grade.

Jeffrey fell right into this category. Only his feelings of abandonment and neglect might have been exacerbated because of the length and depth of his mother's problems with the pregnancy and any lack of resiliency he may have had as a result of his condition. Whereas most children perceive a temporary withdrawal of their mothers' affections and then learn to compensate and accept the new family member because they are taught to feel responsible for the new baby, Jeffrey apparently compensated by withdrawing from the family himself. Friends have described him as engaging in solitary pursuits and in finding enjoyment from the torture of small animals. If he were in pain during this time, he shared the feeling by extending it to other creatures. It was a pattern of immature hostility which he developed into a killing engine.

Before the conclusion of his first year in elementary school, the Dahmer family moved to a bigger house in an exclusive section of Bath Township. Friends described Joyce Dahmer as a very "hyper" person who seemed to have problems with the new house on West Bath Road from the start. The Dahmers' next door neighbor, Georgia Scharenberg, remembered that Joyce Dahmer seemed very upset when the family first moved into the house because she had to share the pond with the Scharenbergs. She had believed the pond was exclusively on the new Dahmer property and was distressed to learn that part of it crossed the property line. "She was just crying and carrying on about it," Georgia Scharenberg said. Eventually the Scharenbergs offered to have her section of the pond filled in with dirt so the Dahmers could have all of the pond on their property. Georgia Scharenberg also remembered eight-year-old Jeffrey and said, "He always seemed to be alone."

Eventually Jeffrey Dahmer found some friends and tried to develop peer relationships. However, during this time he may have experienced an incidence of sexual abuse at the hands of another child. Lionel Dahmer reportedly told a Milwaukee probation officer after his son's arrest for sexual abuse in the Sounthome Sinthasomphone case that he believed whatever his son's problems with sexuality were started with his being abused by a neighbor's child when he was eight. The probation officer, who took handwritten notes of her conversation with Lionel, said that the elder Dahmer wondered aloud about that incident's being the cause of Jeffrey's problems.

Jeffrey Dahmer has denied having been sexually abused as a child, and there is no way to prove or disprove Lionel Dahmer's suspicions. A Bath Township police officer said that he had asked the Milwaukee police to ask Jeffrey Dahmer whether he had been physically or sexually abused as a child. According to Captain John Gardner of the Bath Township police, Dahmer answered that he had not been abused by anyone.

During his elementary school years, Jeffrey Dahmer began collecting animals. His friends said that he would collect dead animal carcasses. According to Eric Tyson, one of Dahmer's older friends who was interviewed for the *Akron Beacon Journal,* "He had a massive insect collection. He had all these large insects, butterflies, dragonflies. Then, he graduated from large insects to road kills." Tyson said that Jeffrey and his friends would walk the country roads of the township looking for rodents and other small animals that might have been killed by motorists.

"He would collect these animals, dismember them, separate them by body parts, and put them in jars." Eric Tyson said that Dahmer would store the jars in a wooden toolshed behind the Dahmer house that Jeffrey always called "the hut." It was an isolated structure way up on a hill on the back part of the property that offered Jeffrey all the privacy he needed to experiment with pickling his animal parts in formaldehyde solution.

"The hut had tons and tons of jars of animals and pieces of animals. He seemed to be fascinated by the decomposition," Tyson told the *Akron Beacon Journal*. He said that Jeffrey once took him and another child into the shed to show them the body parts floating in jars filled with a "murky liquid." He said that Dahmer held one jar up and said there was a raccoon inside it. They didn't believe him. Then Dahmer "took the jar and smashed it on a rock and the smell was so bad that we all vomited."

Eric Tyson, who grew up across the street from Dahmer on West Bath Road, further recalled Dahmer's collection of dead animals that he organized into a kind of "pet cemetery." Tyson told *The New York Times* that Jeffrey had a burial patch for dead animals alongside his house with actual graves and crosses. He was quoted as saying that "A number of neighbors have recalled seeing animals such as frogs and cats impaled or staked to trees." Dahmer had a particularly gruesome habit, friends recall, of burying the actual bodies of the squirrels but impaling their skulls on the little crosses that rose from their graves.

Children from the neighborhood remember that Dahmer would ask them if they wanted to go out and collect road kills instead of playing. They said that he would take his bike and ride around the back roads all alone looking for whatever he could scrape up off the macadam and bring back to his shed for storage. He experimented with his chemical set, figuring out which substances would dissolve away the flesh and fur and leave only bleached bones as trophies.

As Jeffrey grew older, his fascination with dead animals became more complex and involved. He switched from being a passive collector of road kills to an aggressive stalker of animals at some point during his early adolescence. Other people from the neighborhood remember that when Dahmer was about fourteen or fifteen, perhaps during his years at Eastview Junior High, there were reports of missing dogs circulating throughout the area. No one knew whether Dahmer was directly connected to the disappearances, but Jim Klippel, who used to be the Dahmers' next door neighbor, remembered seeing a dog's skull turned into a kind of totem pole in an area only a few hundred yards behind the Dahmer house. Klippel said that he and his girlfriend were walking in the woods when they discovered a dog's head impaled on a stick. The dog's body had been nailed to a nearby tree.

"Somebody must have had a lot of fun with that dog," he said to the *Akron Beacon Journal*, "if that's what you want to call it. It was skinned and gutted. And about a hundred yards away there had been a large fire and thirteen little fires around it. It looked so much like cult worship that it scared us to death."

Klippel remembered the stories of missing dogs and remembered that Dahmer had been associated with them. "I had heard stories in the area," he told the newspaper, "about him going around and doing things to animals. I don't know if he did it. He seemed like such a nice, quiet kid."

Other friends remember stories about Dahmer's fishing expeditions at a local pond near Medina Road. There, most of the local kids fished just for fun and threw back most of the small bass they caught. Dahmer didn't. Friends remember that he would fillet his catch with his pocketknife. Then he would cut it up into little pieces and throw it back into the water where other fish, driven into a frenzy by fresh blood floating down from the surface, would rise to feed on the remains. Dahmer seemed fascinated not only by the fishes' behavior when blood hit the water, but by the very act of paring away flesh from the bone and dismembering the remains.

"Why do you like to cut them up that way?" one of the kids once asked Dahmer as he watched him become totally fixated on chopping up his catch.

"I want to see what it looks like inside," Dahmer reportedly answered. "I like to see how things work."

One schoolmate also remembers another eerie aspect to Dahmer's behavior. He said that Jeffrey liked to listen to heartbeats by placing his ear against someone's chest. He also liked to touch his friends' veins to feel the way they pulsated whenever a new surge of blood was pumped through. This was almost a foreshadowing of what Dahmer was doing to Tracy Edwards on the night he tried to kill him. Edwards remembered that Dahmer put his head on his chest, listened to his heart, and told him that he was going to eat his heart right out of him later that night.

Dahmer's early childhood and his elementary through junior high school years reveal that he exhibited at least five strong patterns of aberrant behavior most often displayed by people who eventually find themselves seriously in conflict with authority or the legal system. In combination and under the influence of other factors, such as alcohol abuse and repeated violence, these people may often develop violent criminal patterns of behavior as well. That, too, is what eventually happened to Jeffrey Dahmer.

1. Parental Neglect

The teacher at the Hazel Harvey Elementary School who noted on his first grade report card that Dahmer seemed neglected may have entered the very first official red-flag warning on Dahmer's personal history. Children who feel neglected often develop dysfunctional patterns of behavior. Other people have said that Dahmer felt abandoned by his mother who was sick at the time and possibly having a difficult pregnancy with her second child, David. Friends and neighbors said that Jeffrey seemed very much alone. If Jeffrey had perceived that he had been abandoned or neglected, even if it was only a perception and not true, he would have been set on a course toward sociopathic behavior.

When he was eighteen, Dahmer said that both parents left him alone in the house after their divorce. Although he was legally an adult at the time and "emancipated" according to court records, he may well have perceived it as part of a pattern in which at least one of his parents had withdrawn from him years earlier. Therefore, Dahmer can be profiled as an adult who reported perceptions of childhood neglect. If that neglect had any basis in fact, he would be a prime candidate for developing sociopathic behavior which he seemed to have done by the time he was in high school if not in junior high.

Simply stated in everyday language, sociopaths are individuals who don't respect other people's boundaries. They may steal, cheat, and lie without any remorse or pangs of conscience, and they may even commit acts of violence if they think they can get away with it. Sociopaths appear not to have any sense of right and wrong, but that is probably only an illusion. More likely, because sociopaths have no sense of personal boundaries, they cannot conceive of the pain they cause when they hurt others and regard all possessions as their own. People can develop sociopathic behavior patterns if they never learned personal boundaries as infants or young children. If their parents neglected them or, worse, abandoned or abused them, their senses of personal boundaries may be impaired. At worst, this could lead to children becoming extraordinarily violent. At the least, they seem completely insensitive to the pain and suffering of others. As they grow older, they seem unable to play by any social rules and ultimately may tend to have no regard for law and may be at high risk for criminal behavior at all levels.

2. Eldest and Least Favored Child

Jeffrey may have perceived himself as a second-class citizen in his own family. His mother's withdrawal due to her illness during pregnancy seemed to have been translated by the six-year-old Dahmer as a withdrawal of her affections from him. He may have perceived that he was the least favored child or the "lost" child because he may have believed that his mother's affections were given without reservation to his younger brother David. This would have made six-year-old Jeffrey involuntarily hostile toward his brother and toward his mother. If his father Lionel were not around the house to become the most favored parent, Dahmer would have grown up in what he perceived to be the absence of affection. He would have developed childhood-coping behaviors to satisfy his feelings of loss, loneliness, hostility, guilt, and shame for not being the child that his mother favored.

If six-year-old Jeffrey Dahmer learned he could cope with the anger, guilt, and shame by asserting control over something else, he might have naturally chosen insects or small animals, especially dead ones. Dead bugs don't protest. By collecting them and displaying them, he was also displaying the one area where he might have exercised control over the world. From small dead bugs, he might have naturally graduated to larger and larger insects until he controlled the beauty of butterfly wings spread out under glass.

The more satisfaction he achieved, the more he sought; until he was killing and chopping up his kills to demonstrate the control he exercised. But there is another side to his coping behavior as well.

A young Jeffrey Dahmer whose boundaries may have already been weakened by the loss of his mother's attention and affection, and later broached by the alleged sexual abuse by a neighboring child, might have developed childhood sociopathic behaviors. Acting out these behaviors may have stimulated him to discover how much he could destroy and how much he could offend others without being stopped. He might also have developed a primal fascination with the "independence" of other life forms such as insects, animals, and fish. His fascination with seeing how animals work (reportedly, his own words) may have been a natural, albeit unhealthy, outgrowth of his fascination with how things could exist independent of his own control. This is a truly dysfunctional behavior, but it makes sense in light of what Dahmer had already experienced by age eight.

In any event, if he perceived himself as having been put in the position of being the least favored child in the family, he would have translated it into a severe sense of inferiority. As an adult, victims of "least favored child" complex sometimes develop hostile attitudes toward authority figures and portray themselves as outsiders. Many serial killers, like Leonard Lake in California and Arthur Shawcross in New York, were least favored children who blamed their siblings for parts of their problems. Lake even murdered his younger brother Donald Lake.

3. Outsider in Family

Another factor in the least favored child pattern is the outsider pattern. Here, a child perceives himself to be formally ostracized within his own family. He's technically a family member, but he believes that the real love, attention, and affection is directed away from him. What should be a primal social situation enhancing the development of a healthy adult now becomes a blueprint for dysfunctional and inappropriate reactions. To gain attention, the outsider and least favored member of the family must indulge in negative behaviors. He withdraws instead of participates and sometimes acts out his most violent aggressive feelings. If unchecked, it results in an adolescent who is incapable of solving his own problems and may seek to medicate himself with alcohol or drugs. This is exactly what seems to have happened in Dahmer's case by the time he entered Revere High School in 1975.

4. Ambiguous Stories of Childhood Sex Abuse, Emotional Abuse, or Physical Abuse

More often than not, accusations of sex abuse circulate around one or both parents in the developmental histories of serial killers. However, many serial killers' life histories are filled with unsubstantiated stories about the neighbor down the street who abused children, including them; childhood friends who abused them, older relatives, and sometimes family friends. In the overwhelming majority of cases, the accused serial killer is unwilling to talk about these incidents because he feels responsible, shameful, and certainly guilty. While not the intrinsic cause of the killer's acts, childhood sex abuse, or the perception of sex abuse, lays important psychological groundwork for later adult behavior patterns. Almost every accused serial killer ever interviewed about his childhood can document personal stories of abuse or neglect. The correlation between child abuse and adult criminal behavior patterns is so high that sex-offender and serial killer profiles at the FBI's Behavioral Science Unit almost always include a childhood pattern of abuse in their descriptions of serial killers. Stories about all types of parental neglect and childhood sexual abuse have circulated around Dahmer from the time that he was first arrested. Even his father cited an incident of childhood sex abuse by a neighbor as one of the causes of his son's behavior even though Jeffrey Dahmer vehemently denied it.

5.   Extreme Cruelty to Animals

Cruelty to animals is one of the clear indicators of early predispositions to sociopathic violence and eventual adult violent criminal behavior. As in child abuse, the correlation is so high that profilers of violent criminals often cite a history of cruelty to animals as a notation to look for in the killer's personal history. Cruelty to animals indicates that the child is looking to exercise control over less powerful life forms. It is an immature expression of rage which will later flower into violence toward other children, teenagers, or less powerful adults. Cruelty to animals may also be a precursor of later hate crimes or homophobic crimes because the criminal seeks to inflict physical violence on people he perceives as weaker than he is.

In Jeffrey Dahmer's case, the cruelty toward animals was an early indicator of the hostility he was feeling as a result of his perceptions of neglect and abandonment. The more alone and abused he felt, the more he sought victims to work out his anger. The ritualistic aspects of the cruelty were especially menacing.

First, Dahmer sought to make trophies or totems out of his animal victims, preserving them in chemicals and cataloging them in jars. For the animals he was assumed to have killed and buried, he organized their carcasses in makeshift graveyards, experimenting with death as it were. He displayed their skulls above the mounds where they were buried. As a gravesite manager for his own kills, this was the ultimate control that the violent Dahmer could wield over the world around him. His small campfire sites and ritual-like burial grounds were a primitive but organized way for him to channel the escalating hostility he was feeling against the world. It was a belief in magical thinking, an external form of intervention in his life that he could not find in his family. His cruelty to animals was a coping mechanism that prevented him from self-destructing when he was very young. Ultimately it was fatal to Dahmer's personality and, of course, to his victims.

By the time he was set to enter high school, fifteen-year-old Jeffrey Dahmer was on a collision course with violence. His patterns of loneliness and hostility were now getting the better of him. His lack of emotional resilience and the gradual failure of his childhood coping mechanisms held him in a stranglehold. It would take only a few more factors to set him on a path of violence.

Those three factors would overtake him in high school: his addiction to alcohol, his parents' divorce, and his abandonment upon his graduating from high school. By the time he was eighteen, he would be almost completely alone in the world and would have become a cold-blooded killer.

Chapter Five

Teenage Alcoholic

"I was always a little wary of him. I was never quite sure what he was going to do. He had this kind of creepy strength about him — an element of danger to him," classmate John Backderf said in an interview to the *Akron Beacon Journal*. "Maybe it was the drinking." Backderf had not seen Jeffrey Dahmer since his graduation in 1978.

According to Backderf, when friends and classmates remember Jeffrey Dahmer from Revere High School, they remember the liquor. Dahmer was always drinking. He was taking slugs at 7:30 A.M. from the beer cans he brought to school slung on the inside of his extra long army field jacket with the ripped lining. The ragged tears in the lining allowed him to hang the cans without giving them away through the telltale bulges on the outside. He would leave the jacket in his locker and sneak back during the day for nips in between classes. He tried to camouflage his behavior as best he could, but by the time he was fifteen, Jeffrey Dahmer was probably a full-blown teenage alcoholic. He was medicating himself with booze to dull whatever pain he was feeling internally.

Other friends remembered that Jeffrey had begun drinking regularly when he was a twelve-year-old in the seventh grade. An acquaintance named Chip Crofoot noted that he had a bottle of gin in his junior high school locker which seemed more than odd for someone so young. Otherwise, Dahmer was so nondescript in his early years of junior high and high school that few people even remembered anything about him. Chip Crofoot explained, "I don't remember much about him other than his drinking. He pretty much kept to himself."

Another friend told reporters that he remembered an adolescent Jeffrey Dahmer as "creepy" but not especially malicious. "I think everybody always knew he was strange," the former classmate told an Akron, Ohio newspaper. "But he was never violent. I never saw him do anything harmful to anyone or to himself with the exception of his drinking." He remembered Jeffrey Dahmer as a strong tennis player who seemed to display more bizarre behavior as he approached his senior year at Revere. In fact, records show that Dahmer involved himself in freshman band during his first year in high school, intramural tennis, and the high school newspaper. Jeffrey also had a job waiting tables at Lanning's Restaurant in Bath and worked out with weights in his basement. Jeffrey was getting big, and he was working out to pump himself up.

Concurrently, his behavior was getting stranger and more daring. He would press his face against the school window during a class so the students could look out and see his flattened expression while the teacher faced the blackboard. In his senior year, a former classmate said, "He traced bodies on the floor in chalk." It was an eerie sight to see the outline of a body on the floor; a foreshadowing, perhaps, of what the police would be doing in his apartment in Milwaukee years later.

* * *

The students might have been repelled by the stale beer odor on Jeffrey's clothing, but school administrators and teachers at Revere High School didn't seem to notice that Jeffrey had a constant smell of alcohol about him. No faculty members reported him for it or even questioned him about it. School officials, who were questioned about Dahmer after his arrest, were struck by the lack of communication they had with him rather than by what he did or said. Jeffrey Dahmer continued to be the same troubled boy that people remembered from the Hazel Harvey Elementary School.

"Jeff was never a discipline problem," George Kungle, his former guidance counselor, told reporters after Dahmer's arrest. He was "a quiet, but not necessarily introverted guy. He never let anyone get to know him well. I would try and talk to him, like you would any kid, hoping to get some insights. He just never said a whole lot about himself." The guidance counselor also remembered conferences with Lionel Dahmer about Jeffrey's academic work. "He was a concerned parent."

About Jeffrey's drinking, Kungle said that he didn't see any evidence of an alcohol problem. "I can't say that I was aware that he had a drinking problem," the guidance counselor told the Akron newspapers. "He was a polite, quiet kid. I can't say there were any signs he was different or strange."

Other acquaintances remember a very bizarre Jeffrey Dahmer who acted out a variety of frenzied behaviors in order to attract attention or amuse his companions. In fact, one former Revere student told the newspapers that by Jeffrey's senior year anyone doing something bizarre or strange in public to attract attention was said to be "doing a Dahmer." Perhaps it was his drinking that reduced his inhibitions so that he was acting with no social constraints on his behavior. For example, classmates remember Jeffrey sitting in the library and yelling out "Mrs. Shepherd" repeatedly without getting caught. Others remember his imitation of the spasmodic, jerking, clenching, and heavily impaired speech of a cerebral palsy victim he said his mother had once hired to decorate the house. This was an act he would pull off in public, in the halls, and in class.

Jeffrey would also bleat in a heavily nasal way that grew more disturbing as he obsessively repeated it. During class or outside of school, Dahmer would start the bleating and his classmates would think it funny. "He would bleat like a sheep," John Backderf told the *Akron Beacon Journal*. "Sometimes he did it loud. He knew it cracked us up."

Most likely, Jeffrey Dahmer was doing something, albeit a crazed antic, to keep himself at the center of attention. Because he might have felt neglected and unloved, he indulged in perverse or outrageous behavior to control other people and keep them close to him. At the outset, his motivation may have been no different from any class clown who wants to command attention. Stories of comedians and performers, who were cracking jokes or acting insanely in high school, abound in show business biographies. Yet, there seemed to be an edge to what Dahmer was doing. He wasn't just being funny for the sake of being funny. His behavior seemed to be anger driven, propelled by a frustration that was consuming him and that he couldn't satisfy. When the effects of his bleating seemed to be wearing off or when his impaired speech and jerking movements didn't get the laugh he expected, he adapted new behaviors.

Classmates recall their class trip to Washington, D.C. On a dare, Dahmer bet that he could talk his way into the White House. Friends might have doubted him, but he picked up the telephone; called the White House; and talked his way into getting a personal, on-the-spot tour of the Vice President's office. His classmates were amazed that Jeffrey could get into Walter Mondale's office, a spot not on the regular White House tour. It was something Jeffrey did to impress others.

One of his most memorable "Dahmers" was his faked epileptic seizure. Classmates recalled that he could fall down, drool, and start shaking at a moment's notice. People were often stunned by this display. He could pull his seizure in the school hallways or in class. His favorite spot was in the cafeteria in front of many students. He became so infamous for his act that students, who belonged to his informal cheering section, paid him up to thirty dollars to do it at the Summit Mall, one of the area's more exclusive shopping centers.

In typical Dahmer fashion, he began by "pounding back" a six pack of beer and then headed for the mall. Then, on an afternoon that few of his former classmates could ever forget, Jeffrey Dahmer bleated, twitched, and collapsed into seizures throughout a number of stores at the mall. He went through O'Neil's and Polsky's department stores, stopping by the counters and then collapsing in a heap and writhing along the floor. He appeared at a lunch counter where he knocked over glasses of water as patrons danced out of his way. "They were jumping out of the way and he sort of bleated at them and ran," Backderf, who was there, told the *Akron Beacon Journal*. At a natural food store, Jeffrey tasted a sample of wheat germ, spit it out all over the floor, and then collapsed in a heap yelling, "I'm allergic." It was a performance that was so memorable classmates still talked about it years later.

Jeffrey Dahmer must have consumed a lot of alcohol during his years in junior and senior high school. To be reeking of alcohol early in the morning and to have downed a complete six pack in order to make a spectacle of himself at the local shopping mall was as physically damaging as it was emotionally crippling. Jeffrey Dahmer medicated himself on a powerful depressant so consistently that he must have been suffering from impaired judgment throughout most of his high school years. If he were a borderline sociopath during this period, his consumption of alcohol only made a bad situation worse. It would be expected that under this kind of social pressure, the personality that was Jeffrey Dahmer probably retreated into a shell.

Jeffrey's date for his senior prom, Bridget Geiger, confirmed the erratic aspect of his personality. She told the newspapers that she felt coaxed into going with him because he was a friend of a friend, but that she regretted it throughout the evening. In fact, Jeffrey didn't even personally ask Bridget to the prom. Dahmer had a friend do it, because he was too shy. The sixteen-year-old Bridget agreed to go to the senior prom with him. She remembered that Dahmer was exceptionally nervous when he picked her up. He seemed actually terrified at the prospect of going out with a girl who might even try to kiss him. Geiger recounted that when he tried to give her the prom corsage, he was so afraid of sticking her with the pin, Bridget's mother had to pin it on her daughter's dress for him.

The evening went from bad to worse. He showed her no attention, she told an Ohio newspaper. "Jeff pulled out the chair for me to sit down and then he disappeared. He didn't even say two words to me the whole night."

He didn't dance with her at all and eventually left her sitting at the table all alone for two hours. Bridget had had enough. When Jeffrey returned to the table, she was already set to leave with one of her girlfriends and her date. "Jeff told me he had been hungry and went to a Mc-Donald's and ate four or five cheeseburgers," she told the newspaper. She said that she believed him, because she spotted the wrappers on the floor of his car. Jeffrey and Bridget left the prom early that night. When he dropped her off at home, she remembered, "He didn't even kiss me goodnight. He shook my hand."

A couple of weeks later in June, 1978, she recalled that Jeffrey invited her to a party at his house. She referred to it as a party for "nerds" with no food or anything, not even music. There were just five or so people sitting around talking when Jeffrey decided that he wanted to invoke the spirit of someone who had lived in the house before them. As if her experience with him at the prom wasn't bad enough, he was now trying to contact the dead. She told the newspaper that "somebody had cooked up this idea of a seance." The group gathered around a round table in the den. Geiger remembered Jeffrey telling her that the house was haunted by an evil spirit which appeared to him and talked to him when no one else was in the house. She remembered that Dahmer claimed the spirit told him "to do things that scare me."

At first she thought he was just "doing a Dahmer," another one of his practical jokes designed to scare her and amuse the group. However, when they turned off the lights and lit some candles she began to worry. Suddenly the candles flared and sputtered, and that was it for Bridget Geiger. If Jeffrey had been trying to frighten her, he succeeded. She said she left Jeffrey's house and never saw him again until his picture turned up in the newspaper as a serial killer.

The two widely different aspects of Jeffrey Dahmer's personality — the class clown who could tear through a local mall on a dare and the shy nerd who ditched his date at the prom to run out for burgers — are nevertheless completely compatible with one another. Dahmer may have been a socially awkward and inhibited teenager who was uncomfortable with heterosexual relationships, but he was also a drunk whose inhibitions would drop under the influence of alcohol. He felt powerless in one-on-one situations when he knew his sexuality was being judged, but he felt in control when he was the clown commanding the attention of an entire group.

Control was also the central issue on his prom date with Bridget Geiger. Dahmer felt he could not exercise control because she represented a threat to him. She might have represented a parental figure because she was judging him as a social companion or because he perceived she was judging him sexually. Inasmuch as he believed his parents had neglected him, he neglected her. It was the only way he felt he could exercise any control over the evening at all.

It was also at about the time of his graduation from high school that his parents Joyce and Lionel Dahmer broke up and went their separate ways. People in the neighborhood remembered that the divorce had been long in coming and was no surprise. Domestic disputes were not uncommon throughout most of Jeffrey's senior year.

Dahmer's classmates said that, probably because of the

problems at home, Jeffrey was hardly ever in class during his senior year. They would see him in the halls from time to time. When he showed up in school, he was usually drunk. By that time the teachers, according to one friend, "mostly just shoved him through."

Friends remember that Jeffrey was caught once with a bottle of scotch in a classroom. When he was asked what he was doing with a drink in class, he replied, "It's my medicine." When one realizes what was going on in his home during this entire period, the story even makes sense.

The real story behind Jeffrey Dahmer's behavior during his senior year might well have been that he was under terrible pressure to choose between his parents who were each threatening to leave. The domestic hostilities became so intense that Lionel Dahmer moved to a different part of the house to be away from his wife. He even set up a Rube Goldberg alarm system: a string hung across the room with keys dangling from it that would jingle if Joyce Dahmer tried to cross into his space. It was an intolerable way to live, and put intense pressure on the seventeen-year-old Jeffrey Dahmer who was already an out-of-control alcoholic.

Lionel finally filed for divorce, citing his wife's "extensive mental illness." He charged her with "extreme cruelty and gross neglect of duty." Joyce, in turn, countersued for divorce, citing Lionel's mental cruelty. Ultimately, Joyce won in court and got a restraining order prohibiting Lionel from "molesting or assaulting or in any way disturbing her or the minor children." She also won custody of Jeffrey's younger brother David along with alimony and child suppport.

The problem for Jeffrey Dahmer was that all during the period up until he was eighteen he was asked to choose the parent he intended to live with. When he reached eighteen, however, he was considered an emancipated child by the court and was excluded from any court settlements. Therefore, although his brother was provided for, Jeffrey was summarily dropped from consideration by the court beyond the legal custody of either his father or mother. It was as if he had been officially removed from the family. At age eighteen, he was actually a legal adult, and no longer a child. It's not farfetched to say, however, that Jeffrey might well have considered himself a child emotionally because in his mind he had been deprived. His brother was provided for, and he wasn't. The whole conclusion to his parents' divorce was quite possibly for him an emotional replay of what happened when he perceived that his mother had withdrawn from him during her pregnancy. He was angry then, but there was precious little he could have done about it. For a child who had claimed to have been neglected when he was younger, what happened during this divorce might have been his worst nightmare.

Dahmer was now a strapping six-footer who worked out with weights, acted out bizarre and aggressive behavior, had dabbled in ritualistic and magical thinking, had experimented with different forms of animal mutilation and disposal, and was a seriously trouble alcoholic who was withdrawn and hostile in private.

Looking at Jeffrey Dahmer's behavior from as objective a point of view as possible, it would be safe to say that, by the time he was graduating from high school, he was in crisis and in dire need of immediate intervention. Alcoholism wasn't his only problem. The divorce scenario was playing out some of his most negative perceptions about physical and emotional abandonment; his dreaded fantasy was taking the form of a frightening reality. In fact, the court legitimized his abandonment by declaring him emancipated and not in need of parental custody. Even for an emotionally stable child — and eighteen-year-olds who have just graduated from high school should still be considered children — such a court ruling can be unsettling. For a child in crisis who had experimented in the past with dismembering and mutilating small animals and other violent forms of acting out, his parents' divorce and the resulting court decision regarding custody could be regarded by some specialists as a significant trip wire.

Jeffrey Dahmer's situation deteriorated rapidly in June, 1978, as his parents' house turned into an armed camp. His father had cordoned off his space in the house and his mother, now with official custody of the younger brother David, retreated to her space. This further pointed up Jeffrey's probable sense of isolation and physical abandonment. To make matters worse, there was no communication between the parents, each of whom was about to move out of the house. Joyce Dahmer and her son David were the first to move.

Lionel didn't even know that Joyce had gone. He decided that he had had enough of living in a war zone and packed himself off to a motel, not realizing that he and Jeffrey were the only inhabitants of the house. As a result, when his parents vacated the premises, Jeffrey Dahmer was left alone in the house with no food, a broken refrigerator, and no money whatsoever.

Whatever structure his life may have had during his senior year in high school was now a bygone memory. It is probably hard for anyone to imagine what it feels like to be abandoned by a family, especially if you've been worrying obsessively about abandonment for ten years. Moreover, because the divorce happened after years of what he perceived as his mother's withdrawal and after over a year of bitter legal proceedings surrounding his father's having filed for a divorce, his being left alone in the house seemed almost like a just punishment.

Children, particularly children who are in trouble, often perceive the divorce of their parents as a direct result of their own problems. This is why most child and family therapists urge that parents going through a divorce take extra special care to make sure the child understands that the issues of the divorce involve the parents and not the children. Feelings of anxiety over abandonment are expected for children caught in a divorce. When the divorce is protracted and especially bitter, as court records show it was in the Dahmers' case, children can feel especially isolated. The divorce only compounded feelings of neglect and abandonment that Jeffrey had had from the time that he was an elementary school pupil. The entire process took its toll on an eighteen-year-old who woke up one morning to realize that both his parents had gone their separate directions and had left him in the house.

There are other issues that come into play which bear directly on the psychological state of someone in Jeffrey Dahmer's position. Children who perceive that their parents have withdrawn from them or who feel abandoned usually blame themselves. They often have dramatic feelings of loss of control and develop overwhelming fears about being alone or losing control of others. They may feel that unless they actively do something to keep people around them, they will suffer abandonment and will blame themselves for it. These obsessions are usually accompanied by unresolved childhood rage at their situation, hopelessness, and helplessness.

It is not out of the ordinary for children who believe they have been abandoned to stop their emotional development at or about the age when they sense the abandonment took place. For Jeffrey Dahmer, that would have been about the age of five or six. Many developmental psychologists theorize that children at that age are first trying to master their own feelings of rage and hostility at not being able to exercise control over the world around them. Children at five or six are entering into peer relationships at this time and face conflicts when they have to conform their own wants to the wants of a group. If Dahmer believed that he was abandoned, these are the very issues he would have difficulty with as an adult.

If we fast forward to age eighteen and imagine a truly abandoned Jeffrey Dahmer alone in his house without food or money, we can also imagine him suffering under fantasies of control or lack thereof. We can imagine that he was hungry for any kind of company, a hunger that was becoming obsessive. We can envision him in the same house where only a few years earlier he had experimented with killing and preserving animal parts. It was on the same property where he had dug his animal cemetery and was thought to have hung bones from trees above the burial mounds. It was also on the same property where he had brought his friends to see his collection of insects and bones. But now he was alone.

He had cavorted his way through high school, pumping up his ego and drowning his inhibitions in alcohol. He had done everything he could to attract attention and get himself surrounded with people. He had always been weird, but it was just his way to exert dominance over a world that was out of control and beyond his comprehension. He played out his games as his parents' marriage disintegrated to the point of open hostility and mutual flight from the house. He might have blamed himself. His attempts at control had utterly failed. Now he was completely and absolutely alone.

He was alone in his basement room with his barbells, passing away the hours by working out his frustration and drinking whatever beer or booze was left in the house. In those days when all of his fears finally came to pass, he must have fantasized what it would have been like to have a friend there to share the time. Maybe if he had a friend, he could make sure that the friend wouldn't leave, wouldn't be like his parents who had abandoned him. If he could have created someone who would not leave him, would it be like the specimens in his insect collection? What could he do to keep a friend in his house for just one night to ease the pain of being alone? What he had done when he was younger?

Young Jeffrey Dahmer had gone after road kills that he later preserved in solution while still in elementary school. Now eighteen-year-old Jeffrey Dahmer was feeling the urge to go looking for whatever he could find again. He set out in his car along Cleveland-Massillon Road to see what he could find. He was just out looking, possibly feeling much the same way he felt years earlier when he set out on his bike, looking for anything. In serial killer terminology he was trolling for something to medicate the feelings of loss and panic that were welling up inside him. And that was when he saw the nineteen-year-old hitchhiker named Steven Hicks.

Chapter Six

The Murder of Steven Hicks

No two people could have been more different than Jeffrey Dahmer and Steven Mark Hicks. Where Dahmer was generally alone and almost obsessive about controlling social situations by thrusting himself into the center of attention, Hicks was trusting and resilient and had many friends. Where Dahmer was terrified at the very thought of being abandoned, Hicks believed that people genuinely liked him and would prefer to be with him. Where Dahmer saw himself as a loner who had to act out many different personalities and strange behaviors to attract friends, Hicks saw himself as a socializer who was confident of his ability to make friends. Hicks seemed to have an innate belief that he was the same person whether he was alone or with friends. People like Jeffrey Dahmer, who are pathologically lonely, do not have that belief. They build their reality from the reactions of those around them and change according to the situation. These two people's fates were about to meet on a morning in June when Steven Hicks said goodbye to his parents and left to go hitchhiking to a rock concert. Jeffrey Dahmer didn't need to tell his parents goodbye. He hadn't seen them since they deserted the house.

On the surface, Jeffrey Dahmer and Steven Hicks came from very similar backgrounds. They were two teenaged boys who had grown up in middle-class housing developments in suburban Ohio and were about to seek their fortunes in life. Like Jeffrey, Hicks had graduated from high school just that June. The boys were neighbors, of a sort. Hicks had grown up in Coventry, Ohio, about fifteen miles away from Bath, but the two had never met during during their years in high school. They were on a collision course, however. On the night of June 25, 1978, a frantically lonely Jeffrey Dahmer would see the good-looking brown-haired Hicks walking along Cleveland-Massillon Road about a mile or so away from the Bath Township police department.

Hicks had left that same morning to hitch a ride over to a rock concert in Chippewa Lake Park. Friends of his had seen him thumbing on the roadside and drove him over to the concert where they spent much of the day together. Then his friends left, but not before agreeing to pick up Hicks later that night. They said they would meet up at an abandoned airstrip near Lockwood Corners and then head to a party after the concert. How would Steven get there? Not a problem, he told them, he would hitch over to Lockwood Corners. He certainly wasn't afraid of anything as he set out from Chippewa Lake Park because he knew the area and felt at home in this part of suburban Akron.

Dahmer was alone in the house on the night of June 25 as he had been since his parents left. Being alone was something he was accustomed to and that other people had recognized about him. Since he was in elementary school, Jeffrey Dahmer had always been perceived by friends and neighbors as a lonely child who was always on the outside. Dahmer told police he believed he was a loner by choice. He said he had no long-term relationships with people. He had been a loner since high school and had never had any best friends he could confide in.

By the time he was in high school, Jeffrey Dahmer also perceived he was very different from the teenagers in his suburban Ohio community. He knew that he was a homosexual. By age fifteen, he was experiencing vivid homosexual fantasies. However, these were bizarre, aberrant fantasies about control, superiority, domination, murder, and mutilation. While still a teenager in high school, he realized that his homosexual fantasies and his fantasies of killing and dismembering human beings were interlocked. He revealed to police in the days following his arrest for murder in Milwaukee that he received gratification from these fantasies, and they occurred many times. Whenever he had fantasies of homosexual activities, he also had fantasies of killing and dismembering people.

Perhaps because he was driven by what some might call a pathological sense of abandonment after his parents deserted him, Jeffrey Dahmer set out in his Oldsmobile to look for something to do or hoping to locate some companionship. He found it when he was driving southbound along the Cleveland-Massillon Road and saw a bare-chested Steven Hicks hitchhiking just down the way from the Bath Township firehouse on a warm late afternoon in early summer.

Jeffrey stopped to let the good-looking Hicks into the car and asked him over to the house for a few drinks. Hicks had been planning to party, friends told police who

looked for him in the days and weeks following his disappearance. Hicks probably decided that having a few
drinks with this kid about his own age would be a fun way
to pass the time. It is also possible that Hicks told
Dahmer that he was looking for a ride to Lockwood Corners and Dahmer promised to drive him over after stopping at his place for a beer or two. Dahmer could be a
charming person when he was trying to engage someone
socially. Hicks must have agreed willingly and gladly.
Not even Tracy Edwards, years later, would have guessed
that Dahmer was capable of a homicidal attack.

Jeffrey Dahmer drove Steven Hicks back to his house
on West Bath Road. The two of them cracked open cans
of beer, listened to some music, and talked in his bedroom. They sat on the bed, then Steven moved over to a
chair. It is here that events which Jeffrey Dahmer related
in his numerous statements to police from Milwaukee
and Bath, Ohio, differ from one another. On the night he
was arrested, Dahmer said to the police that his first
homicide occurred while he was eighteen and picked up a
white male nineteen-year-old hitchhiker on the road in
Bath, Ohio, near the firehouse and took him back to his
house. The report made on Tuesday, June 23, 1991, includes the following: "He states that he took him home
and had homosexual sex with him and was drinking beer
and became intoxicated. He states they got into a physical fight because the nineteen-year-old individual tried
to leave and that during the fight, he states he struck the
hitchhiker with a barbell. He states that the blow of the
barbell caused the death of the individual."

At Dahmer's trial, however, Detective Dennis Murphy read Dahmer's 166-page confession to the court in
which Dahmer specifically said he did not have sex with
the hitchhiker. Murphy testified, "He states the first

homicide occurred around October of 1978 when he saw a white male hitchhiker whom he describes as nineteen, 5'10" tall, skinny build, maybe 150 pounds, having straight collar-length hair, cleanshaven, and he believed he was not a homosexual. He states he did not have sex with this individual, he just invited him in for a drink and when this individual wanted to leave, that's when he hit him with a barbell."

Jeffrey Dahmer also gave a confession to the Bath Township police which was written up in Lieutenant Richard Munsey's report on the missing Steven Hicks whose body had never been found. Dahmer said that in 1978 he picked up a hitchhiker at the Cleveland-Massillon Road. It was warm out that afternoon, Dahmer said, because he remembered that his victim was not wearing a shirt. Dahmer talked about buying or smoking pot with Steven Hicks or just having a few drinks. They decided to go to the Dahmer residence on West Bath Road where they drank beer and talked. After a while, however, Hicks said he wanted to leave. Perhaps, Dahmer had made a promise to drive him over to Lockwood Corners and Hicks reminded Dahmer of this. Dahmer didn't say anything about that, but he did say that he wanted Hicks to stay and couldn't bear his leaving. He didn't want to be alone in the house again. "He wanted to leave and I didn't want him to leave," Dahmer said. Maybe they did have an actual physical confrontation, as Dahmer told police when he was arrested. On the other hand, maybe he just struck Hicks before he realized what was happening. Dahmer told the Ohio police that Hicks was sitting either on a chair or on a bed. Dahmer approached him from behind and hit him with a barbell on the head. Then he used the barbell to strangle him to death. There was no mention of sex.

Jeffrey is the only witness to what happened on the night he picked up Steven Hicks in his car. Only Jeffrey Dahmer knows for sure whether or not he had sex with Steven Hicks on the night he murdered him. He specifically made it clear to police in his first two statements that he had had sex with Hicks. In his later confessions, he insisted he did not have sex with his victim. The later, signed statements were the confessions that were read to the court during Dahmer's trial. In those same later confessions, Dahmer also said that he picked up Steven Hicks sometime in October, 1978, not in June when Steven Hicks was first reported missing. This is another discrepancy between the two statements. The discrepancy in dates was partially resolved in Dahmer's final guilty plea to the murder of Steven Hicks for which he was sentenced to life imprisonment by Judge James Williams of the Summit County Common Pleas Court in Akron. He acknowledged in that plea that the crime took place on June 25, 1978.

All of Dahmer's confessions about the murder of Steven Hicks differ from each other concerning whether Dahmer and Hicks engaged in sexual relations on the night of the murder. This is an important point because the Hicks murder was Jeffrey Dahmer's first homicide. It came at a time when he was most vulnerable to his feelings of abandonment and loneliness. He was also most vulnerable to the fantasies of sex, violence, and murder that he told the police were "interlocked" in his mind by the time he was fifteen. It seems natural, given the pattern of Dahmer's crimes, that he would have been partially motivated by sex urges at some point during the encounter.

If Dahmer did not have sex with Steven Hicks on the night of the murder, it would be one of the few homicides he committed in which he explicitly said he did not have sex with the victim. It, therefore, would not fit the pattern of all of his other murders in which he had oral sex with the victim at some point during the encounter. It's also unlikely that the first of all Dahmer's murders, committed when he was also at his most vulnerable, would not satisfy his complex fantasy of sex, murder, and eventual mutilation.

This murder was also the "imprinting murder," setting the stage for a pattern of murder that Dahmer followed obsessively for the next thirteen years. This "imprinting murder" followed a pattern of animal mutilation that Dahmer had evolved since he was an elementary school child. Furthermore, Dahmer committed this murder after a traumatic event, the loss of both parents from the family home. Among specialists in the psychology of serial crimes, the first crime committed partially as a result of a traumatic event has even greater significance than those crimes which follow; even if those crimes follow much the same pattern as the first crime. Thus, it is even more likely than ever that Dahmer would have either had sex with his first victim, tried to have sex with that victim, or had sex with the victim's body after death. All of these variables would still have been extremely embarrassing to Dahmer after his arrest in Milwaukee. Thus, in subsequent interrogations, he would have been likely to make a point of denying having sex with Steven Hicks. In fact, he did just that only days after admitting that he did have sex with Steven Hicks.

Could Dahmer's memory about the Steven Hicks murder have been faulty? Was Dahmer really not sure whether he had sex with Steven Hicks? Milwaukee police detective Dennis Murphy answered that when he testified that he specifically asked Dahmer if he remembered the name Steven Hicks and Jeffrey Dahmer said he did. "I asked him how he remembered it," Murphy testified, "and he said it was his first one and you always remember your first one."

Moreover, inasmuch as Jeffrey Dahmer told police in the first statement he made within hours of his arrest that he had sex with Hicks, it seems unlikely that his later stories would be more truthful as he more fully adjusted to his arrest and eventual trial. Chances are much greater, therefore, that the first story Dahmer told to the police would be more truthful about specific details concerning the crimes than later stories.

Why is the question of sex an important issue in this homicide? First of all, Dahmer's different versions of the story of his first homicide can help provide a window into his state of mind both during the Hicks murder and, years later, at the time he was arrested. Assuming for the present that he was telling the absolute truth when he revealed to detectives Murphy and Kennedy that he'd had sex with Steven Hicks during their encounter, his subsequent denial shows not only that he was feeling guilty and ashamed about what he'd done, but that he probably experienced guilt and shame in all of his subsequent Milwaukee murders. In West Allis and later in his own apartment, he was angry that he was lonely and ashamed and guilty that his "interlocked" fantasies of homosexual sex and brutal homicide spilled over into reality the night he murdered Steven Hicks. Throughout each of his subsequent murders, the guilt and shame from the very first murder were searing inside him. Dahmer probably felt that only continual consumption of alcohol and more violence kept those feelings in check. He was literally medicating himself on alcohol and violence.

Second, Dahmer's building up of denial about having had sex with Steven Hicks also reveals that the first murder might have "imprinted" a pattern of homicidal behavior so strongly upon Dahmer that it set the pattern for the subsequent homicides. In serial murder cases like this, the first homicide is fraught with so much meaning for the killer that he often repeats the crime as if acting out the shameful events will somehow take away some of the pain that he is feeling. It doesn't work because each new killing carries less and less emotion until nothing the killer does can ease the pain. Eventually the killer finds a way to self-destruct or defuse himself by getting caught. At that point, the overwhelming realization that he is finally identified usually causes him to confess to everything spontaneously to ease some of the pain. It is only later, as the legal system begins to process the killer through a series of hearings and court appearances, that he adjusts to the situation and begins to modify his story. This is apparently what happened in Dahmer's case.

Third, Dahmer's changing his story about having had sex with Steven Hicks is also an indicator that the real issue for Dahmer was his perceptions of homosexuality at the time he committed the crime. He hadn't yet confronted it in high school except by acting out aberrant behaviors. He'd admitted to the police that he'd been fantasizing about homosexual activities since he was fifteen. Now, alone in the house with a boy his own age who probably stimulated him sexually, he probably fantasized about coming on to Hicks. It is very likely that Steven Hicks was not a homosexual and might have been repelled by Dahmer. If so, Dahmer's sexual advances were probably what shamed him the most because it was this seduction attempt that drove Hicks away and so panicked Dahmer that he struck him with a barbell and killed him. Sex, even before loneliness, could well have been the trigger that instigated the murder. But because sex was "interlocked" with violence, Dahmer could have become even more sexually aroused after Hicks was unconscious. Accordingly, it is also highly possible that after Dahmer had struck Hicks, he performed oral sex on him and then was so repulsed by what he'd done, he strangled him and found himself having to get rid of the body. If so, it was a terrible murder in his mind and caused him so much pain that he has been struggling with it ever since.

Dahmer seemed a lot less conflicted about telling the police the story of his disposal of Steven Hicks's remains. In fact, he'd disposed of animal remains so many times during his elementary and high school years that it was a well-rehearsed scenario by the time he got rid of Hicks's body. He said that after he had strangled Hicks, he dragged the body outside and around to the side entrance to the crawl space underneath the foundation of one of the corners of the house. Dahmer had often played in the crawl space when he was a child, and the family had also used it to store items.

Dahmer brought a long kitchen knife into the crawl space and began the methodical process of carving off Hicks's arms and legs from the torso of the body and stuffed the body parts into plastic bags. It was shortly before 3:00 A.M. He was nervous now, still woozy from drinking and heady from the kill. However, he wanted to get the evidence as far away from the house as possible. Dahmer put the plastic bags full of body parts in the trunk of the four-door Oldsmobile in the garage and drove off to dump the bags. However, as he was driving he was spotted by a police car and pulled over for driving erratically. The police officers asked for his license and registration and told him he was driving left of center. They pulled him out of the car and administered a drunk driving test on the spot. However, he passed the test and was allowed to drive away. Ironically, the remains of Steven Hicks were in the trunk of his car the whole time, but the car wasn't searched. Had Dahmer flunked his drunk driving test at the scene, he likely would have been arrested and the car impounded. That would have resulted in the discovery of Hicks's body parts in the trunk and the abrupt end to Dahmer's career as a serial killer. However, Dahmer wasn't arrested and was allowed to drive away from the scene with the mutilated body of his first victim stuffed into plastic bags in the trunk.

Jeffrey Dahmer was in no mood to tempt fate any further, not with a corpse in his car. He turned around and headed for home where he pulled into the garage again and brought the plastic bags back into the crawl space where he sealed them up and tried to forget about them. However, it was hot that June and in a few days, the gasses released from the decomposing flesh were already pushing their way out of the plastic bags. The whole house was putrid from the stench of rotting flesh. His mother or father could have come home any day and discovered the body parts. He had to get rid of them.

Maybe Dahmer figured he'd bury the bags or conceal them in some way. First, he tried to stuff them into a drainage pipe behind the house, but the bones were too rigid and the bags wouldn't fit. Then he tried to dig a grave right alongside the drainage pipe but the ground was too rough and rocky. He tried to scoop out enough soil to conceal the body completely, but there were too many rocks and all he could do was scrape a shallow grave out of the soil. He was tired and still concerned that one of his parents might show up any day. Thus, the shallow grave would have to do for the time being, so he left the bags under the ground behind his house for the next couple of weeks.

But soon Dahmer began to panic again. What if children came to play over in those woods? What if they were digging and found the plastic bags? Dahmer had played right in that same area when he was younger and had dug up dirt looking for bones or flints. Other kids could do the same things. No, he decided, he'd have to get rid of the body once and for all and leave absolutely no chance for discovery. After a couple of weeks of worrying about the incriminating evidence, Dahmer dug the body parts up and set to work removing the flesh the way he'd done when he was younger. First, he cut all the body parts into little pieces, then he pared the flesh away from the bone. He used acid to strip away all the flesh and then put the pieces of flesh and organs into jars of acid until they dissolved into a brown murky liquid. This liquid he flushed down the drain pipe and it was carried away into the township sewage system. Now all he had left were bones: legs, arms, ribs, a spine, and a skull. These he repeatedly smashed with a sledgehammer, pounding them into smaller and smaller pieces until there was no fragment of bone larger than a small person's hand.

There were hundreds and hundreds of fragments, all that was left of the hitchhiker named Steven Hicks. Dahmer told the Ohio police that he then took the bone fragments, climbed up to a rocky cliff area in the back side of his home, and spread the bones around the area. He stood there on a ledge, he said, and began spinning in a 360-degree circle, throwing the bones out over the ground as he turned. It was almost like a ritual, the spreading of his first victim to the four winds, raining down upon the rocky ground in a grisly shower of human bone pieces. When it was over, it was almost like Steven Hicks had never been. Then Dahmer burned Hicks's wallet and all his identification, took the knife and the necklace that Hicks had been wearing around his neck when Dahmer picked him up, and drove them over to a bridge by the Cuyahoga River. He tossed the knife and necklace into the river and they were carried far downstream . . . and out of Dahmer's life for the next thirteen years.

A little over six weeks later, Dahmer's solitary existence in the house came to an end when his father Lionel and Lionel's future wife Shari stopped by for a visit to see Jeffrey and his brother. When they arrived, they noticed the grim condition of the house and the strangely disturbed nature of Jeffrey. Where was David? they asked. Why was Jeffrey acting so strange? Jeffrey told his father that Joyce had taken the younger David and moved in with her family in Chippewa Falls, Wisconsin. Jeffrey was all alone in the house. His mother had made him promise not to tell his father that they were gone. Until Lionel had arrived, Jeffrey had kept that promise. At this point, though, he had no money and no refrigerator. He was completely alone.

Lionel was outraged and filed a motion in court to order Joyce to return David, who was a minor child, to the jurisdiction of the Summit County court. Meanwhile Lionel and Shari moved back into the house and Jeffrey was once again living with a family. In just a few short weeks he would leave for his freshman year at Ohio State University in Columbus. He would try as best he could to return to normalcy, but it wouldn't work. The face and

100

memory of Steven Hicks would haunt him until the very day an Ohio police officer named Richard Munsey would hold a photo of Hicks in front of him and ask him about the nameless hitchhiker he had told detectives Murphy and Kennedy about the night he was arrested. And Dahmer's positive identification of Hicks and his description of the crime would set off another search which would dig up the backyard of his West Bath Road house while officers sprayed Luminol mist into the crawl space. There, thirteen years later, an eerie green handprint glowed on the cinder block and an outline of a pool of green, dried blood glowed in the shadows. The remains of Steven Hicks had been found, and the missing persons report filed by his parents thirteen years earlier was finally cleared.

Jeffrey Dahmer has been sentenced by a court in Akron, Ohio, to life in prison for the murder of Steven Hicks.

Chapter Seven

A Human Time Bomb

Maybe Jeffrey Dahmer believed that his troubles would end when he left his house in Bath Township for Columbus and the sprawling Ohio State University campus in late August, 1978. But if either Dahmer or his father thought that his behavior would change once he moved to the campus, they were mistaken. On the surface, he might have looked just like any other newly graduated Ohio kid joining the thousands of other Ohioans at one of the largest universities in the country. He certainly was as bright as the average entering freshman if not brighter, and he registered for the same required core courses that most entering freshmen take.

There was a huge difference between Jeffrey Dahmer and the average entering freshman, however. Where the average high school graduate might overindulge at Friday night keg parties during the fall rush, or have a few drinks too many and get rowdy at one of the many Columbus bars that cater to the campus population, Dahmer was a full-blown alcoholic who could barely get through the day without having to return to a bottle for another drink. He had been drinking regularly since junior high school, should have been considered an alcoholic by the time he was in senior high, had murdered a young man earlier that summer. By age nineteen, he was in critical need of medical intervention.

Jeffrey Dahmer didn't even make a pretense of trying to keep up with any class work. He came to college, stocked his room with liquor, and simply began drinking day and night. To the students who got to know him, it was obvious that he wasn't one of them. He was a drunk. "He used to take bottles to class with him and came back drunk," his Morrill Tower dormitory roommate Michael Prochaska told the *Ohio State Lantern.* He said that Jeffrey had a serious drinking problem, had no friends, and received no mail. The loner from Hazel Harvey Elementary and Revere High was still a loner at Ohio State. Without the vigilance of teachers and other parents in the neighborhood, Dahmer was now even without the semblance of the safety net he had in Bath. The last time he was left completely alone, he murdered someone. Now, at Ohio State, he was again alone, albeit in a crowd. One could only guess at what might have happened had his father not intervened before the end of the fall quarter.

Booze was expensive and Dahmer was constantly running out of money. It was a situation he would find himself in consistently throughout the remainder of his next ten years. He had spent so much money on alcohol during the first few weeks of his residence at Ohio State, he started selling his plasma to the Columbia blood bank and used the money he made to buy more booze. He was drinking so much, however, that he could never catch up with his expenses. When a watch, a radio, and $120 in cash were stolen from another resident's room at the dorm, the Ohio State campus police questioned Dahmer, but charges against him were never filed. At around the same time, an acquaintance of his from Ohio State recognized Jeffrey unconscious at first and then stumbling around in a drunken stupor on a Columbus sidewalk. He wrote Dahmer off as a college student. He looked like nothing more than a common drunk and not a college student at all.

After Dahmer was arrested in Milwaukee, newspapers profiling his life reported that in fall, 1978, when his father Lionel visited him in his dorm room in the Towers, he was struck by the rows and rows of liquor bottles lining the shelves. This may have been his first serious confrontation with his barely adult son as an alcoholic. "We could see it was fruitless," Lionel told the *Milwaukee Sentinel*. Lionel decided that his son Jeffrey needed to stand on his own two feet. It was time for his Uncle Sam, rather than his father, to teach him how. "Perhaps he could be straightened out by the service," Lionel asserted at the time.

Since Lionel was about to marry Shari, he most probably didn't want to be vigilant about the activities of his adult son. He maintained that he had been lied to by his ex-wife Joyce concerning her taking care of both children while he was living in a motel. She was absent from her older son's life, and now Jeffrey was an undisciplined drinker who was flunking out of college after one quarter. Jeffrey looked as if he was having serious emotional problems as well; he needed discipline and he would get it.

On Christmas Eve, 1978, Lionel Dahmer married Shari Jordan. On December 30, 1978, only a few months after Jeffrey Dahmer had been left alone in the house, murdered Steven Hicks, experienced his parents' divorce, and flunked out of college, he was taken to a US Army recruiting office where he signed his enlistment papers and prepared to ship out on January 12 the following year for basic training at Fort McClellan in Anniston, Alabama.

When Jeffrey Dahmer filled out his enlistment papers, he chose the Military Police as his career. It was all spit and polish, but it required him to complete an especially tough training program. Jeffrey Dahmer washed out of the program and in May, 1979, was transferred to Fort Sam Houston in Texas where he began another training program as a medical specialist. This was a unique twist of fate for the boy who used to delight in brutalizing and dissecting animals. The young man who, according to the psychiatric testimony at his trial, found that the only way he could relate to and feel wanted by his father was to participate with him in filleting fish and learning about the anatomies of small animals, would now be studying the human anatomy and human physiology. The killer who less than a year earlier had murdered and dissected his victim was now taking courses in helping the wounded, dealing with injuries, and combat surgical procedures. It was as if Dahmer were receiving government basic training for the crimes he would later commit on a regular basis.

Dahmer's training lasted about five weeks. He learned the routine hospital procedures of a nurse's aide and the more advanced emergency medical techniques of combat medics who stabilized the wounded under battlefield conditions prior to evacuation. Dahmer learned about drugs, pain killers, sedatives, drugs that paralyze the nervous system, and invasive medical procedures as well. He learned the fine points of human anatomy through diagrams, schematics, and vivid photographs and had hands-on experience with laboratory specimens as well. For a person who had experimented on his own during his elementary years, this program must have been a uniquely satisfying experience. Dahmer satisfactorily fulfilled all of the requirements and received his military specialty qualification. He would soon be shipping out again, this time to his own front-line military unit.

On July 13, 1979, PFC Jeffrey Dahmer received his orders to report to the Headquarters Company in the Second Battalion of the US Army's Sixty-eighth Armored Regiment of the Eighth Infantry Division (mechanized infantry division) in Baumholder, West Germany. This was one of the front-line military units of the Cold War that would continue for the next decade until the Berlin Wall was torn down in 1989. Here was the place, less than a hundred miles south of Frankfurt, where the US mechanized forces would assemble in the face of an attack by Warsaw Pact armor on NATO. Dahmer was assigned to a unit supporting the Army's most advanced tanks, self-propelled artillery, and the Bradley fighting vehicles that form the backbone of any mechanized infantry division. This would become one of the flashpoints of World War III, and Dahmer was there to serve as a combat medic.

In 1979, the Army was still in transition, recovering from the humiliations it suffered in Vietnam. The all-volunteer army in the late 1970s was a haven for many young men, who needed a structure to their lives more than they needed the actual career training the Army offered. This was the case for the deeply troubled Jeffrey Dahmer who set up his bar-in-a-briefcase in his enlisted men's barracks. At first, Dahmer was regarded as one of the brightest and best of his medical unit. He had been to college, had a knowledge of human anatomy that dated back to his childhood, and seemed motivated to learn and succeed. But the Army didn't know that Dahmer was an alcoholic, and soon that pattern began to influence his performance on the job.

Both Dennis Rodriguez and Michael Masters bunked with Dahmer in the enlisted men's barracks. They both remember that Dahmer carried a briefcase that opened up into a portable bar. It was a camouflage for the liquor that was not allowed in the soldiers' quarters on base. But the superior officers also tended to look the other way at their enlisted personnel's habits behind closed doors because almost all of the specialists on base had qualified after a selective training program. If they performed their jobs during the day, the thinking went, maybe they should be allowed to indulge a little during their off-duty hours. Most of that thinking has now changed.

Dahmer's bar-in-a-briefcase was a cleverly designed contraption that held martini mixers, a shaker, stirrers, glasses, and flasks. Dahmer liked to mix himself up a martini after he signed off-duty for the weekend, lie back on his bunk, and play his head-banger heavy metal music into his stereo headphones. "He would drink and have his headphones on, kind of be shut out from the rest of the world," Dennis Rodriguez said. He recalled that after Dahmer had mixed up a shaker of martinis, pounded back a few, and gotten into zone-out position on his bed, there was no communicating with him. "He wouldn't move. He wouldn't even go out for chow. He wouldn't get takeout food. He'd drink until he passed out and then wake up and drink some more. There were a lot of people who used to drink, but not like him."

Other than his drinking during the first year, Dahmer was considered to be a good medic by his unit and its leaders. "He was an average or slightly above average soldier in his first year," Dahmer's Army platoon leader David Goss told the Ohio newspapers in an interview after Dahmer's arrest in Milwaukee. "I was a clinical specialist. He was a combat medic. At the aid station, I'd go back to diagnose a patient and he was right there with me, eager to learn."

Dahmer had a strange personality that other people in his platoon could see even though he went through all the right soldiering motions during his first year in the service. First of all, other members of his unit recalled, he was a loner. That label which had followed him throughout his life and through his one and only quarter at Ohio State was as applicable now as it ever was. In much the same terms that his roommate from college used, David Goss also remembered that Dahmer was unlike other GIs who surround themselves with items from home or photos of their family. "Jeff didn't have that. His room was set up strictly militarily. He didn't have any pictures of his home. I never saw a picture of his parents." Then, in a statement eerily reminiscent of Michael Prochaska at Ohio State, Goss said, "I don't ever remember him getting any mail."

Dahmer never spoke of his family to the other men, and David Goss figured that was also strange. Most GIs overseas tend to speak of their family and background a great deal because the memories form a legitimate basis for establishing a life-style in a foreign country. "I didn't even know he had a brother. He just mentioned his father, mother, and grandmother. The only thing he said about his mother and father, [was] they recently divorced. He said he didn't feel welcome around their houses," Goss recalled. Dahmer didn't talk about girlfriends either, friends said, even though they remember that he would sometimes go into town to frequent one of the local female prostitutes.

Goss said that Dahmer opened up to him sometimes about his family and said that he stayed with his grandmother whenever possible because she was the only person he could relate to. "He could talk to me about anything," Goss told the *Akron Beacon Journal*, "family problems with his mother and father, that he didn't get along with either one, that's why he'd stay with his grandmother."

Members of his unit said that Dahmer sometimes played a chess game or two, spent time at the library where he read books and magazines, and when he was sober never went out of his way to get into fights. He simply did the work that was required of him and slipped off at night into his music. Goss and other members of Dahmer's unit also remember that Jeff could be a literate conversationalist who had opinions and could express them in a friendly way. He seemed "really smart" one of the members of his unit told the press. He was able to carry on "a lengthy and intelligent conversation on any subject."

At first, Dahmer would drink at night and report for work in the morning. He was able to control his habit and not let his drinking interfere with his work. His barracks mates knew that he drank heavily and sometimes kidded about how inebriated he would get in the evenings. However, toward the second year of his enlistment, Dahmer's problems got progressively worse. Michael Masters said that it looked to him as if Dahmer were heading down a long slope of decreasing productivity. But however bad it was getting, Dahmer never let it show.

"He always had that look about him," Masters said. It

reminded him of something that was more "sinister" than angry. "He would never explode. He never showed anger. He would never act it out. He was very calculating. I don't know, he was on a steady decline in life. He was on a losing skid and didn't know how to pick himself up."

Then, toward the very end of 1980, just about a year and a half after he arrived in Germany, the warning signs of danger began to reveal themselves. Dahmer was a fan of heavy metal music and his space in the barracks was decorated with heavy metal trappings and posters. Right above his bed, there was a large poster of Iron Maiden glaring down at him as he lay there with his headphones on. Jeffrey Dahmer began to develop two distinct personalities. When he wasn't drinking, he was still something of the cutup he was in high school. This time, however, "doing a Dahmer" was more like an impersonation of a W.C. Fields drunk than a person having an epileptic seizure. But after he started drinking, he would get surly and belligerent. He would pick fights and indulge in hate rampages against homosexuals and blacks.

People remember that it was as if Dahmer had separate masks. When he became angry and hostile after a few drinks, the dopey smile would drop away and a blank mask of anger would be in its place. After his expression changed, it was as if another part of Dahmer's brain would take over. He would suddenly become explosively angry; he would pick fights. Dahmer would start hurling racist challenges at anybody in shouting distance and his offensiveness turned off all his barracks mates and alienated him from individuals in his unit who could have become his friends. Since he was in a unit of soldiers who were mostly as big and as strong as he was, Dahmer posed no real threat. When the fighting became physical, other members of his unit wrestled him to his bunk until he had a few more drinks and settled back. If he was just being verbally abusive, the members of his unit mostly left him alone to wallow in his own thoughts.

A Dahmer drinking spell usually began with three or so quick drinks and a lapsing back into music. He would slam his headphones over his ears, put a Black Sabbath tape into his cassette, and settle back on his bunk. As he had more and more martinis, he'd start to pick fights with whoever else was around. Eventually, he'd settle down again with some more drinks, more tapes, and pass out. He'd sleep for a few hours, wake up, hit the bottle again, and pass out once more. This was how he spent most of his weekends during the first year and a half. Sometimes he'd take his briefcase away with him and come back early Monday morning, woozy but functioning; ready to report. Toward the beginning of 1981, however, his drinking problem worsened severely.

His racism turned from general obnoxiousness to explicit remarks directed at members of his unit. One soldier in his platoon, Billy Capshaw, remembered how ugly Dahmer became to the black soldiers in the unit after he'd put away a few drinks. He said that Dahmer usually gave him trouble when he was drinking, but when he was sober he once gave him a birthday card. It was strange, but Capshaw knew that Dahmer was a potentially dangerous person. "I knew for a fact," he said, "that he was going to hurt me if he ever got hold of me. He would run after you like a crazy man, like [a] wild nut."

Then Dahmer's two-day binges turned into three-day benders and finally into week-long affairs. "It started to affect his job and appearance," Dave Goss explained to the *Akron Beacon Journal*. "He started missing work. He would come to work at battalion aid station under the influence. You could smell it on his breath. He'd be staggering. Or

111

he wouldn't show up for work."

During his final year, even his barracks mates made fun of his behavior. He had deteriorated so badly that he had become a hopeless sight. David Goss said that Dahmer eventually stayed drunk most of the time. He rarely left his bunk, and when he did he was rarely able to walk upright. The other soldiers in his room made cruel comments about him, took pictures of him while he was passed out, and generally taunted him. Dahmer was unable to respond. He couldn't hit or lash out at anybody because he was almost incapable of holding a thought in his mind for more than a couple of seconds. In fact, during his final months before being placed under a form of house arrest, Goss remembered, "He stayed in his bed drinking, cracking jokes. He was too drunk. He'd screw up the punch line and then he'd laugh."

In the 1970s, and especially after the American experience in Southeast Asia, NATO forces were getting especially vigilant about soldiers who were substance abusers. Pentagon reports about the operating effectiveness of US forces in Asia were extremely critical about the impact of drugs and alcohol on the behavior of Army enlisted personnel. Therefore, in the latter part of the 1970s, the Army instituted new therapy programs to deal with alcohol and drug abusers. Dahmer was a capable specialist, one whose career the Army wanted to salvage if at all possible. As Dahmer's drinking problem worsened and he showed up for duty unable to perform his responsibilities, his superiors sought to place him in an alcohol rehabilitation program.

However, it seemed to those in his unit that Dahmer simply wanted out of the service and might have been using alcohol as his method of choice. More and more frequently during the third year of his enlistment, people would see him hopping into a cab and leaving the base on Friday afternoons. He wouldn't return until Sunday night and would be incapable of functioning. According to David Goss, the Army eventually had enough and began restricting his privileges, restricting him to the base, and forcing him into rehab. Goss said that during the last six months of Dahmer's Army stint, he was put through the military's alcohol abuse program. It was a stern program, in many ways like Alcoholics Anonymous, where the abuser was forced to conform to a strict code of discipline. By forcing the abuser to stick to a precise code of behavior and restricting the person's freedom in other areas, the program was designed to empower the abuser to resume control of his life. It didn't work in Dahmer's case.

As Dahmer resisted the program, the terms and conditions of his behavioral restrictions became harsher. In his last two months in the service, Dahmer might have been sober, but it was at a great loss of personal freedom. Dahmer became a prisoner of the Army under what amounted to nothing less than house arrest. First, he was restricted to his room in the barracks unless he was under escort. Next, the base commander at Baumholder ordered that Dahmer's civilian clothing be removed from the barracks so that he was only allowed to wear his military uniform. He was permitted to use the bathroom, but was only allowed to enter the mess hall three times a day for meals. Twice a week he was physically escorted to the PX to buy necessities such as soap, deodorant, and toothpaste. However, he was not allowed to purchase magazines or chewing gum. During the second year of his enlistment, Dahmer was turned into a kind of robot through this program.

David Goss said that Dahmer was eventually "found unsuitable for military service due to alcohol abuse." He was discharged after two years and a few months, well short of his three-year enlistment. Goss remembers that as Dahmer left, he pronounced what amounted to a dire warning. " 'I may not have made it in the military, but now that I'm getting out, things will be different,' " Goss recounted Dahmer's words. " 'Some day you'll hear about me again. You'll see me or you will read about me, but you will hear about me again.' That was the last thing he said," Goss told the *Akron Beacon Journal*. "Then we finished the ride to the airport."

Goss thought to himself that maybe Dahmer had determined to make something out of his life. However, Goss also remembered Dahmer saying that there was one serious thing that he could not talk about. Dahmer talked about many things, but kept referring to the one thing he could never speak of. Goss would ask him about his secret "thing," but Jeffrey steadfastly refused to divulge what "it" was. "He'd say there was something he could not talk about. I'd say 'There's something bugging you, isn't there?' He'd say, 'Yes, but I can't discuss it with you.' "

Was it the murder of Steven Hicks that was eating away at Jeffrey Dahmer, clawing its way to the surface so that he could confront the terror of his actions? Was his terrible secret the driving force behind his complete collapse in the service?

Dahmer also failed to respond to what should have been a straightforward rehab program. He was calling attention to himself and punishing himself in the Army. He made himself the butt of jokes and placed himself constantly at risk. These behaviors are often typical of some-one who wants to get caught but is too afraid to face the consequences of what he's done. If he can be punished for something else, it might take the place of being punished for the act he really feels guilty about. This "replacement reaction" is also prototypical of serial killers in the very earliest stages of their criminal careers when they're most easily discovered or caught. If they can slip through the wall they begin to build around themselves, their denial becomes stronger, their camouflage more effective, and their killing episodes take on a more routine and methodical aspect to them.

Dahmer was vulnerable in the Army. His negative behavior was so close to the surface that one might have even penetrated his deepest secrets if the probe were persistent enough. He was summarily diagnosed as an alcoholic and a screw up, and let go. With the murder of Steven Hicks still in his mind, he made his dire prediction to David Goss. Soon Dahmer would return to the United States. Within years, he would become a full-blown serial killer acting out his racist and homophobic impulses. Dahmer might have hated himself for the killing of Steven Hicks and might have pitied himself because he was so forlorn, but one he had escaped the traps he had set for himself, there was no stopping him. He was a time bomb whose fuse was growing shorter with every passing day.

Chapter Eight

West Allis

On March 24, 1981, the Army returned Dahmer to the United States from West Germany. Two days later in South Carolina on March 26, he was formally discharged from the Army under Chapter 9 of the Code of Military Justice, the substance abuse clause. Dahmer had no job, no skills, some vocational training in health care, but no real prospects for the future. Despite his high I.Q. scores in the Army, his alcoholism had effectively flunked him out of college in the first quarter and then washed him out of the Armed Forces. At this point in his life Dahmer was like a piece of flotsam drifting with the currents. He was without self-propulsion, without motivation, without the inner drive that most young people have when seeking their fortune in the world. He had failed at everything he had tried not because he didn't care enough about anything to succeed, but because the internal set of psychological switches that controlled his self-motivation motor were turned off. It left him feeling empty and permanently abandoned.

To medicate that feeling of emptiness, that just-below-the-surface pain that never went away, Dahmer anesthetized himself. He tore apart the viscera from animals that he'd killed because it provided him with a sense of control. He also had enjoyed happy memories with his father as they filleted fish together. According to prosecution medical witnesses Drs. Judith Becker and Park Deitz, those fond memories of companionship with his father "imprinted" upon Jeffrey what it felt like to be a wanted child. If Dahmer had associated those particular feelings with actual dismemberment of the fish he'd caught, the simple act of cutting up a fish might stimulate the feeling of being wanted and loved. This may have been the motivation for Jeffrey's cutting up and mincing the small fish that his schoolmates preferred to toss back into the water. When asked why he was cutting them up, Dahmer would say that it made him feel good. That response can possibly stand as an early example of how Dahmer managed to conjure up good feelings about himself and his family in an otherwise emotional void. It was a way, albeit dysfunctional, of combatting the pervasive sensation of emptiness that might have accompanied him everywhere.

Dahmer also medicated himself with alcohol. By drinking until he passed out, he was able to dull some of the pain that haunted him. It was a way to kill the fear that he was not wanted and to distance himself from feelings of anxiety about having no place in the world. Many teenage alcoholics report that they drink because they have no self-image. Drinking simply helps them to fill a disturbing void about themselves. It is not farfetched that the alcohol addiction that eventually unraveled Dahmer's life initially began as a form of self medication.

In addition to his drinking and his morbid fascination with death and dismemberment, Dahmer's apathy toward other people and about life in general was an adult symptom of feelings of having been a neglected child. Apathy is a red-flag symptom because it is actually the flip side of a set

117

of powerful and often violent emotions that the apathetic person truly feels. In this way, apathy is a form of camouflage, a kind of placeholder that often masks the person's misunderstood but all-consuming episodic bouts of rage. Apathetic behavior usually precedes eruptions of intense violence. Families of spree killers or mass murderers usually comment that the killer seemed perpetually apathetic and that his explosion into homicidal violence caught everyone by complete surprise. Dahmer's apparent apathy about himself and his life, in combination with his alcoholism and his inability to motivate himself, was actually a warning sign of imminent danger as well as an indicator that he might have already committed violent acts.

After being discharged from the service, it was an apathetic, destructive, and very troubled Dahmer that set foot on American soil after having spent almost two years in Europe. Rather than returning to Ohio to face his family and try to pick up what was left of his life, Dahmer decided to head for Florida. He was in no condition to confront his father after having failed at college and the Army. He figured maybe he could support himself in Florida for awhile. If he succeeded there, perhaps he could return to Ohio with some semblance of dignity. He left South Carolina and headed south to Miami Beach.

Those six or so months he spent in Florida were almost phantom months in Dahmer's life. Florida police authorities say that Dahmer stayed in Florida for about six months and worked at a sandwich shop near 163rd Street over the causeway in Miami Beach. They have no address for him and say rumors circulated that Dahmer might have lived on the beach itself while working. When he was arrested in Milwaukee, Dahmer told the police that he had stayed in

Miami for about a year. After having confessed to the murdering and dismembering of Steven Hicks, Dahmer insisted that "nothing of this happened" while he was in Miami. It was an answer that had presumably come in response to a police question regarding Dahmer's activities while in Florida because of his admission to murder in Ohio.

The police in serial murder cases, such as Dahmer's, know that killers simply don't stop killing. They also know that serial killers gradually become desensitized to the act of murder as they commit more and more crimes. However, in the early years, the first murders may cause them some feelings of shame and even remorse or guilt. Therefore, serial killers are likely to omit confessions of crimes during their early years if they are still embarrassed by the nature of the murders. Police also realize that often the only person who can lead police to a body dumpsite is the serial killer himself who might be reluctant to do so, especially in a death penalty state like Florida. Therefore, police usually look for crimes that took place in a locality associated with a known serial killer, particularly if aspects of those crimes match aspects of known crimes the serial killer committed. In the case of the Florida police, the most heinous crime committed during the period Dahmer was in Miami was the murder of six-year-old Adam Walsh.

On July 27, 1981, Adam Walsh was abducted from a Sears & Roebuck shopping mall near the Hollywood, Florida, police station. Two weeks later, the child's severed head was found in Vero Beach Canal, less than 150 miles away from Hollywood. The case received national attention, helped spark a national awareness about missing and exploited children, and eventually became the subject of a television special and a movie documentary. Since 1981, other convicted killers, most notably Florida killer Ottis

Toole, have confessed to murdering Adam Walsh. But police found holes in those confessions or discovered that the confessions did not correspond to the facts of the case. Jeffrey Dahmer was different, however. His revelation — coming on the heels of the discovery of severed heads and dismembered bodies in his apartment — that he was living and working in the area where Adam Walsh was killed piqued police interest. Moreover, Dahmer had already killed and dismembered a victim by the time he'd taken up residence in Florida and exhibited bizarre behavior while he was in the army. He was certainly a possibility as a suspect.

However, from his jail cell in Milwaukee, Dahmer adamantly denied ever having murdered anyone outside Wisconsin or Ohio. In a statement given through his lawyer Dahmer said, "I have told the police everything I have done relative to these homicides. I have not admitted any such crimes anywhere in the world other than this state, except I have committed an incident in Ohio. I have been totally cooperative and would have admitted other crimes if I did them. Hopefully this will put rumors to rest."

Although the police were intrigued at first by the possibility that they might have had a suspect in the Walsh murder, logic weighed heavily in favor of Dahmer's early statements because on the night he was arrested he was mentally ready to confess everything. He wanted to get it over with and put an end to the terror of his own existence. Had he not confessed to the Steven Hicks murder, police to this day would not have been able to solve the crime. Dahmer was the only living witness. Therefore, had he committed the Adam Walsh murder or any other murders in the state of Florida or in West Germany for that matter, it was likely he would have admitted them on July 23, 1991.

Another major factor weighs heavily against Dahmer's

having committed murders outside of Wisconsin and Ohio: a secure location where he could bring an unsuspecting or drugged victim. Dahmer's M.O. from the first homicide to the last was premised on his being able to lure the victim back to his apartment where he either lulled him into trusting him, drugged him into unconsciousness, or struck without warning. In some cases, he transported a drugged or semi-conscious person back to his apartment by cab. In the confines of his secure location under the cover of absolute inviolate privacy, he had sex with his victims, dismembered them, and processed or preserved their remains. Everything Dahmer did required a secure and private lair. Neither in his army barracks nor in Florida did he have a secure location where he could return with his victims. Therefore, although he may have been frustrated in both Baumholder and Miami Beach, there was very little he could do to act out his fantasies.

I would even go one step further and suggest that the secure location in which he could act out his fantasies was a part of the fantasy itself. As a child who perceived himself to be neglected, Dahmer built a fantasy world around him, exiting it only to behave in bizarre ways or to exercise control over a group or individuals. A major part of that fantasy was the secure location, be it his own room, a private basement, or a secluded toolshed behind the house where he would have the freedom from the fear of being intruded upon. Young Jeffrey Dahmer had worked up enough denial about what he was doing to protect himself from some levels of shame and embarrassment. For example, he would show off his collection of preserved dismembered animals, would dissect and chop up fish in front of others, and he would involve other children in hunting for road kills. However, it is likely that he was very private about the sexual gratification he was receiving from dismemberment or mutilation. Especially, as he indicated to police, if he had already identified animal and human dismemberment with sexual arousal. Because that shame and guilt were so pervasive, the mere guarantee of privacy could have been like a switch that turned up the heat on these fantasies and helped him translate them into actual behaviors. Therefore, the primary component that Jeffrey Dahmer needed to kill was a secure location. He didn't have it in the army, and maybe that's why he sought to get out of the army any way he could; likewise, he didn't have it at Ohio State. He probably didn't have a secure location in Florida as well, and that's what probably prevented him from undertaking any killing sprees while there. When serial killers don't kill, there are usually external, not internal, factors as causes.

I would take this argument a step further and suggest that once Dahmer killed Steven Hicks and experienced excitement and satisfaction from that murder, one part of Dahmer desperately sought to find a way to kill again while another part of him desperately tried to prevent another murder from taking place. Dahmer was literally running away from the crime, physically and emotionally trying to distance himself from what he had done, while at the same time coping with whatever sexual satisfaction he might have achieved from the crime. Dahmer's later behavior shows that once he started killing and had a secure location in which to kill, he didn't stop until he was stopped. Therefore, his sojourns in Columbus, Baumholder, and Miami Beach were all cut short because even though they provided him with the physical distance from his crime, they did not satisfy his combined fantasies of sexual lust, homicide, dismemberment, and control. Part of him — the part that should have been actively trying to create a productive existence — was consistently shut down by the part of him that needed to be gratified and desperately needed a secluded private location in which to be gratified. Therefore, Dahmer short-circuited what should have been an average, if not above average, college career and then destroyed what could have been a productive experience in the military because he could not get the privacy he needed. He had to get himself back to a place where he could be private. His first thought was to head south to Florida where his family wouldn't intervene, but that proved fruitless because he could never earn enough to buy himself the privacy he needed. Therefore, it is likely that he didn't commit any murders down there and was more than willing to accept his stepmother's invitation to return to Ohio to make another go of it with his family. Subconsciously, however, Dahmer was simply a serial killer looking for the missing ingredient in his life-style so that he could get back to killing.

Lionel Dahmer's second wife, Shari, had been in touch with Jeffrey after his separation from the Army. Lionel admits that he had very little contact with his son, but Shari had tried to monitor his comings and goings from long distance during his stay in Florida. During this period, Shari had tried repeatedly to get Jeffrey to return to Ohio. Maybe she thought that she could undo what she believed had been done to him when he was younger. It is fair to say, based on interviews Shari Dahmer has given to newspapers and on television, that Shari thought she had a handle on some of the problems Jeffrey was experiencing and believed she might have been able to help him straighten out and live productively. Shari told the *Milwaukee Journal* that she knew Jeffrey was melting down animal carcasses to the bone when he was younger. She found that fascination "strange," but attributed Jeffrey's interest to his father's career as a chemist. Lionel Dahmer remembered that Jeffrey showed an interest in bleaching chicken bones with chemicals from his chemistry set when he was ten or eleven. However, neither she nor Lionel could have known about the Steven Hicks murder. Both Shari and Lionel say that the first time they became aware of something that sounded like weird behavior was after Jeffrey had returned to Milwaukee. However, in October, 1981, all Shari wanted to do was to get Jeffrey back to Ohio so she could see what he needed.

This time Jeffrey didn't return to suburban Bath Township but rather to a decidedly more rural townhouse in Granger, Ohio, where his father and stepmother lived. Jeffrey was older now and not the same person who had been left at home by his parents back in 1978. The denial that had been building up in him from the time he had to confront the two police officers who had pulled him over for drunken driving on the night he killed Steven Hicks was now welling up. If he thought that he would have privacy and be able to work out some of his fantasies now that he was back home, he was wrong. All of the old feelings might have still been in place, but Jeffrey Dahmer, like any adult child who returns home, had been hardened by life and was not ready to slip back into childhood acquiescence. His problems started shortly after he got back to Ohio.

On October 7, Jeffrey walked into Maxwell's Lounge at the Ramada Inn in Bath Township holding an open bottle of vodka. He was probably already drunk because he was surly, belligerent, and combative. He refused to leave when ordered out by the management for carrying an open container of liquor. The police were called because Dahmer was behaving in a disorderly fashion in a public establishment, and managers escorted him out into the parking lot to await the patrol car. When the police arrived, Dahmer was still behaving in a disorderly fashion, refused to cooperate with the officers, and even threatened to kick one of the police in the groin. He was confrontational and, when threatened with arrest, he escalated the incident into a near assault. As it was, the police physically took him into custody and transported him to the police station where he was unable to get out of the car without assistance from the officer. Dahmer was charged with having an open container of liquor, conducting himself in a disorderly fashion, and resisting arrest when the police first apprehended him in the parking lot. He was found guilty, fined sixty dollars plus court costs, and given a ten-day jail sentence which was suspended.

If Lionel Dahmer thought his son had changed, he was wrong. He told the newspapers that from the time he was eighteen, Jeffrey had a history of getting drunk and abandoning his father's car wherever he happened to pass out. Lionel would have to retrieve the car the next day from whoever found it. After the incident at the Ramada Inn, Jeffrey's behavior didn't improve.

Lionel told the newspapers that his son would float from local bar to local bar, drinking himself into a foul temper; arguing that he wanted to stay and keep on drinking after closing time; getting into fights; getting hurt. On more than a few occasions, he'd get black eyes or a broken rib. Lionel's and Shari's attempts at rehabilitating Jeffrey had apparently failed, or maybe Jeffrey was too much in rebellion to accept any help from them. It was clear, however, that something had to be done to help this young man with his severe drinking problem. Lionel believed that Jeffrey still needed some form of discipline and needed to have it administered by someone trusted, respected, and loved. That person was Lionel's mother Catherine Dahmer who lived in the Milwaukee suburb of West Allis. Maybe there was hope for his son after all.

Lionel was correct in assuming that his son had strong feelings of love for his grandmother. In his interviews with police and psychologists, Jeffrey Dahmer reiterated that she was the only person in his life that he loved. Perhaps it was because he perceived that Catherine Dahmer loved him; perhaps it was because whatever love Catherine gave him was unencumbered by any responsibilities to perform. Perhaps because Catherine was not a party to the bitter fighting that had split apart Jeffrey's family, he trusted her. She, in turn, trusted in Jeffrey's basic qualities. She believed that a good dose of the gospel combined with hard work around the house and positive reinforcement was all the medication Jeffrey needed to get himself a job and straighten out his life. No one in his family could have ever really believed that Jeffrey had committed a murder and had subsequently torn apart his dead victim limb from limb before pulverizing his bones with a sledgehammer. In their minds, Jeffrey had to get himself off the sauce and on the wagon.

Catherine Dahmer took care of her grandson Jeffrey and made him feel he was not neglected. She said she always sent him greeting cards on his birthday and on holidays, sent him money, and helped him out whenever he needed something. She told newspapers that even after he left her house and moved to the Oxford Apartments, she drove over there when his aquarium apparatus needed repair.

"He had an awful lot of love for me," she told newspapers after Jeffrey was arrested. "He never left without giving me a big hug. He always wanted to do things for me."

Lionel agreed that his mother and his son had a strong relationship even as he doubted his own wisdom in sending Jeffrey there to live after he had gotten into trouble in Ohio.

"They loved each other," he said. "And he'd help her out with the chores." In late October, 1981, Jeffrey moved to his grandmother's house on South Fifty-seventh Street in middle-American West Allis, Wisconsin.

Catherine had a picture-perfect, two-story private house on this quiet street of other similarly well-kept houses in this Norman Rockwell-type suburb Milwaukee. The home had a small patch of front lawn, flower bushes, and a large trellis of flowers beside a side door that led to a private apartment in the basement of the house. Jeffrey probably looked at it and told himself that he now had the privacy that he had been looking for ever since his father came back to the house in Bath in June, 1978 and moved in with Shari. Now Jeffrey could come and go as he pleased with his own key without disturbing his grandmother. It was what he had been looking for for a long, long time.

Catherine asked her grandson to accompany her to church and tried to make sure that he didn't drink. Initially on the surface, it looked as if the Dahmer family plan might have been working. Jeffrey didn't immediately lapse into his old ways, although he did not quit drinking. He began doing chores around the house, cutting the lawn, planting rosebushes, raking the leaves that had fallen during autumn, and trimming his grandmother's shrubbery around the edge of the property.

Although he was having disquieting feelings about being in an entirely new neighborhood and not having any friends, Jeffrey said he tried to adjust. Besides working around the house and taking care of his seventy-plus-year-old grandmother, he also got himself a job at a local blood bank using his combat medic's skills from the army. Jeffrey became a phlebotomist, a blood taker, at Milwaukee Blood Plasma, Inc. He held this job until early 1982 when he was laid off. But at the same time he was working and saying he

127

was living happily with his grandmother, Dahmer had begun to indulge his fantasies about homosexuality much more aggressively. He'd begun frequenting gay bars, clubs, and bathhouses on Milwaukee's south side. The area was referred to derisively by outsiders as the "gay ghetto."

It was in these clubs that Jeffrey began meeting young men who openly advertised their homosexuality and felt comfortable with it. They met to indulge in sexual relationships, have social encounters, and meet one another to set up parties and dates. It was the kind of active social scene that Jeffrey had shunned most of his life. It was also a culture where the people who inhabited it could feel safe from the violent homophobia that raged outside their world and from the discrimination and misunderstanding about their life-style that was pervasive throughout the rest of middle-class Milwaukee. It was a place where gays could feel safe, secure, and trusting of strangers in their midst. Unfortunately the sullen, sad-faced, lone drinker named Jeffrey Dahmer, whom many of them embraced, was not simply an unhappy young man. He was a seething killer with a particular hatred for homosexuals, and he was now free and on the loose with a private apartment. He was what he had been when his parents left him alone in Bath, only now he had already killed. He was a potential serial killer cruising in the very community where he would soon begin killing. The beginning of his spree was only a few months away.

Chapter Nine

The Killings Begin

The City of Milwaukee that Jeffrey Dahmer moved back to when he came to live with his grandmother in West Allis was not the Milwaukee where his father had grown up in the 1950s. This Milwaukee had lost its optimism. It was battered by the recession that had rolled across the midwest rustbelt after 1980, by the loss of jobs due to layoffs at subcontractors and suppliers to the major American automobile manufacturers, an unemployment resulting from the downsizing of companies like Allis-Chalmers. The American midwest was taking a beating from foreign competition in heavy industry and manufacturing, and the local Milwaukee economy was one of the victims.

The Milwaukee that had once publicly prided itself as a city of racial and social tolerance had become many Milwaukees by 1982 when Jeffrey Dahmer returned: completely different cities for the rich and the poor, the black and the white, and the gay and the straight. By 1990, for example, the official unemployment rate for blacks was 16.6%, more than five times the unemployment rate for white residents, according to an article in New York's gay magazine *NYQ*. The unofficial employment rate put the number of blacks out of work at 40% of the African-American population. It was a staggering number.

The economic decline that set into Milwaukee also hit the black and white communities very differently. Even though the loss of jobs was widespread, it was particularly devastating in the African-American communities because of the high numbers of service jobs held by blacks that were among the first to be cut whenever companies had to reduce costs. As tourism declined because of the failing economy, black workers in the service industries were hurt even further. As a result, by the beginning of the mid 1980s, there were at least two separate economies in the Milwaukee area and two very disparate sets of economic figures.

African-American Milwaukeeans could look across the Sixteenth Street viaduct that divided the north and south sides of the city and peer into what amounted to a different country that played by entirely different rules. Maybe they weren't all prosperous over there, but they certainly had food on the table. The poverty, hunger, and growing violence created a sense of hopelessness on the north side of the city which was agitated by seething resentment over the unfairness of it all.

Members of Milwaukee's black community had also expressed their anger over the lack of police protection on the north side and the different treatment received by blacks and whites at the hands of the police. According to *NYQ*, Milwaukee has paid hundreds of millions of dollars in compensation to the families of victims in successful "wrongful death" suits brought against the city. In these actions, the magazine maintained, innocent black men like Daniel Bell and Ernest Lacy were killed by Milwaukee police officers. Other blacks complained of harsh treatment and sometimes brutal confrontations. All the while, however, the police department seemed closed-up tight to members of the black community. Minority applicants found it difficult to penetrate the ranks of Milwaukee's police and fire departments. For years, they had sought intervention from federal courts until the courts ordered the city to seek out more minority recruits. But even as early as 1982, the resentment in the black and Hispanic communities about disparate treatment was running very high.

There was also trouble brewing between the homosexual and heterosexual communities. Milwaukee was a very conservative city despite its protestations that people of all types could live together in harmony. The strong Irish, German, and Polish constituencies were rooted in a conservative political tradition that was historically unsympathetic to the demands of the gay community. Jeffrey Dahmer was a part of that German political constituency and was, according to people who knew him when he was cruising through the gay bars on Milwaukee's gentrifying south side, very conflicted about his homosexuality. He had been taught to hate gays but now was in their very midst and had no way of reconciling the conflict. Dahmer was almost a microcosm of what was happening in Milwaukee itself. As the gay community became increasingly vocal, as well as increasingly wealthy, they posed a challenge to the traditions of the bedrock German and Polish populations.

This growing conflict had already been translated into a number of charges of abuse against the Milwaukee Police Department by the time Dahmer was cruising and killing in the early to mid 1980s. The complaints against the police ranged from what gay activists saw as petty harassment (an aggressive anti-jaywalking campaign, slurs made by police to gays, and an overly zealous flurry of traffic tickets) to serious complaints of gay bashing, raids on gay bars, and a refusal to respond to charges made by gays against people who they said abused them. The complaints of gays against the city of Milwaukee would be objectified by Dahmer himself and the slow response of the police to missing persons reports filed on Dahmer's many victims. But by the time Jeffrey Dahmer first began visiting the gay bars on Milwaukee's south side, the gay community had already characterized itself as having been victimized and deprived of its civil rights by the politically conservative straight community.

Into this bubbling cauldron of animosity cruised Jeffrey Dahmer: confused, conflicted, severely alcoholic, hostile. He was already a killer, and now he was on the loose from the Army and his father, once again looking for trouble. In 1982, Jeffrey stumbled into the "gay ghetto" on the south side of the city and discovered a life-style he had not been exposed to before. In many ways, according to people who worked the clubs and knew Dahmer, the world of transvestites, drag queens, female impersonators, yuppie hustlers, and the fortysomething leather and Levi set were in sharp contrast to Dahmer's dour nerdiness. Yet he insinuated himself into the scene and quickly became a regular at many of the theme bars.

The gay night clubs were more like private social clubs than restaurants or bars. In places like 219, The Phoenix, C'est La Vie, and even the Leather and Levi Rec Room, men who might have been outcasts because of their life-style choices felt a camaraderie that they could not feel anywhere else. In a city where gays were routinely ostracized and sometimes physically attacked, the night club scene was where patrons could feel safe from the outside world and from the predatory attacks of homophobes and gay bashers in the heterosexual community. The regulars who frequented these bars sought more than companionship and safety; they sought understanding and respect. It was ironic that this was the very environment in which Dahmer began to cruise for his victims.

The different clubs had a variety of themes or ethos that defined the types of sexual turn-ons that patrons sought. There were the leather bars, the transvestite bars, the primarily black bars, the disco bars, and Yuppie cocktail bars, where upscale and professionally mobile gays could come out of the closet to express a sexuality that they had to keep repressed during the normal 9:00 to 5:00 business day. People who frequented bars of one particular ethos or another knew, just by the presence of others, that they shared a common bond of sexuality that meant they could trust one another. Dahmer, however, seemed to cruise in different types of theme bars as if he were a man without a country. People who remembered seeing him during the time he was picking up victims remembered that he often seemed more like a yuppie than anything else. Still, Dahmer turned up in places like 219 and La Cage which featured female impersonators, but sometimes resembled neighborhood cocktail bars or black discos. Even the regular patrons said that the local bars could change themes from hour to hour depending upon the crowd. 219, for example, was said to have been a neighborhood cocktail bar in the afternoon, but after 9:30 it changed to a gay bar.

Dahmer patronized different bars at different hours of the day. But wherever he went, the sad-faced, blankly staring Jeffrey Dahmer always stood out because he never seemed to be having a good time. He always seemed to be drinking sullenly by himself unless he managed to get lucky and pick up a young man. He wasn't making any friends in Milwaukee, but he was experiencing for the first time what it was like to mingle among people who openly professed what he had been hiding since he was a teenager. It only created greater conflicts for Dahmer, however, who began to act out the anger and sexual frustration he was feeling.

Dahmer was capably making financial ends meet during this period in 1982 after he moved to West Allis. He was working at Milwaukee Blood Plasma, Inc., where his skills as an army medic had qualified him as a technician drawing blood from donors. He was making a good salary, and had little or no living expenses. He was living with the one person in his life he said he trusted and had all the privacy he felt he needed at the time. Still, there was trouble in his psyche that was waiting to bubble over the top just as it did years earlier in Ohio. It happened again on August 8, 1982, at the Wisconsin State Fair Park.

The Wisconsin State Fair Park had become something of an institution for the middle-class families of the greater Milwaukee and Chicago areas. The Park was so popular that people would travel there from all around the Lake Michigan area for an ethnic celebration of German oompah-pah bands and wurst, polka music, dancing, arts and crafts exhibits, a huge flea market, and the ever-present Milwaukee beer. At the State Fair Park, amidst the festivities and the competitions for farm produce and dairy products, Jeffrey Dahmer started acting out the kind of weird behavior he had been notorious for in high school. For no apparent reason, he dropped his pants and exposed himself in a crowd of women and children. Police arrested him and charged him with disorderly conduct. He was found guilty and fined fifty dollars plus court costs. But more important than the fine or the disorderly behavior itself, this was a warning sign that Dahmer was unhappy, frustrated, and looking for help. It was an outcropping of a severe disorder that would shortly surface again. It was also an example of a public display of indecent exposure which FBI serial killer experts say is one of the basic profile characteristics of the "disorganized" serial killer which is how Dahmer was characterized by FBI experts.

Some months after he was arrested, Jeffrey Dahmer lost his job at the blood bank. During 1983 and 1984 he lived on whatever money he had and on his grandmother's largesse. These were tough months for Jeffrey Dahmer because he was struggling with the monster of his sexuality that was rearing up within him while simultaneously going to church and relying on Catherine Dahmer's contacts to try to get him a job. But he managed to eke through it and on January 15, 1985, his efforts at a job search finally paid off when he was hired by the Ambrosia Chocolate Company on Fifth Street and Highland Avenue in Milwaukee as a mixer for what turned out to be a whopping $8.25 an hour. Dahmer was hired to work the nighttime shift from 11:00 P.M. to 7:00 A.M. in the morning. He had Saturdays off. This allowed him the time to frequent his favorite bars and hangouts and drink to his heart's content in the early evening hours before reporting for work. His Saturday nights remained free for cruising.

During the period from 1985 to 1987 when he killed his second victim, Dahmer was experimenting with various concoctions and sleeping potions at the bathhouses he was frequenting. People who knew him during this period remembered a young man who was sending out serious danger signals that alarmed some of the bartenders and club owners who watched his comings and goings. In particular, Jeffrey Dahmer began to frequent the bathhouses in Milwaukee where he was afforded the privacy of a cubicle in which to serve drug-laced drinks to the companions he wooed back there. The bathhouses were very free environments in which patrons could partner up with one another, have a few drinks, engage in sexual relations, and then move on to other partners. For Jeffrey Dahmer who was looking for anonymity as well as privacy, the bathhouses were almost like an experimental laboratory.

Dahmer told the police that he purchased a variety of powerful drugs that he slipped to his victims. Later in his killing spree, he also tried using ether and chloroform which he had purchased from a local pharmacy, but they didn't work as well as the laced drinks. Even during the early years of his cruising at bars and bathhouses, managers and bartenders began to find patrons passed out in booths and cubicles after having had encounters with the strange-looking Jeffrey Dahmer. Some of these patrons couldn't be awakened at first and seemed as if they might have been poisoned. It wasn't like a simple drunken stupor from which they could be aroused, put into a cab, and sent home. These were near comas in which the victims were so unconscious that they had to be transported to the hospital. In one particular incident, Dahmer was banned from the Club Baths because he had drugged a young man who was ultimately forced to stay in the hospital for ten days after the incident. Paramedics were called to the club to transport the man, and the police questioned Dahmer because he was the last person seen with the young man before he was discovered by other persons.

In another incident, a local Milwaukee female impersonator named "Goldie" recalled that Jeffrey had drugged
someone at a bathhouse called the Tubs. "Goldie" knew
both Jeffrey and the victim, and said that the young man
has remained wary of accepting drinks from strangers to
this very day because of what happened. "He told me a
week after it happened that he was with Jeffrey at the Tubs
and Jeffrey said that he'd get him a soda. So he came back
with the soda. My friend drank it and suddenly he said he
felt woozy like he was going to pass out. Jeffrey was helping him, but then he passed out. Bradley, the Tubs manager, then helped him. He told me later that knowing what
he knows now, he would have been one of Jeffrey's victims
if Jeffrey had taken him back after he passed out," "Goldie"
said. "In fact, the guy hardly drinks his water whenever he
goes out because of the way Jeffrey tried to drug him."

Dahmer was flirting with levels of violence during his
early years in the bars and bathhouses. In August 1986,
four years to the day after he had been arrested at the Wisconsin State Fair Park, he was seen masturbating in the
open along the banks of the Kinnickinnic River which was
a local gathering place for kids. Two twelve-year-old boys
told police they saw Dahmer with his pants dropped all the
way down around his thighs masturbating. Jeffrey saw the
boys, too, because when one of them asked Dahmer
whether he was having a good time, he reportedly answered, "Yeah, I'm having a great time."

Police officers arrested Dahmer who admitted he was
masturbating and, in what might have been a completely
sincere moment of remorse and shame, told them that he
had masturbated in public at least five times over the

course of the previous month. That was an obvious indicator that he was looking for the opportunity to express his conflicts through violence while at the same time he was looking for outside intervention. He must have felt that his sexual malaise was escalating to the point where it would soon be out of control, but he was still too ashamed of his feelings to simply ask someone he knew for help. Jeffrey Dahmer was booked for lewd and lascivious behavior. The officer making out his report wrote that Dahmer admitted "he doesn't know what changed him to make him suddenly start doing this, and that he knows he has a problem and he wants to get help."

Jeffrey's public masturbation and his spontaneous statements to the police reveal that he was in serious conflict. Partly because all of the components were in place for a new killing spree and partly because he was now trolling within the very community where he would soon begin to kill, his psychological pot was boiling over. Dahmer had become sexually potentiated, trip wired as it were, while at the same time he was still angry about his homosexual feelings. He hadn't fully accepted them, and probably never would without some form of therapy. The only safe release, as he edged ever closer to indulging in his own bizarre form of sexuality, was to masturbate. And masturbating in public, especially around little boys, gave him an added thrill.

Jeffrey Dahmer changed his story quickly, however, after he was booked and his case was fed into the judicial system. Instead of admitting to being a chronic sexual offender who had frequently masturbated in public, Dahmer told a probation officer months after the arrest that "I was drinking some beer in an undeveloped wooded area alone. After a few cans of beer I needed to go, so I did, behind some trees. I was sure there was no one else around, but I was wrong. Two boys saw me and called the police." Accordingly, the charge was later reduced to disorderly conduct. On March 10, 1987, Dahmer was found guilty and sentenced to one year's probation by Judge Arlene Connors who also ordered him to undergo counseling. Catherine Dahmer, however, remained unaware of the entire incident, and Jeffrey continued to reside at her house in West Allis as if nothing had happened.

Jeffrey Dahmer's recantation of his original story to the police was his attempt to respin the web of denial around himself when confronted with the seriousness of his actions. Part of him, it must be said, seemed to truly want help. His spontaneous confessions to police at the Kinnickinnic River, and eventually on the night of his final arrest, fall into a pattern in which he admits his crimes, explains that he needs help, and then changes his story in later confessions to omit potentially embarrassing details. It is almost as if he can only tell the truth about himself in the first flash of the searchlight of authority. Once he's used to the glare, he changes his story to protect himself from the feelings of shame and guilt that surround his sexuality. In other words, he never at any time denied he exposed himself to little boys at the Kinnickinnic River; he only changed the motivation from masturbating in public to urinating in public. The former is embarrassing and shameful, the latter is just another version of "doing a Dahmer."

In the months that followed in 1987, Dahmer stayed in touch with his probation officer and answered all the questions correctly that he was expected to answer. He told them that he was still working at the chocolate factory, that he was getting a pay raise from $8.25 to $8.50 an hour. Dahmer was using the money to entice young men at the bars and bathhouses to spend time with him and to show

139

off. Drinks and cabs were also monumentally expensive. Because Jeffrey wasn't driving, just getting around from West Allis to the city was very costly. But Jeffrey could afford it now because he wasn't paying any living expenses and was making almost $17,000 a year or about $340 a week.

During the time he was in probation and dutifully filling out his questionnaires, Jeffrey Dahmer emerged as a full-blown serial killer when he murdered for the second time in his life and kept right on killing. According to the confession he gave to Milwaukee police after his arrest in July, 1991, on a Saturday afternoon sometime during the summer of 1987, he picked up a victim at the 219 Club on the south side and took him to the Hotel Ambassador for drinks and sex. Later on it was reported that the victim was twenty-five-year-old Stephen W. Tuomi who had come to Milwaukee from Ontonagon, Michigan. Tuomi might have been a heavy drinker himself and was looking for the money that Dahmer was offering for posing for nude photos. Although Dahmer told police he remembered very little of the evening, he probably offered Tuomi money and the two of them left the bar and headed for the Ambassador Hotel. "Goldie," who had begun to notice Dahmer at the bars, said that Jeffrey was usually flashing around money and had begun hanging around with hustler-types who were themselves cruising for yuppie-types with ready cash.

Jeffrey told the police that he had been drinking heavily that night prior to his meeting Tuomi and that he was already bleary. After they arrived at the hotel, he gave his victim a powerful drink laced with heavy sedatives and Tuomi fell asleep quite soon after that. Dahmer said that he likewise was very drunk and remembered little after that because he passed out when he saw the sedatives had taken effect. When he awoke, he told the police, the man was already dead, maybe from an overdose of the sedatives. Dahmer had no memory of having killed him. Police specifically asked Dahmer about bruises the man had on his chest, but Jeffrey told them that he did not remember beating him at all. He simply reiterated that when he woke up, the victim was dead next to him. His only problem at that point was to dispose of the body, but he'd been through that drill before.

Jeffrey told the police he left the dead man in his hotel room and went over to the Grand Avenue Mall where he purchased a large suitcase. Actually it was more like a wardrobe valet turned body bag than it was a trunk. He brought the suitcase back to the hotel room where he stuffed the body into it and waited until it was late and he knew his grandmother would be asleep. Then he lugged the suitcase into the elevator and out onto the street where he hailed a cab. Dahmer and the cab driver managed to fit the heavy piece of luggage into the trunk of the cab which he took all the way to his grandmother's house in West Allis. It was now after midnight and his grandmother was fast asleep. He dragged the suitcase down the side stairs into his basement apartment and waited, knowing that he would soon have the entire house to himself.

On the following morning, he told his grandmother that he was tired and would not be joining her for Sunday mass at church. "You go on alone," he told her. "I'll stay in the house." But when his grandmother left, he took the corpse of his victim out of the wardrobe and spread him out on the basement floor. Then he went to work. He first dismembered the body; hacking off the limbs and the head until all he had was a torso. Then he cut each of the body parts up into little pieces of flesh, muscle, and tissue. He minced them ever smaller, much as he had done with the fish he caught at the pond when he was younger. He filleted the flesh from the bones and ground them up as best he could, also. Then he disposed of the bones and the tissue in the garbage. He never kept any parts of the body, he told the police. There were no trophies. He wanted it all out of the house, he said, because he didn't want his grandmother to stumble across anything.

The entire process, he told the police, was started on a Saturday night while his grandmother was asleep and completed on the Sunday when she was in church. It was at this point that Dahmer realized that he had all the privacy he needed. The equation was complete and Dahmer had reached critical mass. He had killed. Now he had killed again. He had successfully disposed of the body in much the same way that he had done with Steven Hicks. Nobody would miss this victim just as nobody had missed Hicks. He had actually gotten away with it. He had had forbidden sex and killed the person who reminded him of his shame. It was all perfect. Now all he had to do was get rid of that foul smell from the rotting corpse.

Chapter Ten

Out of Control

Jeffrey Dahmer had killed again, as he done nine years earlier, and again seemed to have successfully disposed of the body and gotten away with it, he was only reminded of the reasons he was killing: his pathological loneliness.

When left to his own devices in the privacy of his lair, Dahmer acted out his fantasies of incorporating his victims into himself by killing them, having sex with them, and dismembering them. It was almost primitive. By merging himself into the actual disassembly of another human being, he and the victim became joined. However, because Dahmer's murders were not committed out of a passion of the moment but out of an ongoing fantasy fueled by hatred for himself, his own sexuality, and the objects of that sexuality, he was an episodic killer who exploited every opportunity he could to kill, put his mask of invisibility back on, reenter the community, and kill again. Dahmer had found his trolling grounds and like most serial killers, once he established killing and escaping, the pattern itself held him firmly in its grip. It is ironic that most serial killers are actually prisoners of their own criminal behavior.

Imagine Jeffrey Dahmer, an individual who had perceived himself to have been so neglected that he was almost pathologically deprived by the time he was a teenager, returning to the city of his birth after having experienced complete rejection and failure throughout most of his young adult life. Imagine that this individual has become so addicted to alcohol that most of his reactions are completely depressed. In fact, people who knew him and spoke to him confirmed that Dahmer seemed to walk through life completely bleary and in an emotionless and expressionless state. It was as if he were the walking dead. He is also in a very highly suggestible state because most of his logical patterns of thinking and reacting have been depressed by constant medication with alcohol. He is reacting not only to suggestions from the outside world but from internal programming that might have taken place when he was a small child.

Imagine further that this person has already crossed a traumatic threshold by having killed and mutilated a victim when he was essentially a child after both parents had abandoned him in his house. He was traumatized, but he buried it in denial. He is now a walking time bomb who, because he is living in an apartment with someone who trusts him implicitly and where he is given absolute privacy, is for the first time in his life free to explore all aspects of the sexuality that have frightened him. He is arrested for sexual exposure (a red flag) shortly before he loses his job and has to scrabble for money again. Within the same year, he admits to a police officer that he has exposed himself by masturbating in public five times in a single month. Just about a year later, Dahmer sets up a sexual encounter with Stephen Tuomi at a local hotel, kills him, wipes the murder out of his memory. Then he transports his victim's body in a wardrobe back to his grandmother's house, where he dismembers him and disposes of him and actually gets away with it.

He had crossed the threshold. The pattern of escalating violence has reached its critical stage. Jeffrey Dahmer may have been literally transformed into a kind of emotionless killing machine who was reacting to a primary set of fears and hates as well as a profound sense of self-loathing. Once he started killing again in Milwaukee, he became like a human automatic weapon whose recoil from the self-hatred surrounding the crime actually cocked the trigger for another round. This is the way spree-type, control-oriented serial killers propel themselves from killing to killing. They are capable of waiting long periods between killing sprees. But once a spree starts and is not stopped by external forces, as Dahmer's first spree was cut short after one murder by his father's return to the house on West Bath Road, they continue until they are caught or killed. After the murder of Stephen Tuomi, there was nothing to prevent Jeffrey Dahmer from covering his shame with denial and setting up for a subsequent encounter with another victim.

During this period, people who frequented the gay bars and some of the bartenders asked about the missing blondish guy named "Steve" who had always hung around. Nobody seemed to make any connections to Jeffrey Dahmer, but they all wondered what might

145

have happened to him. Also, nobody made any connections to Dahmer who was getting a bad reputation at some of the bathhouses for drugging people in the cubicles. Soon, however, people stopped talking about Steve and Jeffrey was back into his routine of cruising among the bars during the early evening hours, reporting for work at 11:00 P.M. and knocking off at 7:30 A.M. the following morning. On Saturdays, however, he was free to cruise for the entire night, and that was how he met fourteen-year-old James Doxtator.

Dahmer, like many of the other patrons at 219, had noticed the teenagers who congregated at the bus stop across the street to hustle the passersby. For all anybody knew, they could have been male prostitutes or runaways who did whatever was necessary for money to live on. They stood at the bus stop soliciting money from the drivers and taxis that passed by. To Jeffrey Dahmer, they seemed to have no family and appeared alone in the world. One such person at the bus stop was James Doxtator who looked like a Hispanic to Dahmer. In reality, Doxtator was a Native American who lived in the area.

In January of 1988, Dahmer walked across the street from the bar to the bus stop and struck up a conversation with Doxtator. Dahmer asked him if he wanted to make some money by posing for some photos over at his place in West Allis, possibly looking at some videos, and having a drink. It was money, and Doxtator was not about to turn him down; he and Dahmer took the bus back to West Allis.

Dahmer told the police in his confession that he and Doxtator had sex in the basement of the house and Dahmer slipped the young man his sleeping potion.

Before too long, Doxtator passed out. Dahmer began strangling him until he stopped breathing and it was apparent that he was dead. Jeffrey undressed Doxtator and noticed that he had what seemed to be two small scars near the nipples on his breasts that looked like cigarette burns. He remembered that detail and related it to the police in his confession years later. It would help to identify the victim whose body would never be found.

Dahmer told the police that after he undressed Doxtator he dismembered the body and melted down the skin in his acid solution much the way he did with his road kills when he was a child. When the flesh was soft enough to be pulled away from the bone, he cleaned the bones, washed the flesh down the floor drain the same way he did with Stephen Tuomi's remains, and began grinding the bones with a sledgehammer. By the time he was through pounding Doxtator's skeleton into tiny pieces, he was able to dispose of the remains in the garbage.

On Monday, January 18, 1988, Debra Vega, Doxtator's mother, reported her son missing to Milwaukee police, saying that she had not seen him since Saturday, January 16. She told the police that her son had two scars on his chest that looked remarkably like cigarette burns. That was one of the clues that led police to suspect that Doxtator was one of Dahmer's victims when he described the body to police. When they showed him a picture of James Doxtator, Dahmer said that he was 75 percent sure that that was the young man he approached at a Milwaukee bus stop and murdered later that same night in his grandmother's basement. He disposed of the remains the next morning while Catherine Dahmer was in church.

If Jeffrey thought that his comings and goings and the noises in the basement on Saturday night when he brought his victims home had gone unnoticed by his grandmother, he was mistaken. In his fixated state, he had assumed that she could sleep through the conversation in the basement, the struggles as his victims fell to the floor as he strangled them, and the sounds of him storing the body until the following morning when she was in church. Maybe Jeffrey thought that his grandmother didn't notice the smells that came out of the basement, smells of rotting flesh that lingered heavily in the air even after the garbage had been picked up. Jeffrey thought he'd solved the smell problem by loosening the flesh of his victims with acid and flushing it down the basement floor drain, but he hadn't. Of course, he probably couldn't sense the worst of it; not only had he become used to the stench, but like most alcoholics his senses of smell and taste had become dulled. But for Catherine, the odor was overpowering and she was beginning to complain about it to her son Lionel.

The first time, after Tuomi was dismembered and flushed down the floor drain, it was simply the stench that had gotten to her. The second time, when Jeffrey was dissolving away James Doxtator's flesh, Catherine noticed that he had concocted some strange looking brownish black substance in jars in her small garage in back of the house, and the same acrid stench was there as well. That was when she called Lionel in Ohio who said he'd come over to talk to his son about it. Lionel

148

Jeffrey L. Dahmer, 17. (*Courtesy of AP/Wide World Photos*)

Jeffrey Dahmer, 22, after his arrest for disorderly conduct in 1982. (*Courtesy AP/Wide World Photos*)

Jeffrey Dahmer, 31, after his July 22, 1991 arrest for the multiple murders in Milwaukee. (*Courtesy of Cheryl L. Franklin*)

Steven Mark Hicks, 19, Dahmer's first known victim. (*Courtesy AP/ Wide World Photos*)

Joyce Flint, 55, his natural mother. (*Courtesy of the Milwaukee Journal/Sipa Press, Inc.*)

The former West Allis home of Catherine Dahmer, Jeffrey's paternal grandmother. Bobbie Simpson, one of Dahmer's living victims, stands to the left. (*Courtesy of Cheryl L. Franklin*)

A public bathroom in Juneau Park, where Dahmer was seen having sex with men. (*Courtesy of Cheryl L. Franklin*)

Brother John Paul Ranieri, who knew Dahmer through his ministry to the gay community. (*Courtesy of Cheryl L. Franklin*)

Goldie Adams, female impersonator, a barroom friend of Jeffrey Dahmer. (*Courtesy of Cheryl L. Franklin*)

Michele, owner of the Phoenix Club, a regular stop on Dahmer's nightly rounds. (*Courtesy of Cheryl L. Franklin*)

THE MILWAUKEE VICTIMS OF JEFFREY DAHMER
(arranged by approximate date of death)

Steven Tuomi
9/15/87

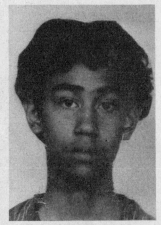

James E. Doxtator
1/16/88

Richard Guerrero
3/19/88

Anthony Sears
3/25/89

Raymond Lamont Smith
5/29/89

Ernest Miller
9/2/90

David Thomas
9/24/90

Edward W. Smith
6/14/90

Curtis Straughter
3/7/91

Errol Lindsey
4/7/91

Tony Hughes
5/24/91

Konerak Sinthasomphone
5/26/91

Matt Turner
6/30/91

Jeremiah Weinberger
7/6/91

Oliver Lacy
7/15/91

Joseph Bradehoft
7/19/91

Jeffrey Dahmer's living room. (*Courtesy of Cheryl L. Franklin*)

The front door and kitchen of Dahmer's apartment after a thorough police search. (*Courtesy of Cheryl L. Franklin*)

The freezer in which Dahmer kept the remains of some of his victims. (*Courtesy of Cheryl L. Franklin*)

The industrial drum in which Dahmer preserved body parts. (*Courtesy of Cheryl L. Franklin*)

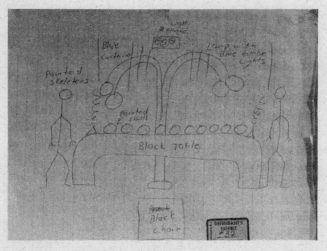

A drawing found in Dahmer's apartment depicting a shrine decorated with human skulls and skeletons. (*Courtesy of Cheryl L. Franklin*)

Excavation in Bath, Ohio for the remains of Steven Mark Hicks. (*Courtesy of AP/Wide World Photos*)

Leononia Raspberry and Rosie Lewis, guards at the House of Corrections in Milwaukee, standing in the room Dahmer occupied. (*Courtesy of Cheryl L. Franklin*)

Dahmer in his first appearance at Milwaukee County Circuit Court on July 26, 1991. (Courtesy of AP/ Wide World Photos)

Dahmer in prison clothes as he is charged with eight additional counts of first degree Intentional Homicide. (*Courtesy of AP/Wide World Photos*)

District Attorney
E. Michael McCann.
(*Courtesy of Cheryl L. Franklin*)

Defense attorney Gerald P. Boyle.
(*Courtesy of Cheryl L. Franklin*)

Dr. George B. Palermo, the first psychiatrist to examine Dahmer for the Milwaukee court. (*Courtesy of Cheryl L. Franklin*)

Shari Dahmar, Jeffrey's stepmother, (left) and Lionel Dahmer, his father. (*Courtesy AP/Wide World Photos*)

Catherine Lacy, mother of Oliver Lacy.
(*Courtesy of Cheryl L. Franklin*)

Shirley Hughes, mother of Tony Hughes.
(*Courtesy of Cheryl L. Franklin*)

Dorothy Straughter, mother of Curtis Straughter. *(Courtesy of Cheryl L. Franklin)*

Mrs. Pablo Guerrero, mother of Richard Guerrero. *(Courtesy of Cheryl L. Franklin)*

Glenda Cleveland, the concerned woman whose call to police resulted in the final arrest of Dahmer. (*Courtesy of Cheryl L. Franklin*)

Carolyn Smith, sister of Edward Smith; Janie Hagen, sister of Richard Guerrero; and Geraldine Martin, half sister of Anthony Sears. (*Courtesy of Cheryl L. Franklin*)

Jeanetta Robinson, local activist and
Director of Career Youth Development.
(*Courtesy of Cheryl L. Franklin*)

Reverend Dr. Leo Champion, local
activist and minister of the Fellowship
Missionary Baptist Church.
(*Courtesy of Cheryl L. Franklin*)

The exorcism performed outside Dahmer's apartment by the Evangelist Gene Champion (left), Evangelist Carolyn Idowu (center) and the Reverend Dr. Ionia Champion. (*Courtesy of Cheryl L. Franklin*)

The Reverend Jesse L. Jackson at a press conference on the controversy over the handling of the Dahmer case by police. (*Courtesy of Cheryl L. Franklin*)

Ernest Flowers, another surviving victim of Jeffrey Dahmer, at the memorial service for Edward Smith. (*Courtesy of Cheryl L. Franklin*)

The candlelight vigil in Juneau Park, to celebrate and heal
the Milwaukee community. (*Courtesy of Cheryl L. Franklin*)

Dahmer's second wife Shari told the newspapers years later after her stepson Jeffrey was arrested that reports in Ohio newspapers about Catherine's having found human bones in her basement were gross exaggerations. She said that when Lionel investigated the foul odor problem and asked Jeffrey what he was doing, Jeffrey replied that he had bought some chickens at the market and had melted them down to the bone with acid. It was an experiment, he told his father.

"When Lionel got there, whatever he had melted down was gone," Shari told the newspapers. All Jeffrey could show his father were the liquid remains of the substance he'd used. "There was some slimy, viscous stuff left," she said. "But we had no idea what it was from." Lionel questioned his son about the residues, but Jeffrey said he was simply fascinated by the way chemicals could melt down animal flesh. It was all very simple and there was nothing to be worried about, he told his father. "I guess I had too much time on my hands," Jeffrey reportedly said to his father, according to an interview Lionel gave to the Milwaukee newspapers. "And I just wanted to see what chemicals would decompose the chicken I bought."

"Jeffrey said that he had free time and that having free time was bad for him," Lionel said. "He's a bus rider and said he saw a raccoon that had died, so he got off the bus and took it home to experiment with, too." Lionel reacted with some concern about his son's experiments, but couldn't remember Jeffrey having shown any interest in dealing with live specimens. "I said, 'God, Jeff, this is strange, this is weird.' " But Shari remembered that her stepson had a history of experimenting with dead animals. "Because his father

149

was a chemist," she told the newspapers, "Jeff used to take animals and melt them down to the bone." It would be the same kind of thing a biology student would do when he dissected a frog. But, she stressed, they were always dead animals, such as road kills. And they were always done under the supervision of Lionel Dahmer, as far as she knew. She did, however, reveal that she thought her stepson's fascination was strange.

Lionel and Shari left Catherine Dahmer's house having apparently explained away the problem of the foul odors and the slimy liquids. They agreed that Jeffrey was doing strange things, but they seemed harmless enough. They didn't know that Jeffrey was still on probation after his disorderly conduct conviction and that he was now heavily cruising among the gay bars on Milwaukee's south side.

Catherine was concerned about noises from the basement and had a feeling he was bringing people over, but she hadn't seen anything. To Catherine and Jeffrey's parents, Jeff might have been troubled, but he didn't seem dangerous. Most people don't realize that an abnormal childhood fascination with dead animals and insects, a fascination that is so powerful the child literally plays with, dissects, or even "poses" the bodies of dead animals, can be a serious warning sign of future dangerousness. Fascination with death among children is borderline abnormal in the best of circumstances, but involvement with the bodies of dead things for the sake of experimenting with them is one of the indicators that a child might be in trouble. In Jeffrey Dahmer's case, this was a fascination that he cultivated into a means of body disposal so efficient that he was able to maintain a serial killing spree in the same area for four years before he was stopped.

On March 10, 1988, Jeffrey filed his final report with his probation officer under the terms of his disorderly conduct conviction at the State Fair Park. He said that everything was as it had been in his life, he hadn't changed his address, and that he was still working even though he'd missed one day at the factory since the last report because he'd been sick. Apparently, the probation officer was satisfied because on March 20, 1988, he was formally discharged from his probation by the Division of Corrections (DOC) of the State of Wisconsin. In a declaration the DOC sent him, they wrote "Jeffrey Dahmer has satisfied all conditions of said probation." Having fulfilled all of his conditions and serving his complete sentence, he was absolutely discharged. Now Jeffrey Dahmer was completely free and he would soon kill again.

Just a little over two months after he had killed Doxtator, Jeff Dahmer met Richard Guerrero, this time at the Phoenix Bar. "Goldie," the female impersonator who knew Dahmer and a few of his victims from the gay bars they all frequented, said that Richard Guerrero had been especially friendly to him. "He was kind of like a cute little brother you never had," "Goldie" remembered. "Guerrero kidded me a lot. He was always nice to me. I think he was really bisexual because I saw him with girls sometimes. I seen him coming from the Lake and he didn't know me out of drag, and I saw him with girls. I saw him in the malls hanging around with girls."

Nevertheless, "Goldie" said, Guerrero was probably hustling for whatever he could make because he had been seen with lots of men and would have been a prime target for Jeffrey Dahmer's offers of nude photos in exchange for money. "Guerrero always was getting in cars a lot. He was always getting into one car and then getting out and entering another. To me, that was always a sign of hustling. Guerrero was a hustler and worked the street. I got to know him on the street. He told me he was twenty-three, but he looked seventeen. He was short—5'7". Short dark hair but he grew it long once to his shoulders then he got a haircut. He was female and macho at the same time. He dressed [in] like blue jeans, leather jacket. He looked tough, but he was nice looking, not movie star."

Richard Guerrero was not a runaway but a young man who lived with his family. As it happened, he only had about three dollars to his name on Saturday, March 19, 1988, when he met up with Jeffrey Dahmer at the Phoenix Bar. "Why don't we go back to my place?" Dahmer asked Guerrero, "Have a few drinks and see some videos?" He said they could have sex and that he wanted Guerrero to pose for some photos that he wanted to take of him. There'd be some money in it for him, Dahmer promised.

According to "Goldie," Richard Guerrero was not the kind of person who'd be put off by this kind of offer. He'd been involved with different people before and already knew Dahmer from the bars. He hadn't heard the rumors about the strange things that had happened to Dahmer's drinking companions at the bathhouses.

He agreed to go along with the tall, sandy-haired, soft-spoken Dahmer who seemed to have money to spend and was particularly interested in him.

They took a cab back to Dahmer's grandmother's house in West Allis where Jeff took Guerrero downstairs and went up to say goodnight to his grandmother. Catherine may have heard the sounds of two people coming in, but she remained in bed. Once downstairs, Jeffrey would later confess, he and Richard Guerrero had oral sex. Maybe it was at this point that Catherine Dahmer started down the stairs and saw her grandson and another man in the basement. She has said that she doesn't remember when it was or who the person was she might have seen with Jeffrey. However, it was reported that as Catherine walked down the stairs, she saw Jeffrey with a dark-skinned man, both of whom were not wearing any shirts, and she simply turned around and went back upstairs. Much later, she and her son Lionel would discuss whether Jeffrey was having homosexual relationships, but neither of them dreamed that her house had become a dumpsite for the bodies of Jeffrey's victims. Her seeing Jeffrey partially undressed with another man would be one of the reasons that she eventually told Lionel that Jeffrey would have to move out. But that wouldn't be for at least another six months.

After Dahmer and Guerrero had oral sex, Jeffrey offered him a drink heavily laced with sedatives. The slightly built Guerrero reacted very quickly to the potion. Once he was unconscious, Dahmer swiftly wrapped a black leather strap around his neck and strangled him until he stopped breathing. Jeffrey kept the pressure up a little longer just to make sure his victim was dead. Then Dahmer waited until no one was in the house before he dismembered him, dissolved away his flesh in jars, in the garage, and then poured the whole mess down the floor drain. As with Doxtator and Tuomi, Dahmer also pounded the bones into little pieces so they could be taken away with the garbage. He told the police that he didn't keep any of the body parts.

The Guerrero family filed a missing person's report with the Milwaukee police department on March 24 in which they said their son had been missing for a few days. He'd left the house to go visit a friend, they told the police, but the friend said he never arrived. The family also put notices in the local newspapers along with pictures of the young man. Dahmer saw those notices and recognized him as the person he'd picked up at the Phoenix. But he had disposed of the body well and there was not a trace of Richard Guerrero left for anyone to find. Pablo Guerrero, Richard's father, said that the family had also printed flyers up with his son's picture and passed them around, hired a private investigator to look for clues into his disappearance, and actually walked the banks of the Milwaukee River assuming that if he'd fallen in and drowned his body might have washed up on a bank somewhere. But they found nothing.

They said they wrote to the television show "Unsolved Mysteries," but the story of the missing Richard Guerreo wasn't picked up for further investigation. Then they hired a psychic who claimed that just by touching the things Richard liked to wear and handling his belongings he'd be able to determine the whereabouts of their son. But the psychic didn't find him either. The Guerreros kept on calling the police every couple of months to see if there had been any progress in the case, but they were told at one point by the officer they spoke to that Richard "was not the only person missing out there." The officer was certainly correct about that. There were now two other confirmed missing persons in Milwaukee, victims James Doxtator and Stephen Tuomi, whose families were looking for them as well.

Jeffrey began cruising for new victims almost immediately after the Guerrero murder. He had established a pattern of looking for likely victims during the week when he only had the early evening hours before he had to report for work. Then he would seize upon whatever opportunity presented itself on Saturday nights when he was off and when he would have Sunday mornings to dispose of the body while his grandmother was in church. If the Saturday night was unproductive, as most of them were, then he would have to wait until the next week until he had another opportunity. Toward the latter part of April, a little over a month after he'd killed Guerrero, an opportunity seemed to present itself.

On April 23, 1988, Ernest Flowers, who lived just over the state line in nearby Zion, Illinois, was in Milwaukee visiting friends and partying at some of the bars in the downtown area. He was at 219 with friends until about 2:00 A.M. and then left for the parking lot. They had arrived at the bar in different cars, and after

Flowers watched his friends drive off into the night he tried to start his Oldsmobile that had been giving him problems lately. The automatic choke was sticking and without the right mixture of fuel and air, the engine wouldn't start no matter how many times Flowers turned the starter. He remembered that it was late and he was tired. He kept trying to start the car, knowing that if the engine were warmed up enough, she just might turn over enough to catch once, and he'd rev it and be on his way. But it didn't work. After a few more tries, he could hear the battery start to wind down and the starter turned more slowly. Eventually, all he could get was the clattering sound from a worn-out battery. Finally, the battery was dead. He needed a jump.

"Then I went to a phone booth on Second Street and Pittsburgh," Flowers told the authorities, "and I started making telephone calls to my friends to see if I could get one of them to come down and give me a jump. No one was home. They were probably still in their cars. I kept calling and calling hoping I'd reach someone. There were probably four or five people standing behind me at the time."

Getting more frustrated and irritated, he kept on slamming the phone down and muttering to himself about his plight. Meanwhile, he could see that the people behind him were getting mad at him as well. Finally, he stepped out of the phone line to "collect my thoughts" and go through his list of friends to see whom he could call. That's when he looked up and saw Jeffrey Dahmer standing over him. "Jeff approached and started talking even though I wasn't paying much attention to him at the time because I was preoccupied with getting my car fixed and getting back. It was more

156

like he just started talking to me and it was something more of an annoyance than anything. After he kept talking and talking and asked me what was wrong I answered him. I told him that my car was broken down and I was trying to find some friends of mine to get it going so I could get home. Dahmer said that he had come down to the bars and he thought that he was going to be drinking so he didn't drive. He took a taxi instead because he thought he might get too intoxicated to drive."

Flowers wasn't even paying much attention to the tall blond guy who seemed to be rambling on. Then Dahmer seemed to say something that made Flowers pick right up. "He offered to give me a ride in a cab to get his car to bring it back so we could jump start my car. Then he caught my attention because he had the solution to the problem that I was trying to work on. Then I began to talk to him. He asked a lot of questions. He told me that he had recently moved to Milwaukee from Ohio. He asked me if I was from Milwaukee and I told him that I wasn't. I was from Racine but lived in Illinois. Then he asked me what I was doing that night and I told him that I was at 219 and he told me that he was at C'est La Vie, La Cage, and the Phoenix. He was able to carry on an intelligent conversation without any incoherent answers. He asked a lot of small-talk questions. He asked about my job and I told him in generic terms what I do. But I have a habit of turning a question back to the person who asked it so if you ask me what I do I ask what you do. I asked him about his job and he told me he worked at a factory downtown and he did electrical work of some kind. He also asked me if I made a lot of money and I told him I'm not starving but I'm not getting rich either."

Flowers, who is black, wasn't really worried about the white guy who had offered to chauffeur him around. He was apprehensive because he didn't know what Dahmer's motives were and didn't want to get caught in any compromising positions. However, Dahmer seemed intelligent and stable even if it was apparent that he had been drinking. Flowers said he "scrutinized" Dahmer very carefully because "when someone who's been drinking offers to give you a ride you tend to scrutinize him." Flowers was also a health care professional who worked with doctors making diagnoses about mentally ill individuals. He had been around the mentally ill, was experienced in working with doctors who treated the mentally ill, and told authorities he did not think that Dahmer appeared to be either mentally ill or insane. He also didn't appear to be so drunk that he would be unable to drive. However, Jeffrey's demeanor did give Flowers some pause. There was something wrong with him, Flowers could tell, because Dahmer kept looking away from him whenever their eyes met. "He didn't hold eye contact. When I looked at him he would look away which was pretty uncomfortable." That was a signal to Flowers that something might be odd, but he felt it was a situation he could control.

Then Dahmer pushed the offer to a new stage and Flowers accepted. "Next he told me that he already called a taxi and that I could share the ride with him to his house. He lived just west of here. Then he was going to drive me back and give me a jump. Because of his insistence that he was being a Good Samaritan I was suspicious of his intentions and made it perfectly clear that all I wanted to do was get my car and get home and that was the extent of what was going to happen. I had no interest in sex or in conversation or in anything else besides getting my car and getting home."

Jeffrey Dahmer said he understood that this was not a sexual encounter. "He appeared to understand what I meant. In fact, I asked him twice during our conversation if he understood what my intentions were and he said yes, he understood them perfectly. The cab showed up and both of us got in the cab. Dahmer told the cab driver Fifty-fifth and Lincoln. The cab ride lasted almost fifteen minutes. We were in the vicinity, Dahmer told the cab driver, just to drop us off on the block. The driver asked him, 'Is it the first house, the next house, where?' But Dahmer didn't give him any specific directions. He only said, 'Drop us off a little farther up here.' Then when we got to the middle of the block, Dahmer said, 'Good, just drop us off here.' "

Dahmer didn't say anything during the cab ride, but began acting strangely once the cab stopped and they started walking. "We got out of the cab in the middle of the block and then I pointed to the house in front of us and I asked, 'Is this the house?' And he said, 'No it's just down the way a little.' I asked, 'Is it at the middle of the block?' I was trying to pin him down a little to figure out just where I was going. He explained that he had the cab driver drop us off just a little away from the house because he lived with his grandmother and didn't want to wake her up by the noise of the car. We walked a block and a half to get to the house."

Flowers was edgy enough at this point to want to wait outside while Dahmer went in for the keys. But

Jeffrey upped their ante once again and once again Flowers went along. "When we arrived there I said, 'I'll just wait for you here,' when he went in to get his keys. He said, 'No, why don't you just come on in, it'll just be a minute.' So he opened the door with his key, punched in some alarm numbers on the alarm system and went upstairs. As he went upstairs I heard a voice that sounded like it was coming from an adjacent room. The voice was an elderly woman's voice and she said, 'Is that you, Jeff?' He walked over to the doorway from where the sound was coming from and he said 'It's me, Grandma, I'm just going to make myself a cup of coffee.' I said to him, 'I don't have time for a cup of coffee. I really do have to go. I have a lot of things to do in the morning, I have to go, really.' I was speaking really loudly and my voice does carry and I believed the person in the next room would have heard me."

Dahmer seemed intent on having his way, and his single-mindedness once again caused Flowers to go along with it. Flowers believed once Dahmer was satisfied on the small things, he would get his keys and take him back to his car. The conversation, the way in which Jeffrey seemed to ratchet up the level of their involvement with each other by tiny amounts until he thought he had him under control, is an almost classic dialogue between a serial killer and his intended victim. It shows that rather than using brute force, Dahmer wooed his victims along by getting them to make a series of tiny concessions to him until they were completely in his power.

Flowers knew that he was giving up as he went along, but the larger picture, the possibility that he could get his car started, outweighed the tiny concessions he was making. It began with Flowers trying to blow Dahmer off at the phone booth, continued when Dahmer made him an offer of a ride and a jump start that he couldn't refuse, and continued with the cab ride. Now Jeffrey had to convince Flowers to drink his specially prepared coffee which, before the victim realized it, would render him helpless. Flowers began by saying he didn't want any coffee. But Jeffrey kept the pressure up.

"Jeffrey Dahmer disregarded what I said, and he said, 'I'm kind of tired, I have to have a cup of coffee,' and walked over to the other part of the kitchen to where the coffee pot was and started to make coffee. Then he got a bottle of Bailey's Irish Cream from the cabinet that was right overhead and offered me a drink. I said, 'No really, I have to go. I don't have time.' I didn't see him reach for the car keys. He was going to supposedly have a quick cup of coffee first. I was standing right behind him in the kitchen. He kept trying to convince me to have some Bailey's Irish Cream. But I said that I had too much to do in the morning to drink now. Then he asked me again if I wanted to have coffee and I said, 'No I have too much to do.' He seemed to be a bit on the nervous side the whole time because he just kept pressing the issue and saying, 'It'll only be a quick one. It won't take very long. As soon as I have a cup of coffee, we'll leave.' Then I decided that a quick cup of coffee probably wouldn't hurt. So I decided to drink a quick one and then we'd be on our way. He asked me what I took in the coffee and I said cream and sugar."

At that point, Dahmer thought he had him. Now all he had to do was get the drugs in the coffee cup and he'd be home free. Flowers noticed that Jeffrey completely hid what he was doing until the coffee was ready. "He was doing the whole coffee thing facing the cabinet and facing the wall and his back was toward me. He was blocking the coffee cups so I couldn't see them. He wasn't talking to me at this time. Then he handed me the cup of coffee. He seemed to have calmed down a little bit. He wasn't talking and didn't seem nervous. He just looked at me. The next thing I recall I was thinking, 'Why is he looking at me like that?' For the first time his eye contact was solid and he didn't look away. It was almost as if he were waiting for something. I asked myself, 'What is he waiting for?' So naturally I started to drink the coffee quicker because I became uneasy and wanted to get out of there. The next thing I remember was that I became extremely dizzy and my head was starting to go down like 'that's it!' I passed out."

For Jeffrey, he had his victim, but he also had his grandmother fully aware that he brought someone to the house that night. Now there was a witness. He had to get rid of the unconscious Flowers as unobtrusively as possible and pass the whole thing off with a plausible excuse. He decided to get a cab to take him to the hospital where he would dump him and say that Flowers had gotten sick. That would be the end of it. For Ernest Flowers, the hours between the time he took the cup of coffee from Jeffrey Dahmer and the time he woke up in the hospital in Milwaukee were simply missing time. On April 24, 1988, Easter Sunday, Flowers woke up to the miracle that he was alive. He wouldn't realize that he had been in the clutches of one of the nation's worst serial killers until years later.

"The next thing I remember is that I woke up in

County General Hospital in the morning. I had suffered injuries. I had an abrasion like a rope burn along the side of my face along the temple and cheekbone. They looked like carpet burns. I had no idea how I got to that hospital and no recollection of how I received those injuries. I was missing all the cash from my wallet, a bracelet on my right arm, and my herringbone chain that I wore around my neck. I don't know if the hospital removed my clothing. When I undressed, I noticed that my underwear was on inside out. I also noticed that I had bruises on my neck and there was a white hair on my public hair." Flowers was shocked and ashamed.

Ernest Flowers had been around too many people who were victims to accept what happened to him without a fight. He was going to follow up. "When I realized my cash and jewelry were taken I filed a robbery and drugging complaint, the whole nine yards, with the West Allis Police Department on that evening around 10:30 P.M. on Easter Sunday when I got out of the hospital." The police followed up by interviewing Dahmer who said that he was drunk and didn't remember anybody named Flowers. That he may have been drinking with someone who got sick and had to go to the hospital. Apparently Jeffrey's criminal record and conviction report did not enter into the police investigation because the West Allis police never filed any charges against him. He was allowed to walk away from what might have been an early short circuit to his career as a serial killer.

Ernest Flowers couldn't let it alone, however, and repaid the miracle of his own life by saving the life of another one of Jeffrey's potential victims almost a year later.

"I saw Jeffrey Dahmer again. That occurred at Club 219 about a year later. I recognized him by his distinctive shoes. They were like tan Hush Puppy type shoes, the kinds of shoes I had to wear and hated. He was wearing them the night he picked me up and he was wearing them again the night I saw him at 219 a year later. It was late that night at the bar and my friend kept telling me that we had to go. So I finished my drink and looked down and saw those shoes. It reminded me of the entire incident and when I looked up, there was Jeffrey Dahmer standing right next to me. I said, 'You remember me?' He said, 'No I don't. My name is Jeff,' and he extended his hand. I didn't shake his hand but said to him, 'You know who the fuck I am.' I was angry. He kept his eyes on me but kept insisting that he didn't know who I was. He said, 'I really don't remember who you are but maybe we could go have a cup of coffee and talk about it.' That made me even more irate. Then he left and went outside and my friends noticed a change in me. I was outside; yelling, screaming, and cursing and threatening to kill him and they wouldn't let me get near him. Then I saw him talking to a black man who was a quarter of a block down. I was screaming and saying horrible things to him. Then a taxi pulled up and they both walked to the taxicab. I started screaming, 'Don't go with him. He's crazy. Stay away from him.' I was just belligerent, I guess. The black guy looked at him, looked at me, looked at him, looked at him again and then he just walked away. Dahmer got in the taxicab and left."

Chapter Eleven

Arrested

The Ernest Flowers incident in April was probably the breaking point for Catherine Dahmer. According to the *Akron Beacon Journal* when Catherine discovered that her grandson was bringing men over to her house, the family reportedly had a discussion about Jeffrey's homosexuality. It was September, 1988, and what with the noises, the strange men at all hours of the night on Saturdays, the foul smells that rose up from the basement and from the garage on Sunday afternoons, it had all gone too far. The family came to a decision: Jeffrey had to move out. Maybe he felt he was being abandoned again as he had been ten years earlier in 1978. Maybe he also wanted to move out because he felt he needed the privacy, although on subsequent encounters he sometimes gave a version of his grandmother's address as his own and still brought victims back to the house in West Allis where he murdered them.

It's more likely that Jeffrey wasn't happy about having to find his own place, but didn't blame his grandmother for getting him to leave. He probably blamed his father because, according to John Paul Ranieri who was running a street ministry among the gay bars in downtown Milwaukee, Dahmer blamed many of his problems on his father. But Jeffrey also knew that he was difficult to be with and knew he had a problem with alcohol despite the fact that he didn't like to be pushed around by his family. However, on September 25, Jeffrey complied with the family's wishes and moved himself to a very cheap one-bedroom apartment on North Twenty-fifth Street in a very bad neighborhood near Marquette University, the place where his father had attended college almost thirty years before. Now Dahmer had his own place and didn't have to measure his comings and goings according to his grandmother's schedule. This time he could work on his own time and conform his pleasures only to his schedule at the chocolate factory. Accordingly, the very next day, Dahmer left his apartment in the afternoon to go cruising. That was how he met thirteen-year-old high school freshman Sounthome Sinthasomphone whose family had moved to the area after having emigrated from Laos.

Sounthome Sinthasomphone remembers the encounter with Jeffrey Dahmer very well because that day he had come within a hair's breadth of losing his life. "On September 26, between 3:00 P.M. and 4:00 P.M. in the afternoon, I was on my way home from school where I was a freshman," Sounthome Sinthasomphone told the court at Dahmer's murder trial years later. "I passed by the area of West Twenty-fifth Street right on the corner. Jeffrey Dahmer came up to me on the corner of Twenty-fifth and asked me if I would pose for a quick fifty dollars. He asked me what school I went to and how old I was. I said I was a freshman and that I was thirteen. Then he said he was asking other kids if they wanted to pose also. I asked him if this was his career and he said no, it was his hobby. He asked me if I wanted to go along with him to his apartment where I would pose and he would give me the money and I said yes. We started to walk to his apartment. We got there after about a block or two walk. We went into his apartment. He asked me if I could strip [so he could take] the photos he wanted with no clothes on."

Sinthasomphone said that he felt funny about taking off his clothes and didn't want to do it. However, Dahmer kept on pressing him and pressing the money on him. Dahmer's relentless insistence, his seeking every opportunity to get the child to make just one more compromise in Dahmer's favor, was the very same routine he'd used with Flowers to lure him into his power.

"He asked me again if I wanted to pose with my clothes on or whether I wanted to strip," Sinthasomphone said. "I told him with my clothes on. He then asked me to lie on the bed, but he pulled my shirt up right to my neck because he said it was a good picture. While I was laying right on the bed with my shirt up to my neck, he took one shot with his Polaroid. I could see the picture come out so that's how I knew it was a Polaroid."

After he got the one snapshot, Dahmer wanted even more. He wanted to get Sinthasomphone to drink his sleeping potion so he could have sex with the boy and get rid of him. But he also had to move slowly so he didn't scare the kid away. Sinthasomphone remembered that Jeffrey didn't rush things. "We stayed in the bedroom for a little while and then he offered me a drink. He asked if I wanted some coffee and I said yes. Then I followed him into the kitchen where he was going to make the coffee. I watched as he put water from the faucet into a pot and boiled it. Then he poured coffee into cups. He put a chocolate colored creamlike substance into the coffee. Then we went back to the living room. He took a little sip of coffee and then I drank about half the cup. He said, 'Why don't you just finish it?' and I drank the whole thing."

This was Dahmer's powerful sleeping potion yet it seemed to have no effect on the boy at all. It was as if the young man's metabolism was either so slow the substance wouldn't act at all for a while, or his system was just different somehow. But Dahmer didn't seem too concerned. Maybe he believed if he took more photographs, the substance would have time to work and he would eventually have the boy in his power. Dahmer coaxed Sinthasomphone back into the bedroom for another Polaroid.

"Then we went back into the bedroom for another picture," Sinthasomphone testified. "He said that I should open my fly for the picture. I told him no, and he said that I should just unzip my fly. I put it halfway down and then he said put it all the way down and show my underwear. He pulled it all the way down himself and then he grabbed my penis. I took my penis away from him and put it back into my pants. That's when he took another picture. Then I said, 'I got to go.' Then he said he liked listening to people's stomachs. I was on the bed still and he started leaning down and he put his ears to my stomach and started kissing my stomach."

It is very significant that at this most critical time of Dahmer's encounter with his victim, right when he was fondling his penis and when he expected that the drugs would kick in and render the boy helpless, Dahmer had the urge to listen to the child's stomach. Escaped victim Tracy Edwards also said that Dahmer listened to his heart when he was handcuffed and on the floor. Moreover, Dahmer reportedly liked to listen to his mother's stomach when he was six years old at the time she was carrying Jeff's younger brother David. He said he liked to listen to the baby's heartbeat or listen to it move around. He also liked to listen to his mother's heartbeat.

It's plausible to believe that listening to life inside another person or feeling the pulse as blood coursed through someone else's body was one of the only acts of bonding, or of affection, that Dahmer was capable of mustering. It always occurred prior to or just after the closest Dahmer ever came to sex and at the time he was about to exert the most control over his victim. In a very primitive and safe way, albeit bizarre, this was Dahmer's act of loving someone else. It was safe because it was one of the only ways he was able to get his mother's attention, and perhaps his mother's affection, while she was pregnant and he was feeling neglected and abandoned. It was primitive because for an abandoned human being, possibly someone in terror of being alone, the sound of another heartbeat was perhaps the most sustaining form of communication. It might well have eased the six-year-old's terror when he felt neglected in his family and remained throughout his life as a way to ease his fears. It isn't farfetched, therefore, to assume that it was one of the climactic moments of Dahmer's especially bizarre serial murder ritual, a signature to his crime that only the living witnesses could attest to.

Sinthasomphone was in terror. Already he had begun to feel the effects of the drugs, but he was so frightened that the natural impulse to flee was overcoming the dizziness he was already experiencing on the bed. Sinthasomphone realized that he was in terrible danger and couldn't let the powerful sedatives overcome him until he got to a safe place.

"I knew right away I had to get out of there," he told police who questioned him later that evening. "I said to him, 'I have to go.' I grabbed my book bag and moved to the door of the apartment. He said, 'Wait, don't forget your money and don't tell anybody that I'm doing this.' I opened the door and he gave me fifty dollars. Then I walked out and I felt very dizzy. I started to walk home and started to feel more dizzy the more I got home. When I got home I slammed the door behind me and couldn't walk straight. I went to bed. I must have passed out because I woke up in the hospital. We left the hospital to go home that night. That's when the police officers came to my home. I told them what happened to me and went with them to point to the apartment and building where this all took place. I picked out the picture that was listed 'Jeffrey Dahmer.' "

As a prior offender who had exposed himself to little boys and had just come off probation, Dahmer's mug shots were in the police books. Dahmer also fit the description young Sinthasomphone had given the Milwaukee police who had only arrested him about a year and a half earlier at the State Fair Park. After Sounthome identified Dahmer, the police went to the Oxford Apartments on North Twenty-fifth Street to question him. Ultimately, they arrested Jeffrey Dahmer and charged him with second degree sexual assault and enticing a child for immoral purposes. Dahmer was sent to jail, but was released on bail a week later. He returned to his apartment and to his work at the chocolate factory while he and his lawyer, Gerald Boyle, got ready for the trial that wouldn't take place until sometime the following year.

On January 30, 1989, Jeffrey Dahmer was convicted of a felony in the second degree sexual assault of Sounthome Sinthasomphone and of enticing a minor for immoral purposes. His sentencing hearing was set for the following May while in the meantime Dahmer was still free on his original bond because the court didn't feel it necessary to remand him to custody pending his sentence. It was a decision, however inadvertent, that ultimately would cost the life of another young man.

* * *

On the Saturday night before Easter, March 25, 1989, Jeffrey Dahmer met twenty-four-year-old Anthony Sears and his friend Jeffrey Connor at the La Cage on Sixth and National. According to Tony Sears's mother, Tony told her earlier that evening that he'd be over for Easter dinner the following day. Sears had wanted to be a model, and his mother said that he loved to have his picture taken. Perhaps that was why Jeffrey Dahmer's promise to take some snapshots of him fell on very receptive ears. Sears's friend Jeffrey Connor said that Tony went out that night to celebrate his new promotion as a manager of a restaurant in town. It was to have been a happy night.

It was at the La Cage, Jeffrey Connor said, that Tony Sears hooked up with Jeffrey Dahmer who was cruising around looking for a drinking partner. The two of them seemed to buddy up. Jeffrey Dahmer told Connor and Sears that he was from Chicago but was in town to visit his grandmother who lived on Lincoln Avenue in West Allis. Jeffrey Dahmer was a regular at La Cage.

"Goldie," the female impersonator who was friendly with Jeffrey Dahmer and many of his victims, said that La Cage was one of Jeffrey's bars of choice because, "He fit in more in La Cage than at any other place." Goldie said that when Dahmer was cleaned up, he matched the La Cage prototype. "La Cage was real Yuppie. Everyone was well dressed and looked successful. That bar was like a 21 Club. This was like the same La Cage that was in Hollywood, and they came out here."

Jeffrey visited La Cage a lot, "Goldie" said, because he liked the clientele that frequented the place and had good luck hooking up with people, especially the hustler-types who were always looking for someone to offer them money. Also, because he was a tall, good-looking blond, "Goldie" said, he hooked up with a lot of young black guys who were doing the yuppie party scene and who may have needed money for drugs. There were a lot of hustlers and hungry cocaine users making the rounds of the yuppie bars, "Goldie" remembered, and Jeffrey Dahmer seemed to attract them all.

Sears's friend Jeffrey Connor remembered that he and Tony closed La Cage on the night of March 25, but Sears still wanted to party somewhere. Connor remembered Dahmer suggesting that he and Tony Sears go over to the house for a few drinks, and Connor volunteered to drive them over. He figured he would see his friend Tony later. But when they got to West Allis, Jeff told Connor to stop the car around the vicinity of Fifty-sixth and Lincoln where Dahmer and Sears got out of the car and walked southbound. Dahmer liked to tell his guests that his grandmother was a light sleeper who was easily awakened by the sound of a car. It was always quieter if they simply walked the final couple of blocks to the house, Dahmer would say. Connor said that he saw them walking as he drove away and remembered that the guy told Jeff that his grandmother lived over on Fifty-sixth Street. Dahmer typically gave false addresses to the people who dropped him off so they wouldn't be able to tell police the correct address of

Catherine Dahmer. He always stopped the cab a couple of blocks away so no one could identify the actual house. This was a type of well-rehearsed plan that almost all long-term serial killers develop to protect themselves from detection. Dahmer might have also been worried that since his arrest in the Sounthome Sinthasomphone case, the police might have been watching his apartment at the Oxford just in case he was bringing anyone else back there.

Dahmer eventually told police that he brought Sears back to his grandmother's house and had sex with him. Afterwards, he gave him a drink with sleeping pills in it, waited until he passed out, and strangled him. The next morning when his grandmother was in church, Jeffrey decapitated his victim and cut the torso and limbs into tiny pieces which he flushed down the drain or left out with the garbage. The head was a different matter. Jeffrey actually liked the looks of Tony Sears, a handsome individual who might have been bisexual because some people said he might have had a girlfriend. Dahmer decided that he wanted to preserve it. He put the head in a pot of boiling water and simmered it to remove the skin. When he had peeled or scraped away the last of the skin, Dahmer painted the skull a grey color and took it back to his apartment in Milwaukee with him. Sears's skull was in Jeffrey's apartment the night he was arrested after Tracy Edwards escaped. It was one of the skulls that the officers found after they searched the apartment.

Less than two months later, Dahmer was back in court defending himself at his sentencing hearing before Judge William D. Gardner. The debate at the hearing between assistant district attorney Gale Shelton and Dahmer's defense counsel Gerald Boyle in retrospect provides a glimpse into how Dahmer's crime and conviction were regarded by the court. In addition, it reveals the factors the court took into consideration in seeking an appropriate sentence for Dahmer who was not only a sexual offender, but a repeat offender as well. Boyle would subsequently defend Dahmer again in the murder trial in early 1992.

Gale Shelton argued to the court that she saw a deeply sinister side of Dahmer that was a clear danger to the community if he were allowed to go free after a short sentence. Both Gerald Boyle and Lionel Dahmer said they saw something very different. They argued that they perceived a young man whose entire life was crippled by alcohol and who wouldn't receive any treatment for his alcohol problem behind bars. What he would receive was a course in brutality which would probably bar him from reentering society in any meaningful way. The judge had to weigh these two arguments against the actual facts of the verdict in the Sounthome Sinthasomphone case.

Gale Shelton argued that Dahmer should be sentenced to prison for five to six years minimum because of the "deeply disturbing picture that the psychologists represented from their interviews with the defendant." She said that everything surrounding the crime itself was also very disturbing and indicated that Dahmer was far more of a danger than he might seem at first. Shelton argued that the community outside of prison provided Dahmer with little opportunity for change or improvement.

"In my judgment, it is absolutely crystal clear that the prognosis for treatment of Mr. Dahmer within the community is extremely bleak," she argued. Her arguments were also quoted in the Milwaukee papers during their coverage of the trial. She said further whatever treatment he might receive on the outside was "just plain not going to work." She said that other people shared her conclusions. "That's absolutely clear from every single professional who's looked at Mr. Dahmer, and the reality is that his track record exhibits that he is very likely to re-offend."

In Dahmer's mind, Shelton argued, the only thing he had done wrong was to solicit a victim who was too young and for whom the law offered special protection. She explained how Dahmer induced Sounthome into going to his apartment with stories of the new camera he had gotten and how he needed to try it out, but could get no one else to pose for him. And she mentioned the fifty dollars that Dahmer threw in as an added inducement. At first, Shelton argued, Jeffrey Dahmer had denied to the police that he had purposely drugged the boy when he put a sedative into his drink. Yet, she told the judge, Dahmer was unsatisfied that Sounthome Sinthasomphone had only drunk half the cup of coffee and pushed him to finish up the rest whereupon he became sick.

"Mr. Dahmer's version is simply not the truth, and that gives me a great deal of concern about his insight into his problems and his ability to work on those problems as an outpatient within a community setting," she continued. Even when he was in therapy after the disorderly conduct conviction, "he only went through the motions." Jeffrey appeared at his sessions, did what he had to and provided the "facade of a very cooperative and receptive appearance. But anything that goes below the surface indicates the deep-seated anger and deep-seated psychological problems that he has, that he's completely unwilling or incapable of dealing with."

She said that the report from the doctor who was seeing him indicated that problems lurked below the surface even though Dahmer seemed to be doing what was asked of him. "The defendant could not have been less cooperative, that he didn't delve into his problems at all, that he denied that he had a problem. The other strain that is constant throughout the reports is the strong predomination of anger and resistance and evasiveness that Mr. Dahmer has displayed, and also his willingness to be very manipulative." The assistant district attorney said she believed that in order to protect the community from Jeffrey Dahmer, any treatment he should receive should take place within a prison setting.

Even though Gale Shelton's comments might have seemed harsh as they applied to a twenty-nine-year-old man who had only been convicted of one sexual offense, they were actually quite perceptive and accurately described the personality of an individual who had already brutalized and mutilated five people in sexual homicides. She was correct that Jeffrey Dahmer was in a complete state of denial about his actions and that he had a tendency (very typical among serial killers) to blame everyone else but himself for his actions. Serial killers rarely accept the responsibility for what they do and lay blame on everybody within reach.

Shelton claimed that all of Dahmer's activities from his drinking to his sexual offense fit into a larger pattern of abuse that seemed to be fueled by a deep anger. Even the anger wouldn't have been so bad, she seemed to be suggesting, had Dahmer only addressed that anger in the treatment program he was asked to undergo. But by walking through the motions of the program and simply not allowing himself to get below the surface of his performance, he had demonstrated a predilection to keep on going in the same direction. In other words, Dahmer had not made a decision to change even though he had faced prison and had been given the opportunity. He had already used up his chance and to give him another chance now would be inviting trouble. The next time, the victim might not be so lucky as was Sounthome Sinthasomphone. Shelton did not know just how accurate she was in her assessment of the defendant.

Like any good defense attorney, and by reputation Gerald Boyle is one of the best defense attorneys in all Milwaukee, Jeffrey Dahmer's lawyer focused the court's attention on only the facts of the present conviction. Everything else — such as larger patterns of criminal behavior, previous offenses, what Jeffrey did or did not accomplish in his treatment program — was all subordinate to the facts of the present case. He said that Dahmer's sentence should be based only on what might be accomplished by sending him to prison or by getting treatment for his alcohol problem in a community-based setting. His state of mind when he committed the crime and his department in a previous treatment program were secondary, too. The facts of the case overshadowed questions of Dahmer's state of mind.

"The reality of it is, as bad as it was, the best evidence before you, your honor, is it happened on one occasion," Boyle argued. "Now, what else do we know? We know pretty well that since that time in September of last year, he has been functioning in this society without any intense kind of psychological or alcoholic help and he hasn't done anything like [that] again." How could Boyle have known that what he was saying at the hearing was dead wrong? In fact, the signature crime that Dahmer had tried to perpetrate on Sounthome Sinthasomphone, if the drugs had worked quickly enough, was exactly the same crime that he had been committing since he moved to his grandmother's house years earlier. He had killed five times and would have killed six times, had Sounthome not had the presence of mind to run for his life as he felt himself getting dizzy. But none of these facts were known to Boyle at the time Dahmer was sentenced.

Thus, Boyle continued to argue that what the court had before it was a young alcoholic who should be considered sick and in need of treatment. Indeed his client's life could be turned around and guided toward productivity if he received the therapy he so sorely needed. Unfortunately, he would not receive it in prison, only in a community-based setting. And prison would make Dahmer's problems worse.

"Now, no matter what you do," Boyle argued, "Some day Jeffrey Dahmer is going to leave prison and be back in society." In other words, Boyle promised the judge, society would have to deal with Dahmer at some point later in his life. If he were savaged by a prison experience in which he received no therapy, nothing would be gained except for the inevitable unleashing of a hardened criminal upon society. Right now there was a chance to avoid that future and rehabilitate Dahmer. The court, he urged, should take that chance.

"He's very alone in the world," Boyle said of his client. "He really is monastic and Spartan, the way he conducts the affairs of his life which is probably nobody's fault but his own." And, he incorrectly, but inadvertently, pointed out, "We don't have a multiple offender here. I believe he was caught before it got to the point where it would have gotten worse." Thus, the attorney suggested, the court should give Dahmer a long suspended sentence which would always be there, hanging over the defendant's head, in case Dahmer didn't complete whatever treatment the court ordered. And, in fact, the court ultimately invoked the long suspended sentence still on Dahmer for not completing his treatment and for violating the terms of his probation by getting drunk, associating with minors, and being a habitual criminal. Unfortunately for his victims, however, his violations of probation came as a result of the very multiple

homicides his attorney was concerned a̶
plea to Judge Gardner.

The tragic aspect about Jeffrey Dahmer's case̶
the cases of most serial killers, is that they are v̶
often arrested on charges that are only a small tip o̶
the iceberg in relation to the rest of the crimes they
are concurrently committing. Jeffrey Dahmer was arrested for a sexual offense when a sexual offense was
only a small part of the entire picture. Therefore,
when a bizarre aspect to the crime comes before the
court, courts should look for a "signature aspect" to
the crime, a particular moment in the offense that
seems to carry some psychological weight for the perpetrator. If such a signature is present, a much more
thorough investigation into the defendant's behavior
and a real search of outstanding warrants should be
conducted. It is likely that a signature criminal is already committing crimes far more serious than the
offense for which he's been arrested. Had such an investigation been conducted on Dahmer and his
whereabouts since his arrest at the Wisconsin State
Fair Park, the police might have tied him to some of
the missing persons reports that had already been
filed for individuals in whose company Dahmer had
been seen by witnesses. At the time of his sentencing
hearing, the pieces of evidence were already in place
to tie Jeffrey Dahmer to three of the missing persons
and the drugging, sexual offense, and robbery of
Ernest Flowers who had reported the offense to the
West Allis Police Department.

addition to Gerald Boyle's plea to Judge ᵈner, Lionel Dahmer also spoke at the sentencing ᵃring. He begged the court to find some way of ᵢving Jeffrey the treatment he so desperately needed. He asked that if there were a choice between prison and treatment, and he assumed there was such a choice, that his son be given treatment and the opportunity to rehabilitate himself.

Then Jeffrey Dahmer spoke to the court on his own behalf. First, in fielding questions from the bench, Dahmer admitted that he was an alcoholic and a homosexual with sexual problems. "I'm an alcoholic," he said. "I'm not the sort that has to have a drink very single day, but when I do drink, I go overboard. The prosecution has raised very serious charges against me, and I can understand why. What I've done is very serious. I never meant to give anyone the impression that I thought otherwise. I've never been in this position before. Nothing this awful. This is a nightmare come true for me. If anything would shock me out of my past behavior patterns it's this. Please give me a chance so that I can tread the straight and narrow and not get involved in a situation like this ever again. I can't stress enough that I desperately want to change my conduct for the rest of my life. This enticing a child was the climax of my idiocy. It's just, it's going to destroy me, I'm afraid, this one incident. I don't know what in the world I was thinking when I did it. I know I was under the influence."

For someone who did not know that Dahmer was already a serial sex killer, this might have sounded like a sincere plea for help and understanding. But Dahmer had become so accomplished at denial that he was able to stand up in court and pull this off in the face of the prosecution's very accurate portrayal of him as an unreformed potentially violent predator. Denial is the main component of a serial killer's camouflage, a camouflage that can hold up even when the killer is arrested for another crime. In case after case, serial killers have bragged to investigators about how they were able to defend themselves against lesser charges when the serious crimes they had committed simply went right past the authorities because warrants hadn't been searched, evidence was lost, or the police simply didn't know where to look. In Dahmer's case this is exactly what happened, and the judge bought everything the defense had told him.

Judge Gardner sentenced Dahmer to five years in prison on the sexual assault charge but put him on probation for five years instead. As part of that probation, the judge ordered Dahmer to spend one year in work release in the House of Correction and to complete a program of psychological treatment. On the second charge of sexual enticement of a child, the judge sentenced Jeffrey Dahmer to three years in prison but stayed his sentence and ordered an additional five years probation to run concurrently with the first five years. Finally, the judge prohibited Dahmer from any contact with juveniles and ordered him not to loiter near schools, parks where children gathered, or playgrounds.

Dahmer had done it. He stood right up there in front of a court and lied his way right through to a suspended sentence and probation. He'd done probation before and it wasn't so bad. He'd even managed to keep on killing right through the whole process. Now, despite his previous killings, he'd convinced a judge that he could control the monster that was eating him up from the inside. The court had only seen a tiny portion of the horror that was Jeffrey Dahmer and had let him walk right back onto the street. Now, having successfully beaten the system for a second time in less than three years, Dahmer was once again free to kill.

Chapter Twelve

On Probation

With the words of Judge Gardner ringing in his ears, Jeffrey Dahmer was remanded into custody. The judge told him that he could have made it far worse for him had he so chosen. "I could send you to prison and you wouldn't get any treatment for the problem. You'd come out probably worse than you are right now," he said. The judge was also aware that Dahmer was doomed to repeat his offense over and over because it was likely he couldn't control himself unless he was taught how. "You are going to repeat," he foretold, "because it's a drive. It's almost a biological urge that you have." But with treatment, Judge Gardner thought, there was hope for the man standing before him, and he wanted to use that hope rather than discard it. "This is the kind of thing that the prosecutor would just ask the judge to throw away the book. . . . But if there is an opportunity to salvage you, I must make use of that opportunity."

Unlike Dahmer's trial for murder in 1992 where

the victims' families were invited to make a statement to the court and to the defendant prior to sentencing, the Sinthasomphone family was not present and had no input into the judge's deliberations. By the time Judge William Gardner had effectively gaveled Dahmer's sentencing hearing to a close, unbeknownst to all, the fates of the next series of Dahmer's victims had been sealed. The courtroom was emptied and Dahmer taken away to begin serving his twelve months.

Jeffrey Dahmer had been originally sentenced to do his time at the House of Correction, but that was later changed to the Community Correctional Center (CCC) on North Tenth Street right in his old neighborhood in Milwaukee. He was in walking distance from his job at Ambrosia Chocolate Company where he was still on the night shift, and only about fifteen blocks from his old apartment. In effect, although he was confined to a bed in prison during the day, he had completely resumed his travels during the night going to and from work.

Dahmer fit into the system of rules at the CCC quite well, even though he was unhappy there. In fact, prosecutor Gale Shelton's analysis of Dahmer's uncanny ability to camouflage himself within the rules of a system and play those rules to keep himself out of trouble proved to be prophetic as Dahmer navigated his way through the prison system. The rules were very specific inside the prison environment, but Dahmer learned to follow orders in the army and he showed up on time for bed checks and was able to adhere rigidly to his work-release schedule. Dahmer also learned that you didn't have to be a perfect prisoner to earn time from the system (days subtracted from your sentence) for simply following the rules. This was a game which anybody who understood how the system works could win.

Dahmer was miserable in prison, however, and his hatred for minorities surfaced whenever he felt safe enough to let it surface. He once told an inmate about how he hated blacks and fantasized about killing black people once out of prison. But the inmate didn't take him seriously. No one did. Dahmer, after all, was a nerdy type of guy who had molested a kid. He was, in prison parlance, a "short eyes" and fair game for any convict in the dorm. Dahmer told his family that he was raped by black prisoners on at least one occasion, but was probably terrorized by the other prisoners throughout his sentence. His grandmother said in an interview that she believed Dahmer had been assaulted more than once and had developed a deep hatred for the black prisoners at the Community Correctional Center. All of his was ironic because while Jeffrey was complaining about being the victim, he had already murdered four black men and sexually assaulted a fifth. But, nevertheless, Catherine Dahmer said that she believed her grandson's attitudes hardened as a result of his time behind bars.

Dahmer also created an incident when he broke the rules on the day he was given a twelve-hour pass to spend Thanksgiving with his family in West Allis. As one of the conditions of his release, Jeffrey was not allowed to consume any alcohol and he had to be checked back into the correctional center at 10:00 P.M. that night. However, when he showed up at the gate after 4:00 A.M. in the morning, the smell of alcohol heavy on his breath, guards administered a balloon sobriety test which Jeffrey failed. He admitted that he had consumed a quart of Jack Daniels over the Thanksgiving holiday. In fact, Dahmer reportedly confided to an inmate that he had not spent Thanksgiving Day with his family at all but had gone out on a drunk and polished off an entire bottle of bourbon all by himself.

One of the corrections officers noted in his report that "Jeffrey claimed to have drunk a quart of Jack Daniels on Thanksgiving Day. It also appears from a review of the presentence that Jeffrey is not motivated toward any type of treatment. Essentially, that could be a problem area." The prison reprimanded Dahmer by taking away from him two days of the "good behavior" time he had earned when he was following the rules.

Jeffrey told a very different story to the psychological experts who interviewed him for their subsequent testimony at his murder trial. Jeffrey said that he was so frightened of facing his father, his stepmother, his brother David, but ultimately his grandmother Catherine, at Thanksgiving dinner that he didn't go to the house at all but got drunk, stayed in Milwaukee, and hooked up with an older man. Dahmer said that the man sexually abused him after he passed out from drinking too much bourbon. When he awoke, Dahmer told the experts, he was hanging upside down from a hook in some food packing plant. He was dazed, in pain, and so disoriented that he didn't remember what had happened. He only knew that he was experiencing an overwhelming sense of shame and rage at having been sexually abused, which was an ironic reversal of fortune for him. He made his way back to the prison and tried as best he could to cover up the story from the prison officials and from his family. The "imprinting" had been made, however. The next time his family saw him, when he was released from prison, they said they saw a person who looked as if he'd been through a terrible experience and would be forever hardened and changed.

By way of a disclaimer, it's important to make clear that Jeffrey Dahmer's story of having been abused sexually on his Thanksgiving release has no independent confirmation whatsoever even though it was entered into the court record during the trial testimony of the medical experts. As in the cases of most serial killers, what the killers say to authorities is important because it represents his perceptions even if those perceptions cannot be independently confirmed as true. Dahmer's story may well be true because it has taken two years for him to talk about it and deal with it. It may well be true because members of his family said that he came out of prison changed and hardened. However it may also be a pretext, invented by Dahmer, to explain away his actions and possibly bolster the defense theory that he was insane at the time he committed the crimes. Without independent corroboration, we will never know.

Whether Jeffrey Dahmer was raped the night he was on holiday release or whether he just got drunk and passed out somewhere, Dahmer was not about to give up after receiving his reprimand. He launched on a campaign to win back some of the time he had lost. It was a kind of gambit, to be sure, especially in light of his being reprimanded for drinking after he reported back late to the correctional center. Nevertheless, he must have sensed that a response to the Thanksgiving Day reprimand was called for. On December 10, 1989, he wrote the judge who sentenced him a direct letter pleading for a reduction in his sentence.

"My name is Jeff Dahmer," the letter began. "On September 20, [sic] 1988, I was arrested in Milwaukee, WI for taking pictures of a 13 yr. old minor. On Sept. 27, 1988 I was released on bail from the Mil. co. jail. On May 25, 1989 after having entered a plea of guilty in your court, I received my sentence. It was as follows, one year on work release at CCC, and five years of probation. I have, as of this date, served six months and four days of my sentence. Sir, I have always believed that a man should be willing to assume responsibility for the mistakes that he makes in life. That is way I entered a plea of 'guilt' to the crime of which I was charged.

"During my stay at CCC, I have had a chance to look at my life from an angle that was never presented to me before. What I did was deplorable. The world has enough misery in it without my adding more to it. Sir, I can assure you that it will never happen again. This is why, Judge Gardner, I am requesting from you a sentence modification so that I may be all wed to continue my life as a productive member of our society." The letter was signed "Respectfully yours, Jeff Dahmer."

In typical Jeffrey Dahmer fashion, which Milwaukee Assistant District Attorney Gale Shelton had so eloquently pointed out to the court at his sentencing hearing six months earlier, Dahmer failed to acknowledge and take responsibility for the full seriousness of what he did. It was as if Dahmer had simply wished away the assault he perpetrated on the child and only referred to having been charged with taking photographs of a minor. His letter did not say that he fondled the child or even that he tried to drug him. He also didn't mention the second count of the charge which was the enticing of the child for immoral purposes. It was as if in that letter, Jeffrey Dahmer simply rewrote his past history in a public demonstration of the behavior the prosecutor had said was the most dangerous aspect of his criminal personality.

Whether the letter worked or not or whether

Dahmer simply had earned enough days of good behavior time to shorten his sentence considerably is a matter for debate. The record shows, however, that after serving only ten out of the twelve months in work release, Dahmer was up for parole in March, 1990, as the result of an early release program. Unfortunately for him, however, Dahmer had managed to get through ten months of prison without having participated in a recovery program. And this made his father Lionel Dahmer angry and fearful. Lionel believed that alcohol had been his son's ruination. He also believed that were his son to be released without having had the benefit of some recovery program with a substance abuse professional, an even greater misfortune would befall him. Of course, Lionel could not have dreamed in his worst nightmares that his deepest fears had already come to be and that Jeffrey had been a serial killer since 1987 who had used Lionel's own mother's house as his body dumping ground.

On March 1, 1990, a frustrated Lionel Dahmer made a desperate plea to the court that his son not be released without completing the substance abuse program that the court itself had mandated. In a letter to Judge Gardner he pointed out to Judge Gardner that there had been no coordination whatsoever among the various state agencies responsible for providing an alcohol abuse program for Jeffrey and as a result he had received no treatment. Lionel also pointed out that after his son's previous conviction the treatment he had received for his alcohol addiction was not conducted by an experienced substance abuse professional and therefore it was as if he'd received no treatment at all. It simply made no sense to him that his son should reenter the very same environment under the very same conditions that he had placed him and the young boy he had abused at peril.

He implored Judge Gardner that Jeffrey be kept behind bars until the root cause of his problem had been addressed. It had not been addressed in the past and the parole system would be incapable of handling him, Lionel wrote. "Based upon this and several conversations with Jeff's prior generic caseload parole officers, I have tremendous reservations regarding Jeff's chances when he hits the streets. Every incident, including the most recent conviction for sex offense, has been associated with an initiated by alcohol in Jeff's case. I sincerely hope that you might intervene in some way to help my son, who I love very much and for whom I want a better life. This may be our last chance to institute something lasting," he concluded in an ironically dramatic phrase that could not have been more accurate in its prediction.

However, despite his explicit warnings, the day after Lionel sent his letter to Judge Gardner, Jeffrey Dahmer walked out of prison and into a serial killing spree so furious that he would write himself and the city of Milwaukee into the true crime record books.

Something had changed about Jeffrey Dahmer

during his incarceration at the CCC, Shari Dahmer noticed when she saw him again. She agreed with her mother-in-law Catherine that this was not the same Jeffrey who had entered the correctional center ten months earlier. "Something happened to him in prison that he would never talk about," she told a Cleveland newspaper in an interview. "We all know what can happen to a child molester in prison. He had no light in his eyes. Jeff lost his soul in there. He said he'd never go back to prison."

In fact the serial killer Jeffrey Dahmer, who had gone into prison possibly with the chance to make himself whole again, had emerged from prison a bitterly angry human being who was determined to inflict as much violence on the world as he could. Jeffrey believed he had been abandoned since the age of six when he perceived his mother had withdrawn from him and the family in order to have her new baby. Since that time his parents had fought bitterly. Now, having gone to jail, he had returned to face his family again, with an even greater shame. Because for Jeffrey Dahmer and for many pathological people like him, shame usually generates a pent-up fury that results in explosive and often homicidal violence. Dahmer's return to society would mark the beginning of a terrible killing spree in the gay community where Dahmer sought to take out his revenge on homosexuals because he was still in deep and violent conflict about his own homosexuality.

Jeffrey Dahmer began his probation assignment

almost immediately upon his release. He would have a strict line to walk because his probation agent Donna Chester had laid down what seemed to be absolute rules for his continuing freedom. She said that he was obligated to meet with her twice a month for the remainder of his probation. She said that he had to undergo a substance abuse treatment program for his alcohol addiction, and she categorically forbade him to have any unsupervised contact with a person under the age of eighteen unless she had approved it first. The latter stipulation was also a condition of his earlier probation and he had violated that almost as soon as probation ended. This time the probation department planned to enforce it.

There were additional conditions attached to Jeffrey's probation. He was supposed to participate in a psychotherapy program specifically to address the issues of his conflicts over his sexuality and the reasons he expressed those conflicts in a sexual offense perpetrated on a minor, and he was not to contact the child he had abused.

Finally, as a part of his alcohol abuse treatment program, Dahmer was forbidden as a condition of his continuing parole to consume any alcohol. To engage in drinking of any sort would have been a violation of parole and technically he could have been so charged and returned to prison. For someone like Dahmer, these were tough conditions.

Dahmer signed a lease at the Oxford Apartments

only a couple of months after his release from the CCC and moved into apartment 213 on May 13, 1990. He continued to work at Ambrosia Chocolate Company just as he had done without interruption since 1986. By the end of May he was also back in the Milwaukee bar scene, back into his old habits again, and technically in violation of his parole requirements. On May 29, he encountered Raymond Smith, also known among his friends in the gay community as Ricky Beeks, at 219. Raymond Smith had a ten-year-old daughter and was living in Rockford, Illinois, where he had grown up. He had served time in jail in the past and had a criminal record which dated back over ten years, but had come to Milwaukee to live with his half sister, Donita Grace. She had told police that because it was not unusual for Ricky Beeks to disappear for weeks or months at a time, she didn't call the police when he didn't turn up at the house. In fact, she said, she had heard rumors that Beeks had been shot in 1990 and was surprised that his remains turned up in Dahmer's apartment.

Dahmer said that he struck up a conversation with Beeks at the 219 and offered him money to come over to his new place to be photographed, have some drinks, and watch some videos. When they got to North Twenty-fifth Street, Dahmer followed much the same procedure that he did at his grandmother's house. They walked the final block to the apartment complex and entered through the alley in the rear of the building. But at this point,

Dahmer's M.O. changed in a major way and indicated that at least for this first homicide after his release from prison his sexual dysfunction had moved even farther off the scale. Dahmer specifically didn't have sex with Beeks as soon as they got to the apartment and sat down. Instead, he immediately mixed him a spiked drink which knocked him out. At that point, Dahmer strangled Beeks and, once he was dead, removed all of his clothes. Then, in a departure from the pattern of his recent series of murders, Jeffrey Dahmer performed oral sex on the dead man's body before dismembering him for disposal. Dahmer seemed fascinated with Beeks's skull, however, and wanted to preserve it. He boiled the flesh off the bone, dried it, and painted the skull so that it looked like a plastic model which he kept as a trophy to join the skulls of Anthony Sears and a subsequent victim.

Donita Grace commented that her half brother's death was more grotesque than real. "It was something out of a horror movie," she told the newspapers. Beeks's grandmother, Thelma Smith, told the newspapers that she blamed the system that allowed Dahmer to roam free as much as she blamed Dahmer. She said there were a whole series of missing persons reports filed by families in the black community in Milwaukee that the police didn't investigate. She also said that had the probation department followed up on Dahmer, he wouldn't have had the ability to have kept on killing for so many months. "People had been calling them and they

197

didn't investigate. You just can't lay it all on Dahmer. I believe he's sick, but if his probation officer had been keeping up on his case, maybe some of this could have been avoided."

On a Wednesday, June 14, just about two weeks after Dahmer killed Raymond Smith, Eddie Smith disappeared after spending the night dancing at a number of local bars, ending up at the Phoenix Club, and then going off to a private party with Dahmer after the bar closed. Eddie Smith, sometimes called "The Sheik" was a regular patron of the gay bars in the area. He was tall, taller than Jeffrey Dahmer, and very handsome. He had dreamed of becoming a model and liked to cavort as if he loved the spotlight. Smith had grown up in Milwaukee and had been a member of the gay community ever since he was in high school. The female impersonator "Goldie" remembered him from their school days together and knew that he and Jeffrey Dahmer had become friends who partied together in the weeks before Smith disappeared.

"Eddie Smith was called 'the Sheik,' " "Goldie" said, "because he looked like he was wearing an Arab headpiece. He was playing ball, but he couldn't stand it so he'd wear a baseball cap with a piece of fabric over his head. That was how he got his name. Eddie was around twenty-six. He had been a drag queen at one time six or seven years ago during disco. He used to do Donna Summers.

198

He also hustled on occasions when he needed the money. I also know that he drank pretty heavily on occasion, but I don't know if he was an alcoholic. There was a story about Eddie that circulated around the Phoenix Club that he could walk into the bar, buy himself a fifty-cent draft beer and wind up getting a blow job out of it. That was what people believed about Eddie."

"Goldie" said that like many of the men who cruised the bars, Eddie was able to conform himself to whomever he was with. It was something that went along with the whole party atmosphere among the bars and the people who had frequented them for years. Most importantly, though, "Goldie" said, Eddie Smith knew where he could find money. "He hustled when he was out of money. Maybe he had low self-esteem. A lot of who he was and what he did was dependent on who he was with and whether he was doing drugs. He would do coke on occasion. Eddie and Jeffrey were at a party together on the night he disappeared. Friends of mine who were at that party said that Jeffrey and Eddie were at that party together on the north side. There were drugs at that party. From what I heard, lots of friends told me there was—kind of like 'Hey you missed a good party last night. There was a lot of coke there.' Things like that. And that was the very same night that Eddie Smith disappeared."

"Goldie" and Eddie Smith had been friends for years, he said, and that's what made it even harder to deal with Smith's murder. "I knew him for a long time," "Goldie" said in an interview for this book. "We met in junior high, but there was nothing ever sexual, I can tell you that right away. There was a whole group of us. We all knew who we were and why we were different. We'd show up in school and just check right out the door; wouldn't even stay. We knew how different we were from the rest of the community. I was coming out, in effect. We'd meet a bunch of other kids from other schools and we'd do the same thing. We'd hang out in General Park all day, then we'd go downtown. We were all aware of the same things about ourselves and were dealing with it as a group. This park was one of the cruising parks in Milwaukee, so we went to a place where we would feel comfortable. You could get anything you want there. The whole city knows about this place. There've been murders there, everything. Jeffrey Dahmer was seen at this place all the time. He cruised this park. I've observed him getting head there. There are holes in the bathroom stalls — the public bathroom stalls — and I've seen him through the holes getting head from other people. I've spoken to other people who were down there with him, not necessarily in the bathroom but in the bushes. I've known people who were with him at the Tubs. The Tubs was right behind the Dunkin' Donuts between Seventh and Eighth and people told me how they'd be there with him."

"Goldie" said he often saw Eddie Smith and Jeffrey Dahmer together. They had become regulars among the different bars. "The night that they went to the party Jeffrey and Eddie Smith had been drinking, playing music, doing drugs. People all saw them go out together. It was a houseparty, nothing more than that, but there were drugs and there was the kind of music and the scene that accompanies drinking and drugs. There was nothing out of the ordinary about this kind of party. Every night on the weekend, you can walk into one of these bars and get an invitation to about ten or fifteen of these houseparties. They're all part of the scene here — the after-hours scene after the bars close. Sometimes you have to pay to get in. Eddie wasn't seen after that. In fact my friend told me that he actually saw Jeffrey and Eddie leaving together. He saw them making out at the party. Kissing one another, getting intense, and the they left."

Jeffrey Dahmer said he had offered Eddie Smith money to pose for pictures and Smith readily agreed to go back to Dahmer's place with him. They took a cab to the Oxford Apartments, went upstairs, and had oral sex with each other before Dahmer offered Eddie a drink. After Smith passed out from the sleeping pills in the drink, Dahmer strangled him and then dismembered his body. During the entire process of dismemberment, Jeffrey kept taking Polaroids of the process. Then he put the parts of Smith's body into garbage bags and disposed of them. Later on he disposed of the garbage bags, too.

Eddie Smith was quickly missed by his friends in the gay community, "Goldie" remembered. They were also very concerned because there were rumors about other people missing as well. Nobody actually connected the missing persons to Jeffrey Dahmer directly, "Goldie" said, but there were also rumors spreading about Dahmer's being a dangerous person who tried to drug other people. Dahmer had already been thrown out of a couple of bathhouses years before, "Goldie" said, because people he'd been with had passed out and couldn't be aroused. Thus, there were warnings circulating around the bars about Dahmer, but nobody had ever actually accused him of being responsible for anyone's disappearance.

Eddie Smith's sister Carolyn reported him missing on June 23, 1990. She said that the police seemed concerned at first about her brother and very thorough in the questions they were asking until she told the officer that her brother was gay. "His whole attitude changed," she said. "I really think that once he left, he tore up the report. The police later said the report was either lost or never filed."

Carolyn Smith and Eddie's friends would not give up on him, however, and began a campaign to spread the word about his disappearance through the neighborhood. "Goldie" remembered "that after two or three months after Eddie disappeared, people were coming out with pictures 'Have you seen this person?' These were people who knew Eddie. They said that he would call. He was the kind of guy who would always call. He has sisters, family, he would always call them. Eddie was not the guy who would disappear. Even when he went with someone, when he wanted to go, he just got up and went. He wasn't the kind of person who would drop out of sight for extended periods of time. After two months, you knew something was wrong because he never checked in with any of his friends. He would call and say, 'I'm here, don't worry.' It struck Ted, his roommate, really funny, too, because Eddie was just not there at all which wasn't like him. He would always call. But now no one could find him. He always stayed in contact. So for him to disappear even for like two weeks, was way out of the ordinary, and people were getting worried."

Then, "Goldie" remembered, a very strange thing happened. Jeffrey Dahmer, who had been gradually becoming more and more agitated as the months wore on, mentioned Eddie Smith in conversation as if he actually knew what had happened to him. This made "Goldie" very suspicious because he knew that Dahmer and Eddie had been together on the night that Smith disappeared.

"I remember it was last January or February, somewhere in there when me and my friends were having this discussion outside a bar," "Goldie" remembered. "My friends said that Eddie just wanted to be alone. Another one of my friends said, 'No, that wasn't like Eddie to take off like that. He always calls.' Then Jeff Dahmer walks out of the bar and says that he was looking for Eddie too. So we said, 'What do you mean? Like weren't you guys dating?' You see everybody who knew Eddie and who knew the people who were at this party saw Eddie and Jeff leave together and that was the last time they saw Eddie. But they saw Jeff. And Jeff stands with our group and says that he was looking for Eddie now. He said, 'I called the Racine police and they told me that they found Eddie Smith in three pieces over in Racine.' My friend Allen got really upset because he was good friends with Eddie and he started screaming at Jeff, 'You liar! What do you mean three pieces? Tell me what three pieces in Racine means.' I mean, Jeff actually stood thear and told us that Eddie was in three pieces over in Racine. We were really afraid because we thought there was going to be a fight outside the bar. So I told Allen, 'We don't want no fights here,' and I took my friend inside the bar. Now I wonder if that's where he took Eddie and that's why the police couldn't find any remains of his body. Maybe Jeff did things down there in Racine that we don't know about. We didn't here anything more about Eddie or about Jeff and Eddie until the summer when the whole thing came out. That's when we knew what happened to Eddie."

About a month later, Carolyn Smith reported that she had gotten a call late at night from someone she didn't know. The voice on the phone said to her, "You don't have to bother about looking for your brother." Distraught over the sound of this guy's voice, she asked him why.

"Because he's dead," the strange, answered.

"How do you know?" she asked.

"Because I killed him!" And the stranger hung up.

Dahmer killed Eddie Smith in June, 1990, just about a week after he had opened up a private portion of his life to his probation agent Donna Chester and told her that he was severely conflicted about being a homosexual. He said that he was really "down" about the things that were happening in his life, especially his not getting any sleep and his not being able to talk to his father or his grandmother. He was feeling especially isolated from his family even though he didn't have that much contact with his father any more. But, he said, the worst thing was that he felt so guilty about being a homosexual he didn't know what to do about it.

By the end of that summer, Jeffrey Dahmer had found his next victim and continued to express his conflict in the form of homicidal violence.

Chapter Thirteen

Another Missed Opportunity

Jeffrey Dahmer was depressed and complained constantly of deeply despondent feelings when he saw probation officer Donna Chester on June 25, 1990. Things weren't really breaking right for him, he told her. His life was a mess. He had to work such intolerably long hours at the chocolate factory, he hadn't even set his new apartment up and wasn't even sure that he wanted to stay there. But even if he wanted to move, he was stuck in a lease until the following May. He said he liked the neighborhood, though, because it was easy for a white guy to maintain his anonymity in a completely black community.

It was also the time, Donna Chester noted, that someone pay what the department called a home visit to Dahmer's apartment. However, it would require two probation officers instead of one because, she wrote, "the subject lives in a very bad area." She also reported that Dahmer was keeping all of his scheduled appointments, he still had his job, and he seemed willing to talk about his problems, even though he tended to embellish them to get sympathy. But Dahmer always seemed to be down on himself, and she kept on urging him to pursue his required psychotherapy treatment program. She told him to report back to the office on July 9.

On July 8, however, the Sunday before he was to report, Jeffrey had been frequenting the bars along National when he met an attractive fifteen-year-old boy in the street. The young man said that he was living in a foster home with an Hispanic family and readily picked up on Jeffrey's standard offer to pay cash for a nude photo session. Jeffrey had promised him two hundred dollars, and they took a taxi which brought them back to the Oxford Apartments in less than fifteen minutes.

Jeffrey and the young man didn't waste any time once they were inside. The boy took off his clothing right away and Jeffrey began taking pictures with his Polaroid. Suddenly the young man said he wanted to leave and Dahmer panicked. Having run out of money to buy sleeping pills, he bought a rubber mallet to club his victims unconscious. Therefore, when the young man said he was leaving, Dahmer grabbed the mallet, and hit the teenager in the head. As the young man sagged to the floor, not unconscious but certainly defenseless, Dahmer grabbed him by the throat and began to strangle him. The child began screaming in terror, pleading for his life, and swearing that he wouldn't call the police if Dahmer would only spare him. Then he began to resist Dahmer and the two of them got into a vicious fight.

Perhaps it was the screaming that frightened Dahmer the most because the last thing he wanted was for busybody neighbors to call the cops who would arrive to find him standing over a teenager in a virtual repeat of the crime he was already on probation for having committed. Dahmer released his grip on the kid's neck but stood menacingly over him while trying to calm him down. The kid stopped screaming and in turn tried to calm down Jeffrey Dahmer. Both of them, for entirely different reasons, were in mortal terror for their own lives. The teenager didn't want to die and Jeffrey did not want to return to prison again.

"I didn't want you to leave," Jeffrey said to the teenager, the boy later told his foster parents.

"But I won't tell anybody about this is you let me go," the teenager said to Dahmer. "I promise."

The kid wasn't drugged, Jeffrey didn't have the advantage of surprise, and he didn't have an effective blunt instrumet that would knock the kid out with a single blow. There were neighbors with big ears all over the whole complex. It would only take one phone call to bring the cops. The easiest solution was simply to take the kid at his word and hope for the best, assuming all the while that he could talk himself out of a tight situation as long as no witnesses showed up to finger him.

"If you talk to the police, I'll find out about it and come back for you," he threatened the young man. "And when I find you I'll kill you."

The young man promised that he wouldn't tell anybody, and Dahmer called a cab to pick him up. That might have been an incriminating piece of evidence also, but it was better than either of the two remaining alternatives he had: letting the kid wander around the neighborhood himself where he would surely come in contact with the police or walking the kid out of the neighborhood himself under the watchful eyes of potential witnesses.

When the young man reached his home on the south side of town, he immediately told his parents what had happened. He gave them a description of the man who had propositioned and then beat him with a mallet. He explained how he had screamed for his life and then talked his way out of the apartment. The man even called a cab for him, the teenager explained. His foster parents rushed him for an examination to the Sinai Samaritan Medical Center and reported the incident to the police who met them back at their home. The teenager gave the police a description of the man who had assaulted him, the address of the man's apartment, and his first name, "Jeff." However, despite this information, it appears that Dahmer was not contacted about the incident.

The following morning, Jeffrey showed up an hour late at his probation agent's office for his scheduled appointment. Donna Chester noted that Jeffrey seemed more than usually depressed and he was unkept in his appearance. She rescheduled him for that same afternoon at 1:45 P.M., concerned about his unhealthy demeanor.

She wrote that Jeffrey looked "very rough" that afternoon; her first piece of advice to her client was to move away from his neighborhood. Dahmer replied by complaining about money. It was bad enough that he had to borrow just to pay the previous month's rent, he said, so he certainly could not afford to move to a more expensive place. But none of that made sense to Donna Chester. She had a copy of his pay stub that showed he was making almost $250 a week after taxes. He was on the payroll at $8.75 an hour, having gotten two $.25 raises since he began working at Ambrosia and putting him up at $18,000 a year. In addition, he claimed that he was working overtime at the plant and that should have added substantially to his pocketbook at time and a half. There were many people she knew who would be thankful for a base pay of $18,000 a year with Dahmer's living expenses.

Jeffrey told her that he had lots of medical expenses, especially after falling down a flight of stairs. He also had severe financial problems, he said, because there were many unpaid bills that had to be satisfied. Food was expensive, he said, and he was overwhelmed with depression. Chester promised Jeffrey that the two of them would work out a payment plan for his outstanding bills if he brought them to the office next time. As for his food expenses, Donna Chester gave Jeffrey a list of places where he could get free meals. That would take care of him for the present, but Donna had to get to the bottom of this financial problem Jeffrey was supposed to have. Perhaps Jeff's fall might have been a mugging in which he had lost his money or perhaps he was spending his money on something else . . . like booze.

During August, Jeffrey paid two more visits to the

probation department. On both occasions, he complained of severe depression and a host of physical symptoms that ranged from stomachaches to headaches. Many severe alcoholics are chronically depressed because alcohol is a drug that depresses the nervous system. Alcoholics also suffer from frequent stomachaches because the intestinal linings are being eaten away by alcohol and from headaches because the brain is reeling from a chronic condition of oxygen deprivation. In other words, if a doctor had examined Dahmer and did a routine urine or blood serum test, Dahmer would have displayed the symptoms of alcoholism. However, no such examination was required by law.

In his conversations with Donna Chester during August, 1990, Jeffrey hinted that his problems were so severe and his options so limited that "the only way he can see out is to 'jump from a tall building.' " For people who have a record of violence, and Dahmer had such a record, an absolutely deflated sense of self is often a precursor to even greater levels of violence because the consequences of that violence are less frightening to the individual than the day to day misery of going forward. In Dahmer's case the complaints about worthlessness and depression were constant and so were Dahmer's continuing serial murders.

What Dahmer was unconsciously describing was a condition that many serial killers experience in the penultimate stages of their careers. Rather than exploding the way many mass murderers and apocalyptic suicidal killers do, taking scores of people out with them as they end their misery in a burst of lethal violence, serial killers tend to implode, taking up less and less space in the outside world. The darkness inside them becomes even more dense and impenetrable as they attach themselves to victims' lives one after another in sequence and snuff them out in silent anonymity. That's what was happening to Jeffrey Dahmer even though it was not readily apparent to those around him.

When Jeffrey complained further about his financial situation, his probation officer suggested that he look into bankruptcy protection with a lawyer competent to advise him financially. Dahmer, however, was resistant to all suggestions. He was stubborn about the way he felt. Instead of making any attempts to recover his life, he seemed to be looking for reasons to fail. No matter what suggestions Donna Chester offered, Dahmer found reason after reason to deny their validity for his life. When she tried to encourage him by showing him that he had a positive side to him, he said that there wasn't anything good about his life at all.

On September 2, Dahmer finally did make another connection. This time Ernest Miller, who was raised in Milwaukee but was living in Chicago at the time of the murder. Jeffrey Dahmer told police he was intrigued by this guy's looks but found he had to murder him in a different way because the victim had such a special musculature.

The last Ernest Miller's family saw of him was on September 2, 1990, after he had attended Sunday services at the Golden Rule Church of God and Christ.

Ernest Miller worked as a busboy in Chicago, but was a dance student who was saving up enough money to back to dance school in the fall. He had a very well developed body, and was proud of the way he looked and moved. He had come up to spend Labor Day in Milwaukee before the fall quarter started and would have to go back to Chicago to balance his dance studies with work.

Very late on Sunday evening, Ernest Miller had gone for a walk over to the crowded shopping district at North Twenty-seventh and Kilbourn. That area was only a few blocks away from where Jeffrey Dahmer lived, and Dahmer sometimes walked over there at night to scope the action. There were always a lot of young people hanging around the area, especially gays, that he could get into a conversation and eventually try to solicit. So it was with Ernest Miller.

He and Dahmer met one another by chance in front of a bookstore on North Twenty-seventh, where they started up a conversation. Dahmer was always affable when he was on the hunt, and he especially seemed to like the shining and healthy-looking Ernest Miller. For a man like Dahmer who was focused on death and the gradual decay of all living things, Miller seemed to be brimming over with life. Maybe that was what Dahmer wanted to internalize somehow. Jeffrey offered the twenty-four-year-old Miller money if he would come to his place for sex. The two of them walked over to Dahmer's place where the typical pattern began to unfold itself: they had sex, Jeffrey offered Miller a sedative-laced drink, and Miller passed out. Then the pattern changed. Instead of strangling him to death with his strap, Jeffrey killed Ernest Miller with a knife. Dahmer told the police that Miller was so muscular and he was coming out of the sleeping potion so quickly, he believe he would be unable to strangle him to death. Therefore rather than wrestle with a reviving victim, Dahmer took his knife and slashed Miller's carotid artery, causing blood to splatter about the whole apartment and Miller to go into shock and then death from loss of blood.

As Ernest Miller lay bleeding to death on Dahmer's bed, Jeffrey took a series of Polaroids of him. Then he cut up the body and disposed of the flesh in acid. He boiled the flesh of the skull and painted it. He bleached Miller's skeleton in acid and preserved that as well. Dahmer also took special care to carve away Miller's biceps which he then placed in the freezer, possibly to wear around his own shoulders and arms as an act of bonding with the man he seemed especially fascinated by or maybe even to eat at a later time.

Miller's skull, his skeleton, and his biceps were all totems that Dahmer expected would bring pleasure and excitement to him and stimulate the feelings of passion he experienced when he originally committed the murders. A serial killer's totems also provide a level of validation for the killer that he does not necessarily have in the real world. Serial killers view themselves deep down as worthless individuals who barely exist. The more they kill, the more they puff up their visions of themselves (hypergrandiose statements) while at the same time they collapse psychologically upon themselves.

Nonconfrontational or avoidance-type serial killers like Jeffrey Dahmer simply kill more furiously the more they collapse. For Dahmer, the further along he proceeded in his serial killing spree, the more he felt he needed to collect totems to confirm the existence that he described to his parole officer as gradually slipping away from him.

A few weeks after Miller's disappearance, someone called Ernest Miller's grandmother and made choking and gurgling noises into the receiver, possibly mimicking the sounds Miller made after Dahmer had cut his throat. Another time the caller made groaning noises as if the person on the other end of the line was in extreme pain. Finally, on a different occasion, the caller simply whimpered "Help me" over and over again.

If indeed these calls were made by Jeffrey Dahmer, they mark a further escalation and extension of his violence from the victims to their families. On one level, with the victims dead, the logical extension of the excitement of having the victim is in touching the chords of the people who still love him and probably miss him. On another level, by communicating with the victim's family, the murderer is also interacting with the living victim because only the killer—and not the family—knows the victim is actually dead. It's another way to preserve the excitement of owning the living victim. Finally, the murderer is also experiencing a direct thrill in crossing the boundary to expose part of himself to the victims' families. As the killings become more routine and the excitement level declines, touching the chords of the families reinvigorates the entire thrill of the crime.

On September 10, 1990, Jeffrey Dahmer discussed his problems with Donna Chester at a scheduled meeting. According to her notes, Dahmer told her that he was not interested in children or in young males sexually at all. He said that he felt the major part of his offense was alcohol and that was it. Two weeks later, Jeffrey had another meeting with Donna Chester. During this session, she replied to his question about the progress of his probation that he still had a lot of work to do to resolve his emotional problems. His probation officer told him point blank that she didn't think he was working hard enough on resolving his problems at all.

That was the same day that the Milwaukee police received a missing persons report on David Thomas from Chandra Beanland, David Thomas's girlfriend. She said that the family was used to his coming and going at strange times of the day, but he always would return home. This time, she said, he didn't come home and she was filing the report.

Only a few days before Beanland called the police and during the time Dahmer told his parole officer that he had been bedridden with a head cold and on vacation from the chocolate factory, Jeffrey Dahmer met the twenty-two-year-old David Thomas near the Grand Avenue Mall. He and Thomas got into a conversation and Dahmer suggested going over to his place for a few drinks where he would give Thomas money to pose for pictures. Dahmer told the police that Dave Thomas wasn't his type. After he gave him the drugs and Thomas was unconscious, Dahmer didn't feel like having sex with him at all. Rather, Dahmer said, he might have been willing to let the guy wake up and go on his way, but he was afraid he'd be made that Dahmer drugged him and he'd go to the police. Therefore, Dahmer said, he killed Thomas while he was unconscious and disposed of the body.

Dahmer had disposed of Thomas's body so thoroughly that there was simply nothing left of him to bury. The only way he was identified as a homicide victim was when Dahmer said he recognized a photo of Thomas supplied by Thomas's sister. Other than that identification and Dahmer's uncorroborated story of how he met and murdered Thomas, the police have no evidence in that case whatsoever.

Thomas was the last person Jeffrey killed in 1990 and, for all appearances, Dahmer seemed to go on a kind of hiatus from murder. What he did and why he did not kill during this period are still a matter of speculation, even for the psychologists who interviewed him because Dahmer had a habit of changing his story many times. We know from parole officer's records that Dahmer was mugged at gunpoint on September 25 and robbed of ten dollars and a bus pass. His father and stepmother came to visit him from Ohio on Thanksgiving in 1990. According to an interview Shari Dahmer gave to a Milwaukee paper, she described Jeffrey's one-bedroom apartment as depressing after seeing the house he'd grown up in. However, she said, there were no indications that anything was amiss in Jeffrey's life. There were certainly no indications that any crimes had been committed in the apartment.

On December 5, he and Donna discussed the possibility of his communicating with his mother Joyce in California. Chester asked Jeffrey if he was mad at his mother, and Dahmer said no. It was just, he explained, that he hadn't taken the initiative of communicating with her in five years. If the experiences of adult children who've perceived themselves to have been abandoned by a parent are any indication, Dahmer was in fact deeply furious with his mother. That fury was reinforced after he graduated high school and his mother moved away with his younger brother David to Chippewa Falls, and translated into the murder of Steven Hicks.

When the thought of contacting his mother came up, deep feelings were stirred within him.

At his December 12 meeting with Donna Chester, Dahmer said that the Thanksgiving holiday actually went "okay" and that he had "no major confrontations" with his family. On December 17, however, Dahmer said that he'd been robbed again and wanted to buy a four-hundred-dollar security system. Donna Chester remarked that Dahmer was showing indications of inappropriate spending and that he might experience some difficulty with the upcoming holidays and his family.

Those difficulties would lead to his final spree of blood lust killings.

Chapter Fourteen

Crisis

"Just say Hi," Donna Chester had suggested when the idea arose to send Joyce Flint a Christmas card. Then Jeffrey Dahmer retreated to his apartment to spend a Christmas for the most part alone. He had said that he wasn't particularly interested in seeing his father. He was also ashamed about seeing his brother. Thus, he would probably just stay in his apartment and work over at the factory. He kept his appointment with Donna Chester on January 3 at which point he complained again about money problems. Then on January 22, his next scheduled visit, Donna Chester noted that her client sought to reassure her that he wouldn't commit a new offense because of the prospect of jail. Jail was his deterrent, Jeffrey said, "and I don't want to go to jail." He also indicated that he had thought long and hard about his homosexuality and finally admitted to himself that he was gay and that was all there was to it. In her notes, Chester wrote "told agent that's the way he is so 'fuck it.'"

Toward the end of January and early February, Jeffrey picked up the flu but still, according to his statements, had to work more than full-time shifts at the factory. By the time he staggered into the probation office on February 2, he looked terrible. "Client's appearance is again disheveled, unshaven, dark circles under his eyes. He says this has to do with having the flu and working twelve hours a day."

On February 18, a day of pouring, freezing, wind-driven rain, Jeffrey Dahmer crossed paths with his next victim at a bus stop shelter across the street from Marquette University. Eighteen-year-old Curtis Straughter, who called himself Demetra, had dropped out of high school and was a member of Gay Youth Milwaukee. He wanted to be a model, but had just lost his job as a nurse's aide. He was hustling for whatever money he could get when he met Jeffrey Dahmer. Straughter's grandmother, Katherine, with whom he lived said that the kid was very wild and was always out partying and hanging out with different people. Other people said that Straughter had had a tough time coping with his homosexuality. He was unhappy about it and estranged from his family. He was looking to pick up a modeling job on the day that he stood in the rain waiting for a bus on Wisconsin Avenue. He needed money, but he felt he had a future. Dahmer would bring that all to an end.

Dahmer offered Curtis some money to come back to his apartment which was only a few blocks away. It would also give them some respite from the rain, Dahmer said. They got to the apartment, and Dahmer mixed him a drink right away to warm him up. After

Curtis passed out, Dahmer immediately strangled him with his strap and then took off all his clothes. Dahmer performed oral sex on him. He then began cutting the body up and took Polaroid pictures of every step. Then he severed Straughter's head and boiled off the skin so that he could preserve the man's skull.

After the murder in March, Jeffrey Dahmer missed an appointment with his probation officer and had neglected to call. When he finally did show up at the office on March 25, 1991, he said he had been "still sick, tired, and exhausted the last couple of weeks." However, he had some big news. The contact he had initiated with his mother Joyce over Christmas had apparently paid off; his mother had called him from California and this was the first time they had spoken in five years. It was a momentous day.

To most people whose parents had not disappeared from their lives, the return of a parent would normally appear to be a cause for celebration. On the surface, that's what it must have seemed like for Jeffrey Dahmer and perhaps even for his parole officer who might have seen the first glimmerings of hope in the otherwise bleak misery of Dahmer's life. However, there could have been much deeper feelings that were stirred with Joyce Flint's phone call. Jeffrey told Donna Chester that he and his mother had talked for a bit over what she was doing in Fresno as a counselor at an AIDS clinic. They talked about the contacts that Joyce had with the gay community there and how her working with people with AIDS had aroused in her a great sympathy for her clients, for people suffering from and under the threat of AIDS, and for homosexuals in general who lived under the burden of misunderstanding and hatred. Joyce said she was aware that he was gay and that she accepted it. Not only did she accept it, she said, he was her son and she loved him.

Far beneath the surface of Jeffrey's outward demeanor, even beneath a level of his immediate awareness, much deeper sets of emotions and memories were being stirred. Primal love, developmental psychologists now know, is only one half of the mother/child equation. Primal rage is the other. The two coexist and are part of each other in a representation that can shift from moment to moment. Infants, even newborns, can scream at their mothers through tears and can be quieted in an instant. Those same emotions don't go away as the child grows; they develop. Words are attached to them; descriptions of feelings become associated with them; memories, tastes, smells, and sensations may define or evoke them. But they never go away. In normal functional relationships, we learn to recognize primal emotions and deal with them within an elaborate and heavily reinforced social structure. But in dysfunctional situations those primal emotions aren't socialized into acceptability. They remain just as infantile, as unmediated, and as potentially violent as they ever were. They are also still well beneath a level of conscious understanding which can make them even more mysterious.

Therefore, when Jeffrey Dahmer was experiencing a sense of shock over his mother's call, which then may have led to real feelings of warmth that he had not experienced in years, it also opened the floodgates to all the feelings of primal rage he had about his childhood.

222

These were infantile perceptions, sensations, and fears that might have gone all the way back to the time he was six. These were inextricably linked to the feelings of primal love and primal loss he had with respect to his mother. Most people organize their primal emotional morass into adult perceptions about the world. Children do not, and Jeffrey Dahmer probably had the emotional developmental skills of a seven-year-old child. He had no adult definitions for these feelings because they were all unresolved. Unfortunately, they were also neurologically linked ("imprinted") with the brutal murder of Steven Hicks. Thus, immediate feelings of love for his mother also brought in the terrible perceptions he might have had of loss, abandonment, and rage. He had no way to separate his primal emotions logically. He was not enrolled in a formal psychotherapy treatment program which might have helped him sort out the conflicting feelings his conversation with his mother might have legitimately evoked. His reactions to his mother's reappearance, which came upon him unawares, stimulated a whole set of neurological reactions over which Jeffrey Dahmer had no control.

Jeffrey Dahmer had been reacting to a powerful set of unconscious motivations from the time he was six. He was fighting the terror of his perceived abandonment. When he killed Steven Hicks, he was still fighting that terror. And in each and every one of his murders, whether they were as calculating as Jeffrey said they were when he confessed to the Milwaukee police or as reactive as some people speculated afterwards, it is likely that he was reacting to the terror of loneliness. Those emotions of pathological loneliness and the panic of being abandoned might have been reignited in him as a result of speaking with his mother. In Dahmer's mind, her pregnancy with his brother David, when he was six, might have been the source of whatever happened to him afterward. This is only supposition at best. The record does show that after Dahmer's conversation with Joyce Flint, he went on a final killing spree of seven murders and one attempted murder between early April and July 22, 1981, the night his final victim escaped.

On April 7, 1991, nineteen-year-old Errol Lindsey left his mother's house on Twenty-fourth Street right around suppertime to get a key made. He'd been over at the Grand Avenue Mall earlier in the day. On his way to get the key, he walked past the shopping area on Twenty-seventh Street and Kilbourn where he crossed paths with a cruising Jeffrey Dahmer looking for a victim of opportunity. Dahmer had told the police in his confessions that whenever he went out in the evening, he knew whether or not he was planning a homicide for later that night. Before going out, he would prepare his knockout drugs by pulverizing them into powder and leave them in a glass on his kitchen counter. Evidently, Jeffrey had planned to commit a murder the night he saw Errol Lindsey coming his way.

Dahmer began a conversation in which he ultimately offered the young man who had sung in the choir at the Greater Spring Hill Missionary Baptist Church money to pose for some photos. Jeffrey Dahmer's approach to his young victims was as consistent as it was cunning. He said, as he said to both Konerak and his brother

Sounthome, that he was a photographer looking for photo subjects so that his new camera could be tested out. He was willing to pay photo subjects for their time. If interested, he would invite the subject back to his apartment where he would either induce them into taking off their clothing or invite them to have a drink. The drink was, of course, drugged and would render them unconscious long enough for Dahmer to strangle them. Then they were his. If the victim were obviously gay and looking for more than just a photo session fee, Dahmer sometimes had sex with them before drugging them. In either case, it was a well-rehearsed pickup and victims usually went along. So it was with Errol Lindsey who went back to Jeffrey's apartment on the promise of money.

Once inside the apartment, Dahmer told the police, he offered Lindsey a drink he had drugged, waited until he passed out, strangled him, and then performed oral sex on him. He said that he then dismembered the body and preserved the skull. Errol Lindsey never returned home that night, and his family had no clue to his whereabouts. His mother Mildred wondered how somebody could disappear on his way to get a key. "It was like he vanished from the world," she had said. Nothing made any sense until July when the news broke about the discovery of bodies only a few blocks away from where they lived. Then Dahmer identified Errol Lindsey from a photograph his mother provided, and the mystery of his disappearance and whereabouts was resolved. The only question remaining was why, and that's going to be debated for a long time to come.

* * *

Six weeks later, Jeffrey would murder his companion the popular and friendly Tony Hughes, whose disappearance would shock and infuriate the Milwaukee gay community. Anthony Hughes was an especially protected member of the community because he was deaf from a childhood disease and also mute. He was very literate, however, and communicated by lip reading, gestures, and writing notes. Hughes was also a dancer who was described as being able to feel the beat and the bass through the floorboards of clubs like 219 and La Cage.

Although Hughes was a regular at the clubs, he was actually living in Madison, Wisconsin. He had told his family that Milwaukee had become too dangerous a city. There were too many people disappearing from his community, especially Eddie Smith, and he was worrying about himself. In May, 1991, he had come back to Milwaukee to visit his family. On the night of May 24, when he was killed, he left his sister's home after 10:00 P.M. to meet up with friends at the 219. That was where he ran into his friend Jeffrey Dahmer, whom he had known since 1989.

Female impersonator "Goldie" knew Tony Hughes and had seen him and Jeffrey together on many occasions. Like other members of the gay community, "Goldie" liked and respected Anthony Hughes.

"I only talked to Tony Hughes in writing because he was mute. Tony was a light-skinned black guy who was really nice and was always smiling. He was average height, maybe smaller, and was always very well groomed and attractive and clean. He wasn't a hustler like some guys around here. He had a job, had money. Dressed like he came out of *GQ*. Really a nice guy who dressed sharp and seemed to like himself. He always had other friends who were hooked up with other guys. I think Tony was seeing another guy, too, some guy with a mustache who was taller and was a blond. The guy was a darker blond than Jeffrey Dahmer, I think, but definitely a blond and taller.

"Goldie" saw a kind of attraction between Tony Hughes and Jeffrey Dahmer because both of them, in their own ways, were yuppie types even though they had opposite attitudes about life. "There's that pull, that chemistry. I think there was an attraction there," "Goldie" observed. "I have no idea why Tony went with Dahmer other than maybe there was a little bit of attraction. It certainly wasn't for the money because Tony had money. Richard Guerrero, I think, went with Jeffrey for the money. But not Hughes. I would see Dahmer and Hughes talking in the bar from time to time. You knew when they were together, but it wasn't for money. Also, they had been friends for quite a while. I saw Tony and Jeffrey together well before Tony disappeared, so he must not have been afraid of Jeffrey at all. Tony was always nice to people. He was never rude to somebody. He had his own 'type,' that was his lover — blond/brown hair, taller, well-dressed. You could say that Dahmer would have been Tony's type when Dahmer was cleaned up and not scruffy. Jeffrey could get cleaned up and look like a well-groomed person."

"Goldie" doesn't remember Hughes as a heavy drinker. He socialized, but never became bleary-eyed like Jeffrey. "He was more like a weekend drinker. I mean you'd see him with Jeffrey in a bar, but you didn't really see him drinking at all during the week. On the

227

weekends he'd drink. He'd be at the Wednesday shows; Tuesday night shows. But these were for entertainment and not to get drunk. He certainly didn't drink the way Jeffrey did."

tony and Jeffrey first met at the party scene and carried their relationship over to the bar scene, "Goldie" speculated, because he saw them together in public at people's apartments as well as at the bar. "I saw them together at 219, but there was a whole party life going on in the community where people who were going together went. Tony and Jeff went to parties together during this time."

Jeffrey told the police that he had written Tony a note at the 219 club on May 24 inviting him to come over to his apartment where they would watch videos, Tony would pose for photos, and Jeffrey would give him fifty dollars. Tony let his friends know that he was going out for awhile, but that he'd be back. This was a departure for Dahmer because, for the first time since the Eddie Smith disappearance, Jeffrey was taking someone with whom he had been publicly identified. Whether this mean that Jeffrey was calling attention to himself or whether he was going to be more aggressive and more open in the community is a matter for speculation. All that can be said is that where most serial killers try never to be seen with their victims, Jeffrey had gone out of his way to be seen on the last night with a companion that he'd known for two years. It would have been normal in any follow-up investigation for the police to have investigated all of Tony Hughes's acquaintances and to have found Jeffrey's name in Tony's address book. At that point, a records check on Dahmer and the discovery that he was currently on probation for a sexual offense on a minor might have prompted the police to pay a visit to his apartment.

Tony Hughes never returned to 219 on the night of May 24. Jeffrey said that after the two of them got up to his place, he gave Hughes a drug-laced drink. When Tony fell asleep, he killed him and dismembered his friend's body. Jeffrey also said that he preserved the skull.

Tony's family tried to follow up his disappearance as best they could. They checked with his friends at the 219 Club, distributed flyers, and posted a reward. Their activities involved the entire community. "Goldie" remembered that after Hughes disappeared, the community reacted not only because of the disappearance but because of the police reaction. "The police didn't even go down and talk to them after he was missing. I didn't know exactly how long he was missing. It seemed like a while, but I wasn't sure. I only remember hearing about Tony and thinking how he was like family to me. You could say he was more like a sister to me. I have a reputation of being well liked and we got along. I gotta look good and have a smile on my face all the time and talk to people even the ones who are real nasty to me."

The family only found out the truth about their son after July 22 when Jeffrey was arrested. At about the very same time, the police questioned "Goldie" about identifying some of the victims. They showed him a photo of what they think Dahmer might have done with his friend's skull.

Goldie remembers the police saying to him, "We don't know if you can handle this" as they held up a stack of photos. "He had a stack of photos of Jeffrey's victims and showed me one. I saw in the photo that Dahmer had made a statue out of the head of Tony Hughes and the hands were cupped under the head, like they were just under the head and the head was off. I just freaked out. The picture was in black and white. What looked like Tony's head was right on a table, on Dahmer's table. It was one of Dahmer's own pictures that he took. I didn't know whether to cry or get sick. I was shaking inside. I was trying to figure out how someone could do something like that. In the other picture the police showed me there was a plastic or metal keg of beer with the top cut off and there were bodies in there. A keg of bodies and you could see hands sticking out and fingers in there and that's all [you] could see."

About two days after he murdered Anthony Hughes, Jeffrey went to the Grand Avenue Mall. He'd mixed his powders, and murder was on his mind as he cruised through the area looking for someone he could induce to come over to his place. He found a bouncy fourteen-year-old Laotian child who had come back from a soccer game and was window shopping through the mall on the Sunday of a Memorial Day weekend. The exuberant kid caught Jeffrey's eye, and Dahmer began a conversation with him. Even though Dahmer might have been able to tell that he was talking to a minor and was potentially violating his parole requirements, he approached the Laotian. What he also probably did not know was that the kid, whose name was Konerak Sinthasomphone, was the younger brother of Sounthome whom he'd abused just about two years earlier. That case was the reason Jeffrey was on probation.

Sounthome had been tragically shaken by his encounter with Jeffrey Dahmer years before and reportedly told his little brother not to speak to strangers. Konerak, however, was indeed speaking to Jeffrey Dahmer on that Sunday and agreed to go with him to his apartment to pose for photos taken from his new camera. Jeffrey had promised to pay Konerak fifty dollars for the alleged photo shoot. Once they got to his apartment, Jeffrey took a couple of photos of the boy and then gave him a drink just as he said he was getting ready to leave. While Konerak was drinking, Jeff told him that he wanted to look for a videotape that the boy might like to see. That was long enough for the drink to take effect and for Konerak to pass out. Then Jeffrey had oral sex with the child and decided that he wanted to have a beer. It was now nighttime. Checking to make sure that Konerak was going to be unconscious for a while, Jeffrey went out to the store to buy a few beers.

When Konerak awoke and found he had no clothes on, he was dazed and disoriented. It was after midnight. He looked around for the man who had gotten him up to the apartment and saw that he, too, was gone. Then he wandered outside, still incoherent and woozy from the drugs, where he met a number of people who saw him staggering around. They immediately realized that he was a young boy and said that they saw a stream of blood on his leg. Nicole Childress placed a call to 911 from a pay phone. Sandra Smith, Nicole's cousin, attended to Konerak who, she said, was bleeding from his anus. She said she also noticed that he had bruises on his body. While she was trying to help the child, Nicole Childress got through to Operator 71 on the other end of the line. The conversation was transcribed and released by the police. It was published in a number of newspapers, including *The New York Times* on August 2, 1991.

911 OPERATOR: Operator 21.

CHILDRESS: Hi, I'm on Twenty-fifth and State, and there is this young man. He's butt-naked. He has been beaten up. He is very bruised up. He can't stand up. He has no clothes on. He is really hurt. I got no coat on. I just seen him. He needs some help.

OPERATOR 71: Where, where is he at?

CHILDRESS: Twenty-fifth and State. At the corner of Twenty-fifth and State.

OPERATOR 71: He's just on the corner of the street?

CHILDRESS: Yeah, he's in the middle of the street. He fell out. We're trying to help him. Some people are trying to help him.

OPERATOR 71: Okay. And he's unconscious right now?

CHILDRESS: They're getting him. He's bruised up. Somebody must have jumped on him and stripped him or whatever.

OPERATOR 71: Okay. Let me put the fire department on the line. They'll send an ambulance. Just stay on the phone, okay?

CHILDRESS: Okay.

The phone rings and a man answers: Fire Department.

CHILDRESS: Can you send an ambulance to

the corner of Twenty-fifth and State?

FIRE DEPARTMENT OPERATOR: What's the problem?

CHILDRESS: This butt-naked young boy, or man, or whatever. He's butt-naked. He's been beaten up real bad and he's fell out and people are trying to help him stand up. He can't stand up. He's butt-naked. He has no clothes on. He is very hurt.

FIRE DEPARTMENT OPERATOR: Is he awake?

CHILDRESS: He ain't awake. They're trying to get him to walk. But he can't walk straight. He can't even see straight. Everytime he stands up, he falls out.

FIRE DEPARTMENT OPERATOR: Twenty-fifth and State?

CHILDRESS: Yeah, a one-way.

FIRE DEPARTMENT OPERATOR: Okay, Bye.

Milwaukee police officers John A. Balczerak, Joseph Babrish, and Richard Porubcan were dispatched to cover the call. At the same time Jeffrey Dahmer returned from the store and saw Konerak being held up by Sandra Smith. He went to grab the boy's arm away from them, but Sandra Smith wouldn't let him go. "He's my lover," Jeffrey reportedly said to the young women holding the boy, but they still would not let him take the boy away. Then the police car arrived, then the fire department unit arrived, and Jeffrey Dahmer was suddenly in the middle of a commotion in the middle of the street. He reached out for the boy again, but the girls held him back and the police stepped in to sort things out. In the meantime, the fire department unit had arrived and put a blanket around Konerak.

Sandra Smith yelled at Jeffrey Dahmer not to hurt the boy and then started explaining what had happened to the police when she was told to back off. "We'll handle this," she said the police told her when she tried to explain what had happened. Then she asked that she and her cousin Nicole be listed as witnesses and remembered that the police said "I've been investigating for seven years, I don't need an amateur telling me what to do."

Nicole Childress remembers that when she tried to speak up, the police brushed her off as well. "They was listening to Jeff. They wasn't listening to me. One of them told us to get lost or he'd take us downtown," Childress remembered. She said she believed that if the police had taken the boy away, he'd still be alive.

Dahmer explained that the young man was his lover and that the two of them had had a fight after which time the man ran into the street. This wasn't the first time he'd done this. But Jeffrey said that he had IDs for both of them and that if they went back to his place just down the street, he'd show them ID. Konerak was still incoherent and disoriented. Everytime he tried to speak, it came out gibberish. Everytime the young women tried to speak, the police brushed them off. It was Jeffrey they were listening to.

Back at the apartment, Jeffrey reportedly told the police that the two of them were friends and were taking pictures when the guy drank too much and began wandering about. Jeffrey even had the Polaroids of the awake and aware Konerak Sinthasomphone to show the police officers. They didn't react immediately to the foul stench in the air. Although they admitted later they were aware of it, they didn't search the apartment. Had they gotten a search warrant or run a warrants check on Dahmer, as police officers Rauth and Mueller would do under similar circumstances three months later, they would have found that Jeffrey was on parole for a sexual offense. Had they looked through the apartment, they would have found the body of Anthony Hughes murdered from the night before.

The police made one final visual scan around the room and left. Once in their patrol unit, they radioed back to dispatch: "Intoxicated Asian, naked male. Was returned to his sober boyfriend." (There was the sound of background laughter on the police radio tapes.)

Then just before they went off to their next call, one of the police officers in the car said: "10-4. It'll be a minute. My partner is going to get deloused at the station." That was the end of their transmission.

Meanwhile back at the apartment, Dahmer turned to Konerak who was now looking at him intently. As the police unit pulled away, and with Konerak Sinthasomphone completely helpless because of the drugs, Jeffrey strangled him until he stopped breathing. Then in a familiar routine, he took off the boy's clothes, performed oral sex on his corpse, and began the process of dismembering him and Anthony Hughes in the next room. He kept Konerak's head in the freezer, he told police months later, but he put his torso in the fifty-seven-gallon drum in his bedroom. That container would hold such fascination for Tracy Edwards, him-

235

self having been lured to the apartment for a photo session.

While Jeffrey was dismembering Konerak, Sandra Smith's mother, Glenda Cleveland, simply couldn't let the matter drop. Sandra had gone back home and told her mother what the police did. She said she saw blood running from the boy's anus and knew that Jeffrey had handled him roughly. Yet the police wouldn't listen to her, and Nicole had been the one to place the emergency call. Instead they took them both back to Jeffrey's apartment. Something was very wrong. Glenda Cleveland was going to follow up on this herself. She now dialed 911 and the police released the following transcript which was also published in *The New York Times* on August 1, 1991:

CLEVELAND: A moment ago, ten minutes, my daughter and my niece flagged down a policeman when they walked upon a young child being molested by a male guy. And no information or anything was being taken but they were taken downtown. I was wondering, I mean I'm sure further information must be needed. The boy was naked and bleeding.
OPERATOR: Okay.

The call was transferred by the dispatcher to another police officer, where Mrs. Cleveland repeated her story.

CLEVELAND: I wondered if this situation was being handled. This was a male child being raped and molested by an adult.

OFFICER: Where did this happen?

(She was transferred again to another police officer.)

OFFICER: Hello, this is the Milwaukee Police.

CLEVELAND: Yes, there was a Squad Car No. 68 that was flagged down earlier this evening about fifteen minutes ago.

OFFICER: That was me.

CLEVELAND: Yeah, uh, what happened? I mean my daughter and niece witnessed what was going on. Was there anything done about the situation? Do you need their names or information or anything from them?

OFFICER: No, not at all.

CLEVELAND: You don't?

OFFICER: It was a young, intoxicated boyfriend of another boyfriend.

CLEVELAND: Well, how old was this child?

OFFICER: He was more than a child. He was an adult.

CLEVELAND: Are you sure?

OFFICER: Yup!

By the time the conversations were completed, it was certainly possible that Konerak was already dead. As he dismembered the body, Jeffrey Dahmer took photos of the process until he finally put the torso away in the drum.

When the transcripts and the story of Konerak Sinthasomphone came to light, community leaders and gay activists were outraged. The *NYQ* cited a Wisconsin law that calls for the mandatory arrest of someone perpetrating domestic violence regardless of sexual orientation. "Even if the cops thought they had intervened in a domestic dispute between two men," the magazine article said, "they were required to separate the parties and arrest the aggressor. They did not."

After Dahmer was arrested and the transcripts were released, Milwaukee Police Chief Phillip Areola suspended the three officers and began an investigation into the handling of the Sinthasomphone case. He was immediately criticized for his actions by the Milwaukee Police Association which claimed that he should have been supporting the officers before reacting so quickly.

The ironies, however, in comparing the Konerak and Sounthome Sinthasomphone cases abound. Both brothers were accosted by the same individual for the same purpose and drugged with heavy sedatives. Both had the presence of mind to fight their way out of the apartment. Sounthome made it out of the apartment because the drugs were too slow in acting. Also, Jeffrey was early in his career and not aggressive enough to stop him. Konerak made it out of the apartment because Jeffrey wanted to get some beer before he killed him. Yet even though both Sounthome and Konerak made it out of Jeffrey's apartment alive and into the street, no one interfered with Sounthome's escape. He made it all the way back home. Unfortunately, in the case of Konerak, he was picked up by the police who didn't listen to witnesses Sandra Smith and Nicole Childress. The police returned Konerak to Jeffrey Dahmer's apartment where he was murdered that same night.

* * *

The day after he killed Konerak, Jeffrey kept an appointment with Donna Chester. She wrote in her notes that her client was still down about everything. In the previous meeting, he'd said that his only problems were financial and he would soon be working them out. He'd figured that he was in debt to the amount of $2000 and would soon work with an agency to help him develop a budget and pay off what was due.

On May 27, "He continued to complain about everything." Then he told Donna Chester that his grandmother was ill and that he was going over there to help her out.

Two days later a strange voice telephoned Sounthome Sinthasomphone and said into the receiver, "Konerak is in danger right now."

Jeffrey Dahmer had already moved on to his next victims.

Chapter Fifteen

The Final Spree

Jeffrey Dahmer had been playing it closer and closer to the edge with every success he achieved. He had escaped an almost certain arrest by talking his way out of a jam with those cops during the Konerak Sinthasomphone incident, but his life was still in shambles. He was still shaky from the whole experience. His drinking had gotten worse, and even people in some of the bars were telling him to get into recovery before he dropped dead from too much booze. His grandmother was sick and she might have to go into the hospital; he was running out of money; all the latenesses he'd piled up at work and the unexplained absences had gotten him into trouble. He told Donna Chester that if he kept being late or absent he would lose his job. If he lost his job, he'd lose the apartment before the summer was out. If he had to vacate the apartment, somebody would have to notice the human bloodstains from the victim's throat he'd cut and the smell that everybody in the building had been complaining about. Jeffrey Dahmer was staring blankly at a dead end.

His problems had no solutions; they only posed more and greater problems.

Jeffrey Dahmer staring at one of the prototypical flypaper traps that serial killers wind up in as they near the end of their careers. Nothing they do makes them feel any better. The more they kill, the deeper they seem to be burrowing into the ground. Eventually there's no way out, and they wind up making a stupid mistake just to break the pattern. That's when they get caught in spite of themselves. In Dahmer's case, he was getting angrier and angrier at his situation, but couldn't break out of the loop of medicating himself that killing young men was doing for him. It was as if he were feeding his hate, only to find that it was more consuming with every new kill. There was no way out.

In June, 1991, as he was crashing through bar after bar looking for new experiences, Jeffrey Dahmer crashed into Brother John Paul Ranieri, of the Ecumenical Order of Charity who ran a kind of street ministry and counseling service for the gay people in Milwaukee. Ranieri, who held court in a leather bar known as the Wreck Room, believed that Jeffrey Dahmer was not a troubled gay person at all but a heterosexual who had serious problems relating to women. He was so mad about that, Ranieri recalls, and so angry about the ease with which gays seemed to accept their sexuality, that he was consumed with hatred toward them and that's what motivated all of his murders. "When I first saw Jeffrey Dahmer walk into the Wreck Room," Ranieri said, "I thought he was just another Yuppie. He wasn't dressed in any of the kind of outfits that you would normally find at the Wreck Room."

The young, clean-shaven Dahmer on the make was in

stark contrast to the older, bearded, hippie-ish patrons of the Wreck Room. John Paul noticed that Dahmer seemed ill-fitting as he sat at the bar. "He looked out of place. He looked like he'd come over from one of the bars down on South Second Street and just was out of place. He'd come in late afternoon and early evening. I never saw him pick anyone up, but I did see him mingle with a couple of people. They were late 20s to early 30s, usually black or Hispanic."

Dahmer had the reputation in 1991 of being a favorite among the hustlers who worked the South Second Street strip because of the money he was flashing. It was usually in the company of hustlers that he came into the Wreck Room. "There were a few hustlers and at least on one occasion he was mingling with one of them," Ranieri said. "That person was white and he had known him from the C'est La Vie which was known as a chicken bar because of the young age of the kids. You do get hustlers and male prostitutes going up and down the whole strip. Because the Wreck Room is far away from where the hustler bars are, a person coming into the Wreck Room is looking for something more than hustling. He's looking for something stable and more [like] companionship. He's also looking for quiet because that's what the Wreck Room was. There's no loud rock music here, more country."

Jeffrey Dahmer was always stumbling around drunk, Ranieri remembers. it was notable because he was a young man who looked like he was in terrible trouble because of how drunk he appeared to be. Even in the early hours of the evening when other people would be just setting up and ordering their first beers, Dahmer was already drunk.

"I never saw him sober," Ranieri remembered. "You could tell he was drunk by his demeanor. You can tell when someone's had too much by the way they get bleary eyed or lean against the bar or no longer walk in a straight line. I didn't feel I was being cruised by Dahmer who had walked out of here a couple of times drunk. On club nights or at a beer blast, he'd just walk in here, stay a couple of minutes and walk out. There is no sexual activity allowed in the Wreck Room. There's a code of ethics in that bar which you don't find in a lot of other bars. Also there's not a lot of Yuppie traffic in the Wreck Room, although many young people come in to look at the leather crowd and laugh at them. You don't necessarily find people in here looking for daddy types because you find that at the C'est La Vie and the Phoenix."

John Paul said that he had become the confidant of many people not only in the Wreck Room but along the whole strip because of the counseling he was doing. His ministry, he said, was one way he had of trying to resolve the sadness among people in the community. John Paul explained that he had experienced many of the difficulties younger homosexuals had when he was younger and was now trying to help the people he was bumping into at the bars. Now, at this point in his life, he said, people were willing to seek him out with their problems and he was willing to help. It was in that capacity that he first noticed Dahmer, and Dahmer first came up to talk to him.

"I was playing one of the video games and Jeff was already in the bar. It was a late afternoon. he was relatively coked out, talking and moving around the bar but had had a significant amount of alcohol in him. He broke the ice. I was playing this game and he turned around and said, 'How do you get such high scores?' I turned around and said, 'Jeff, look, the first thing you got to learn [is] how to turn yourself around and stay sober. If you ever want to sit down and talk, we can do that. We can deal with it if you

243

want to get off the alcohol.' So he just sat there on the bar-stool and watched me get high scores. I asked him whether he wanted to deal with his alcohol problems. And he was having another drink. I said, 'Why don't we go out onto the patio and we can talk about it?' And that's how it got started. I asked him, 'Is there a reason why you drink so much? If you want to turn around and get off the stuff, we have to find out what motivates you to drink.' I asked him if he was on drugs and he said no and I believed him. We made small talk, nothing heavy-duty. I told him that I had been dry for nearly twenty years and that if I could do it, he could do it. I was able to confront him about his drink-ing because I had seen him in that kind of a condition be-fore. There are others like him, similarly drunk, but most of them will turn around and tell me to bug off. Jeff didn't. I think he was incredibly depressed. He was down in the dumps. And it wasn't what he said, it was his attitude. Jeff seemed to walk around without emotion, as if he had no hope. I think he trusted me. I think he needed to trust someone. I let him know that he could trust me because whatever he told me would be held in confidence."

Then, in that conversation, Dahmer did a strange thing. He was usually guarded about himself, especially to strangers. But it was as if some of the hatred toward homo-sexuals and blacks that had been building up inside of him before and during his murder spree just burst right out over the top. Dahmer seemed as if he were losing control. It would be one of the last conversations he would have with anybody before he was arrested a month later.

"At the time a lot of people were camping it up in the front bar", Ranieri remembered. "They were boisterous, affected. There was lavish behavior that they were putting on. It seemed to get to Jeff. He was mad about it and made derogatory remarks about black queens. But we hear remarks about queens and fags all the time. This was different, there was more of an edge to it. Jeff was angry that they didn't know how to behave. I asked Jeff, 'Do you have a problem with blacks?' And Jeff snapped back, 'What do you mean? According to the Biblical stories, they should be all subservient to the whites anyway.' 'Where do you come up with that?' I asked him. 'It's in the Bible,' he said and he quoted some scripture. He seemed to be well-schooled in the Bible and intelligent as well. In fact, whatever he said to me about Biblical sanctions was right there in the chapter and verse where he said it would be. The guy knew his Bible. But when we talked, he was just angry and depressed. He seemed to be walking in a basic fog but he could hold an intelligent conversation for a half an hour before he started to spin off."

Then, in a strange part of the conversation, Dahmer began to talk about his problems not as a gay, but as a straight person who was unable to have a relationship with a woman. John Paul didn't know, of course, that the man he was talking to was responsible for all of the disappearances along the strip. He believed in that moment, he was talking to an individual who wasn't gay at all, but a heterosexual trying to find out why he was failing as a straight by exploring the gay community. It was very bizarre in retrospect, John Paul said, but now it all fits.

The main problem that John Paul saw plaguing Dahmer was not his conflicts over his sexuality, but his drinking. "Jeff referred to having gone to a treatment program for alcoholic problems. I told him he needed to get help and I wanted to motivate him. Then we talked about how Jeff couldn't get it on with women. He wanted to be with girls and because he couldn't, he found it incredibly frustrating. He had gone to straight bars, he said, where he had tried to get a relationship going with any girl he could find. It was always a flop. I said to him that the reason he failed all the time was that he drank so much. 'No girl's gonna go out with you,' I said. 'You've got to straighten your act out.' I don't think Jeff was conning me. I think he was really concerned. He saw that he had a major problem in that he couldn't have a relationship with a woman, and I thought that was the major reason he was drinking. Initially I thought of him as a bisexual. Then I could see he was straight. The more I talked to him about anal in those few minutes, the more I thought he was officially 'raw' and that he didn't belong in the bar."

Then John Paul became aware of the level of violence lurking in Jeffrey Dahmer right below the surface. It was menacing, he said, not because he hadn't seen it before but because in Dahmer it was a significant, meaningful violence. Dahmer may have looked nerdy, but there was a pointedness to him that other nerds and conflicted young men didn't seem to have. "I had assumed that Jeff was gay because he was hanging out in the gay bars," John Paul said, "but it was clear after talking to him that the guy was looking for trouble. You can tell when a straight person walks into a gay bar and is either looking for trouble or wants to start trouble. It sends up signals. When you talk to that kind of person who's angry and who's making derogatory remarks, you know there's trouble afoot. Jeff was that kind of person. He kept on making remarks about the gays' responsibility for the AIDS epidemic. I told him that his drinking was going to get him in trouble, especially if he were cruising into the bar looking for safe sex. A few drinks later, he'd forget all about safe sex. We got into the issue of AIDS and he said, 'You know, all of these gays should be dead anyway from AIDS. None of them should live. This is a plague sent by God on the gay community.' That was one of the signals that [told] me that a straight person is in here looking for trouble."

John Paul fished for some more answers from Dahmer. This was the first time that the strangely sullen young man who'd sat stone-faced at the bar so often had voluntarily opened up. John Paul was as curious as he was astonished to hear the levels of hatred this person was spouting. "I said, 'Jeff, if you don't like these people, what the Hell are you doing in the bars here? What are you walking around here for?' He could have been here for a lot of reasons, social or anything. Nothing Jeff said to me was especially new, assuming that he was gay. There are gays who walk into this bar filled with hate about blacks and gays who will cruise the very people they're hating and say that all gays should be dead from AIDS. And that AIDS is a curse. But Jeff was different. The way he said it, it had more of a punch to it, it scared me. He meant it, and that's why I asked him. But what bugged me the most was that Jeff didn't even answer my question. He simply looked at me with a flat expression and didn't say a word. It made the hairs stand up on the back of my neck because it was chilling. What he did tripped something in me that told me this man was dangerous."

Now John Paul had to push for answers because this person seemed paradoxical as well as dangerous. He didn't look particularly threatening, John Paul remembered. In fact, he mostly looked pathetic. But there was something in his demeanor and in the flatness of his eyes that told people who dealt with him that he was capable of far more danger than the person who looked like he was going to fall facedown like any hapless drunk.

"He didn't look especially dangerous," Ranieri explained. "In fact he looked like a wounded basset hound and that evoked compassion. It was my impression that he got himself boxed into such a corner with what he was doing that there was no escape. He was sad and hopeless. But at the same time he gave off the impression that he was dangerous. There was something so conflicting in his personality that I didn't how to deal with it. Jeff didn't have one single trait or mannerism that would clue you that he was gay. He looked and acted completely straight. The weird thing about Jeff was that when I saw the photographs of him in the paper after the arrest, he wasn't wearing any glasses and I didn't recognize him at all. He was a complete stranger. When they put the glasses on I said, 'Oh, shit, that's him. This is the guy I was talking to.' It looked like he hadn't gotten sleep in ages. He was so broken and pale, He looked pathetic, but when you put alcohol in people they say a lot of things they wouldn't normally say. It breaks down barriers — but it brings out the personality."

Knowing what he now knows about Dahmer, Ranieri said, he was appalled that he was able to get so much to drink from the bartenders along the strip. John Paul believed that much of the fury Dahmer was able to muster was due mostly to the alcohol that he was consuming. The booze had so depressed him that he blew off any abilities a normal person might have had to deal with the violence and hatred. In Dahmer's case there were no abilities and the guy was just pure emotion that could explode at any time. The more John Paul probed in the conversation, the more he realized that he was talking to a potential time bomb who needed some form of intervention right away.

"What pisses me off is that Jeff was being served double and triple shots of liquor while he was pacing back and forth between the front and back bars. Something was on his mind and gnawing at him from the inside. Jeff was so frustrated that I thought that he was impotent, that he couldn't do anything. His impotency, I believed, was a result of alcohol. I told him what I thought and he didn't respond. I think he was most upset about not being able to have a decent relationship with a woman while he was trying to do so. I didn't ask him about female prostitutes and I didn't ask him about drag queens because of his comments against blacks and queens in the front bar. I thought at first, beside the drinking, he was simply having a major problem with trying to have heterosexual sex. He was a straight who was all conflicted. But there was more. His attitudes also told me that he had problems with his dad."

Because of his experience in dealing with people uncomfortable about their homosexuality, John Paul said that he was able to figure out just where the trouble lay. Often guys would start talking about a member of the family, a parent or some authority figure who made growing up very difficult for them, and that would be translated into their behavior. Dahmer was no exception, John Paul explained, but he was also more angry and closer to exploding than other people he'd spoken to. During their conversation, layer after layer of anger in Dahmer seemed to peel back like the layers of an onion. Finally, as John Paul reached the nuclear core, both he and Dahmer could see, just for a moment, the fury that was burning there. Dahmer pulled back. It was too difficult for him to confront it. In fact, it was the psychological nuclear reaction that was fueling all of the murders, but there was no way John Paul could have known that. All he saw was the white-hot anger.

"I was fishing for some reasons about this alcoholism. I shared with him that I had had a lousy relationship with my dad, that I had dealt with physical and emotional child abuse, that my father and I never got along very well, and that it was a very conflicted kind of relationship. And I asked him if that was his problem. It was my opinion that it was part of his alcohol problem. . . . Our conversation, however, got close to the mark when we started dealing with problems in his childhood and his growing up. I also touched on the point of religious sentimentalism and guilt feelings. And he talked a little bit about the issue of [how] gays should be dead, there was no reason for them to exist as if they were a pariah. He felt the gay community was totally useless.

"It was my opinion that his father had a lot to do with his behavior. He said his father did hate gays. He called them queers. When he talked about his father's feelings for queers, his voice even dropped. He had this monochromatic voice when he talked about his own feelings. When he talked about his dad, his voice dropped much lower. . . . It's my opinion that I think he really hated his father with a passion. It's my opinion from the final minutes of the conversation I had with Dahmer that if Jeff had had a chance he would have killed him. I asked him how much he hated his father, and that was the opinion I drew from his answer. Then we were so close to something critical, Jeff just pulled up stakes and left."

That was the last time John Paul Ranieri and Jeffrey Dahmer would talk to each other about anything substantial. It was as if Jeffrey had looked inside himself, let more of the rage out that he had only just hinted at in conversations with his parole officer, and then closed it down. He medicated himself with more and more alcohol, gradually poisoning himself until he could barely walk around. He told his parole officer Donna Chester at their June 24 meeting that the reason he looked so terrible was that he was working twelve-hour shifts again. It was killing him, making him so tired he could barely stand up, but he needed the money. She wrote in her notes that Dahmer simply denied having any problems. It was his work schedule that was on his mind. In reality, however, Dahmer's drinking had become more aggressive than usual. He was almost always drunk when he wasn't working or having to make an impression on his parole officer. And it was in a falling-down drunk condition that John Paul saw him the next time.

"I saw him again the following weekend in the afternoon. He was so sick he was passed out on the back bar. He didn't look well at all. He was so wasted he didn't even recognize me. He turned around and said, 'I think I'm going to throw up.' I asked him if there was anything I could do, and he started to vomit right there. I took him into the bathroom and put his head over the toilet. He threw up. Then I told him that he had my number and name and he could call me any time, but that he was making himself sicker and sicker by drinking like this. I said there was no way I was going to talk any sense into him now. So I cleaned him up and told him to sit there in the john. 'If you get sick again outside you're going to throw up all over the place.' He leaned up against the wall and I got a cab for him."

The Jeffrey Dahmer that John Paul Ranieri stood upright on his feet and put in a cab was about to embark on an out-of-state hunting trip in Chicago. The situation in Milwaukee was becoming too hot for him. Everyone along the strip was talking about the missing gay men, Anthony Hughes, Eddie Smith, and now Errol Lindsey. Flyers were going up and people had begun to mention Dahmer's name in connection with Hughes and Smith. Dahmer had been seen by neighbors Nicole Childress and Sandra Smith with Konerak Sinthasomphone who would soon be listed as missing. At some point, even Jeffrey Dahmer could have seen that anybody putting two and two together would have associated him with enough of the missing persons that an investigation would be inevitable. Now, even John Paul was warning people about him. The heat was on.

"During the two weeks, and specifically that night after our first conversation, I warned people about him and told them that he was dangerous," John Paul revealed. "In fact there was this one thirty-two-year old light-skinned black kid that Jeff was cruising and I warned him about Jeff. He was a photographer. The two men he cruised in the bar were a lot more trusting of who they met here. They were not overtly feminine but were emotional sponges who fed off people. The kids he had cruised were people who would suck the emotions out of you. They were very needy — excessively needy. I told the one kid to stay away from him. The kids were basket cases after Dahmer's arrest."

Jeffrey Dahmer decided to take a ride to Chicago to see what relationships he might find down there. He was forbidden to leave the state unless he had permission from his parole officer, but he took the trips anyway over the course of a couple of weekends. He went down on the weekend of June 30 for the Gay Pride parade to see who he could meet and whether there was any chance of picking someone up who didn't know him from Milwaukee. He was in luck. He met Matt Turner at a bus station, and the twenty-year-old man seemed to pick up right away on his offer for a professional photo session up in Milwaukee. Turner was a natural for Dahmer's pitch because the young man was trying to break in as a model and had performed in a number of lip-synching contests for prizes. With a portfolio of photographs from this man, Turner may have thought, his chance to break into modeling might even be easier. He agreed to pose for the nude photographs and went along with Jeffrey.

Dahmer told police that they took a Greyhound bus back to Milwaukee and a city cab to the apartment from the bus station. When he got the victim to his apartment, he offered him a drink right away. Turner quickly fell asleep and Dahmer used a strap to strangle him. Then he dismembered the body, put Turner's head in a plastic bag which he tied with a twist tie and put in the freezer. He put Turner's torso in the fifty-seven-gallon drum in his bedroom and made plans to head back to Chicago the following weekend.

On Friday night, July 5, Dahmer met Jeremiah Weinberger at Carol's Speakeasy, a gay bar on Wells Street with lots of dancing. Jeremiah was a Puerto Rican, Dahmer told the police, and he offered the good-looking, twenty-three-year-old man money to go back with him to Milwaukee to pose for a few pictures, spend some time, and watch some of his favorite videos with him. Weinberger, reportedly, thought about it and then agreed to go along. The two of them took the bus back to Milwaukee and a cab from the bus depot to the apartment. Weinberger agreed to stay the whole following day with Jeffrey. Dahmer told police he took photos of him, had oral sex with him, and they watched videos together. However, Dahmer revealed, on the second day Weinberger said that he had to get back to Chicago. But Jeffrey told the police that he didn't want the guy to leave. He couldn't stand being alone again, not after having spent two days with this guy. So he offered him a drink laced with drugs. After Weinberger passed out, Jeffrey strangled him with his hands, took photos of him, and cut his body up so that his torso would fit into the fifty-seven-gallon drum. He took Polaroids of the dismemberment process, too, and put Weinberger's head in the freezer.

That week, Dahmer went to his parole office for another meeting again. This time he complained that because of a variety of reasons, he had been late to work a number of times. Of course, Dahmer didn't reveal that the latenesses were caused by his drinking and cruising. He only said that if he got fired, he would be in severe financial difficulties. That, he confided in her, might be the very reason for him to consider suicide. Donna Chester noted in her observation notes that Dahmer had again raised the option of suicide.

Jeffrey Dahmer also paid another visit to John Paul over at the Wreck Room and mentioned that he'd been down to Chicago to see some of the action. That, too, caused John Paul some consternation as he realized that there had been another, deeper, darker change in Jeffrey's demeanor. Whatever had gotten hold of him had sunk its teeth deeper into what was Jeffrey's psyche, John Paul said. "Dahmer told me he had gone to Chicago and bummed around. He never mentioned any places or names. But the way he said it was expressionless — without emotion. Dahmer behaved as if he were on mood altering prescription drugs. People who have been taking mood changing drugs walk around sometimes as if they're zombies."

By this time, word of Weinberger's disappearance had begun to spread through Chicago's gay community. According to an article in the *Milwaukee Journal*, people noted that Jeremiah Weinberger had disappeared and that he'd been seen leaving Carol's Speakeasy with a man they didn't recognize but who they later said fit Jeffrey Dahmer's description. The witness said that Jeremiah told him he was leaving with the stranger for Milwaukee. Other people in Chicago said that rumors were abounding about missing gays in Milwaukee. There was speculation that the missing Weinberger might have met with the same fate as the people in Milwaukee, especially because he had told a friend that he was going to Milwaukee right before he disappeared. Before Dahmer's arrest, photos of Weinberger were being circulated around Chicago's gay community.

On July 14, Jeffrey Dahmer was fired from his job at Ambrosia Chocolate Company because of continual lateness and unexplained absences. He was disconsolate and panicked. He had no source of income and didn't want to turn to his family for help. He felt that it was unfair that he was fired. During that period, he would later tell his parole officer, he was actually helping his grandmother Catherine who was sick and had been hospitalized. He had gone out to the house in West Allis, he told Donna Chester, but had overslept. When he got to the factory, he was fired. Jeffrey was frightened and anxious during the whole week because he had no idea where his next money was coming from, and he was already behind on the rent. He would soon have to vacate the apartment. But rather than solve the problem, he would medicate his fears away with the one success he could achieve: a sexual homicide.

On July 15, according to Dahmer's statement to the police, he encountered his next victim, Oliver Lacy. He said he met Lacy on Twenty-seventh Street and Kilbourn while the man was going over to his cousin's house. According to the newspapers, Lacy had a two-year-old son and had moved to Milwaukee from Chicago to join his son and Rose Colon, his financée. Dahmer said that when he met Lacy on the street, he told him that he was a photographer looking for models. He was paying good money, and Lacy might enjoy it. Oliver Lacy agreed and walked over to Dahmer's place with him. At first, Dahmer said, the two men got undressed and gave each other body rubs. Then he gave Lacy a sleeping potion which knocked him out. Afterwards, he strangled him and then had anal sex with the man's corpse. He then dismembered him and put his head on the bottom shelf of the refrigerator. That would be the head that Rauth and Mueller would find when they first opened the refrigerator to check out the source of the foul smell.

Jeffrey called Donna Chester the following day on July 16 to tell her that he'd been fired. This was it, he said. There was no place for him to go and he would probably lose his apartment by the first of August. "Taking action to get him psychological assistance," Donna Chester wrote in her notes. Then on July 17, the next day, Dahmer failed to show up for a meeting. He called, Donna Chester's notes say, and told her that he'd overslept. She set a meeting for the next day. Dahmer showed up, they talked, and he was told to call her by July 29 if he was unable to find a new place to live.

It was a phone call that Dahmer would never have to make because he was arrested the following week and the nation went into shock.

Chapter Sixteen

The Trial

There would be one final young man who would fall victim to Dahmer's rage before Tracy Edwards escaped from Apartment 213 to tell the whole world about the horror he'd experienced. That man was Joseph Bradehoft who was married and had three children between the ages of two and seven. He had come to Milwaukee from St. Paul to look for work. According to the *Milwaukee Journal,* Bradehoft was originally from Greenville, Illinois, and living with his brother while looking for a job. Bradehoft was a white man who met Dahmer on Friday, July 19, the day after Dahmer met with his parole officer. Bradehoft was waiting at a bus stop with a six-pack of beer on Wisconsin Avenue across from the Marquette University Campus when Dahmer spied him from the window, got off the bus, and struck up a conversation with him right then and there. Jeffrey told police that he offered Bradehoft money to pose for some pictures and watch videos with him; the man readily agreed, and they walked off to Dahmer's apartment.

Dahmer told police that once in his apartment, the two

men engaged in oral sex and then he gave him a sleeping potion. After Joseph Bradehoft passed out, Dahmer said, he wrapped his rubber strap around the man's neck, strangling him until he was dead. He then dismembered Bradehoft, putting his head in the freezer and his torso in the 57-gallon drum. Dahmer, however, kept Bradehoft's identification card which the police found along with Oliver Lacy's when they searched Dahmer's apartment on the following Monday, the night of his arrest.

One weekend separated the murder of Joseph Bradehoft from Tracy Edwards's wild escape into the street where he flagged down the officers, Rauth and Mueller. This time, the complaining witness had a long story to tell about being theatened with murder, being handcuffed, and assaulted with a knife. This time when the police went back to the apartment and banged on the door in the waning hours of July 22, the horror of what was happening behind the door of apartment 213 would become apparent. This time, Jeffrey Dahmer wouldn't talk his way out of a tight situation as he had in Bath, Ohio, in 1978, when he was stopped for drunk driving with the body of Steven Hicks in his car. Nor would he elude the police as he had done when West Allis police detective Don Yockey questioned him about the April, 1988 charge filed against him when he drugged and robbed Ernest Flowers.

Dahmer's explanation to Yockey that he had met the complainant at a gay bar, took him back to his West Allis apartment in the home of his grandmother where the two men got to drinking and fell asleep, woke up, and put the man on a bus seemed to wash for the detective. He was quoted in *The New York Times* as having testified at Dahmer's trial that "He seemed normal. He wasn't hesitant. I felt there was no problem. I believed his story."

Nor would Dahmer's story pass muster the way it did on the night that Konerak Sinthasomphone went staggering into the street, and Dahmer was able to convince the Milwaukee police officers who responded to the 911 call that Konerak was his adult lover. While the body of Tony Hughes lay decomposing in the next room, Dahmer was able to lie his way out of the situation by describing Konerak's problems as a "lover's spat." The police officers, according to *The New York Times,* were later dismissed.

This time Rauth and Mueller, the officers, were almost overwhelmed by the pervasive smell, saw the Polaroid shots of Dahmer's victims in plain view around the couch, and called in to dispatch for a records check on the man in Apartment 213. From the point forward, all of America became fixated on Jeffrey Dahmer, the man who kept severed heads in his refrigerator, a fifty-seven-gallon drum full of torsos in his bedroom, and arms and legs scattered throughout his dresser drawers.

Each and every day following his arrest, there were new revelations about his crimes. As the victim count jumped and more families were notified that identification cards of their family members were found in Dahmer's apartment, an entire community began to come alive with grief. After the immediate notifications in the hours after the arrest, the circle of Dahmer's terror became wider. Police asked families who filed missing persons reports to come forward. This was especially difficult for families who had been waiting for word on missing relatives for months. Eddie Smith's family, Tony Hughes's family, and the Sinthasomphones all had been pushing the police for information regarding their missing children. All of them became worried when the discovery of human skulls in a northside apartment hit the newspapers. Finally, the revelations of Dahmer's crimes stirred an even greater concern among all the families of missing persons when the police asked them to provide photos of family members so that they could be shown to the mysterious suspect who was in custody. The request for photos, the large numbers of bones and skulls that had been reported in the paper, and tales of a gruesome chamber of horrors in a Milwaukee apartment set the stage for what would be the most talked-about serial killer case in over a decade.

Then Jeffrey Dahmer confessed and provided the police with the horrible details of the relentlessness of his pursuit of victims. He described how he left first his grandmother's house and then his own apartment to go cruising among the gay bars and clubs along North Second Street or National. He explained how easy it was for him to lure unsuspecting young men, teenagers, and even adolescents to his apartment with promises of money for a photo session. And in almost matter-of-fact language, he described how easy it was for him to pulverize or "powderize," as he called it, the concoction of sedatives necessary to render an individual unconscious just long enough for him to strangle him to death or cut his throat. Then he described these dead victims as sexual partners who would never leave him. They would never abandon him in death as they would in life. Their memories would always be a part of him because he "owned" them by causing their deaths.

* * *

In each daily revelation in the *Milwaukee Journal* and the *Milwaukee Sentinel* readers were fascinated about the stories of a man who seemed more like a predatory beast than a human being. Like an animal driven by the most primal of impulses, Dahmer stalked, camouflaged, lured in an elaborate mating ritual, trapped, and then murdered his quarry. Dahmer seemed worse than Ed Gein, the *Psycho* killer who used the skins of his dead victims as lampshades and slipcovers, worse than Chicago's John Wayne Gacy who buried his victims in the soft dirt beneath his house, and worse than New York's Arthur Shawcross who confessed to cannibalizing some of his victims by eating their genitalia. No, Dahmer seemed much worse.

Then in the continually breaking story, Milwaukee residents learned Dahmer was already on parole when he killed and under the management of a probation officer. Then they discovered that police officers had actually been in the Dahmer apartment only a few feet away from a decomposing corpse in the next room and had been smooth-talked into believing the man's story while his adolescent victim sat there incoherent on a couch. Then Milwaukee readers found out that Dahmer had killed this adolescent victim only moments after the police left and stored his torso in a fifty-seven-gallon drum right in his bedroom. They learned that this victim was the younger brother of the child that Dahmer had abused a couple of years earlier in a crime that resulted in probation in the first place. This was too much to comprehend, but there was even more.

In Dahmer's earliest confessions to the police, he described a homicide he'd committed in Ohio when he was only eighteen years old; a homicide, police realized, that had been an open case since 1978. So the Ohio law enforcement authorities searched where Jeffrey Dahmer told them to search, and that's when they found the bone fragments that Dahmer said they'd find. Then people from the gay communities in Milwaukee and Chicago came forward and described their fears of a homophobic stalker in their midst, who had been causing the disappearances of patrons from gay bars and clubs for the past two years. Reports had been filed, people said, but no one had listened. Now the perpetrator was apparently identified, and the story he told was more horrible than their worst nightmares.

Soon, Ernest Flowers, Tracy Edwards, and Sounthome Sinthasomphone, Dahmer's living victims came forward, to describe what it was like to have been in the clutches of a fixated killer and to have escaped. The three men had been victims and were traumatized by Dahmer, yet they kept their heads about them and planted the seeds for their own escape. Fortune was on their side, and they were able to seize upon the mistakes that serial killers inevitably make.

People who knew Dahmer in Milwaukee came forward. The female impersonator "Goldie" and Brother John Paul Ranieri, E.O.C., said that they actually warned others to stay away from this sullen, sadfaced drunk who seemed headed for disaster and would bring anyone near him disaster as well. Both "Goldie" and Brother John Paul readily explained that his malevolence was overwhelming, focused as it was upon members of the gay community and upon African-Americans. These were hate crimes, people said, propelled by whatever it was that usually propelled serial killers.

Newspapers were abuzz with the rumor that Dahmer would argue the issue of sanity. Under Milwaukee's strict laws governing insanity pleas, Dahmer would not challenge the facts in evidence; he would only challenge the interpretation of those facts. He'd already confessed. Now he would plead that he had a mental disease at the time he committed the crimes, and that disease prevented him from conforming his actions to the accepted definitions of right and wrong under the laws of the State of Wisconsin. Dahmer was arraigned; and indeed, he announced that he would plead guilty but insane to the charges against him. The facts were in evidence; the jury would now have to decide his culpability on the basis of medical testimony. The stage was set for the sanity hearing of the decade: Who was Jeffrey Dahmer and why did he kill?

In fact, as is the case in many serial killer trials, there was much more at stake than a simple debate over mental disease. Dahmer had selected the overwhelming majority of his victims from the African-American community. According to witnesses who had conversed with him about this, Dahmer had gone on record that he hated black people. But he went further. In a conversation reported by Brother John Paul, Dahmer said that black people were created for the sole purpose of serving white people and that the AIDS epidemic was a heavenly scourge to wipe out homosexuals. This person seemed more like a hate killer than a serial killer, especially to members of the African-American and gay communities who had a long list of complaints about unequal treatment from the police. Now, in their very midst, was a bizarre homophobic hate killer who had been targeting mostly black men for the past few years. He had actually been questioned by the police on a number of occasions and released. Tempers were running high.

When the Milwaukee police released the transcripts of a series of 911 calls placed by Glenda Cleveland as she tried to get information regarding Konerak Sinthasomphone, it was as if everything believed about the city's treatment of black people was borne out. What had happened is that despite the protests of black witnesses who said that the boy the police brought back to Dahmer's apartment was a minor, the police believed a coherent white man over the statements of two young black women whom Dahmer referred to in his confessions as "hysterical."

Unfortunately, it's easy to sound hysterical or overwrought when you perceive your statements of truth are being set aside by peace officers whom you also perceive are making determinations on the basis of race. Suddenly the Dahmer case took on the implications of a bias crime in Milwaukee. That created an additional issue for the community leaders.

As the Jeffrey Dahmer case was prepared for trial, Milwaukeeans began to learn something about "living" serial killers: they become a focal point for the communities in which they are tried. Rarely are the perpetrators of particularly heinous crimes treated in the same way ordinary criminals are treated. Serial killers are the best example of this, because they are usually so brutal and merciless in their crimes they embody the deepest fears people have about strangers and about themselves. They also represent an attack on the entire moral structure of a community. Therefore, communities spend an inordinate amount of time and money making sure that a local serial killer will get extra-special treatment before the eyes of the law. Many people also anguish over what is the worst possible punishment a serial killer can receive, and they anguish even more when the state does not have a death penalty. The Jeffrey Dahmer trial fell squarely into this category for a number of reasons, and these helped determine the type of trial Dahmer received and the type of verdict the jury returned.

First, Dahmer came from what might be construed as a typical, all-American middle-class family. His father Lionel was a chemist, a Ph.D. who had grown up in Milwaukee and had gone to college at Marquette University. Second, Jeffrey was born in Milwaukee; he was a native son of native stock. Third, Jeffrey had family in Milwaukee and had lived with family while he was committing the first murders. Fourth, Jeffrey apparently did not come from an impoverished or deprived background. He had had the benefits of relative affluence, the benefits of good counsel when he was convicted of a sexual offense, and, it was perceived, he was given special treatment in court because of the pleas entered on his behalf. Yet at the same time he was able to camouflage his career as a serial killer and he emerged from jail only to kill again. What had gone wrong? What would Milwaukee do about it?

For leaders in the African-American and gay communities Jeffrey's pleas of insanity had an all-too-familiar ring at first. It was interpreted on the streets and in the gay clubs and bathhouses as just another pretext for comitting crimes against the communities least able to defend themselves. Activists pointed to popular statistics which showed that black perpetrators of crimes against whites tend to have higher conviction rates and serve longer sentences than white perpetrators of crimes against blacks. And perpetrators of crimes against gays tend not to be prosecuted at all, gay activists claimed. Jeffrey Dahmer embodied all of these preconceptions and fears. His plea of insanity combined with the experts and their assistants assembling around the courthouse like a gathering of the clans seemed like the beginning of an elaborate show.

There were all kinds of threats made in the newspapers about the need for violence to effect change. Black activists called for calm but recognized that if Dahmer was perceived to have gotten away with punishment for killing black men almost at will because he was judged to be insane, then there might be no controlling younger members of the community who already felt powerless and disenfranchised. Dahmer was an example of the fear that it was "okay to kill blacks." Suddenly, the stakes of Dahmer's insanity plea became uncomfortably high for the community.

The Milwaukee police department was already enmeshed in enough scandal before police officers walked away from an incoherent Konerak Sinthasomphone slumped over on Jeffrey Dahmer's livingroom couch. They were still dealing with the backwash of charges and countercharges in the Lawrencia Bembenak trial and the issues raised by her compromising photographs of Milwaukee police officers and claims that she was framed for murder by members and former members of the police department. They didn't need additional heat from the press about their treatment of blacks and gays. Yet there stood Dahmer, an example of a person who claimed to have smooth talked his way out of trouble with the Milwaukee police and the West Allis police. Now he was pleading insanity, adding possible insult to the damage his case might have already inflicted.

In this way, Jeffrey Dahmer suddenly found himself a political entity as well as just a defendant in a criminal case. Depending upon whose opinion one relied upon, Dahmer was the embodiment of community fears; the example of a criminal justice gone haywire; the reason the state needed a death penalty law; the reason the parole system didn't work; or, the general of a new race war, as the sick hate mail pouring to newspapers described him. Jeffrey Dahmer became public property as well as a public enemy, and the disposition of the case suddenly had a whole host of political implications that most criminal cases do not have. This was now a hornet's nest of issues.

As both sides continued to prepare for a January, 1992 trial, the community groups and victims groups were also organizing. Victims, as district attorneys around the country are beginning to realize, claim that they have rights in addition to the rights of the accused. In the Dahmer case especially, some attorneys speculated upon arguments that the civil rights of the victims' families had been violated by Jeffrey Dahmer and those rights needed to be considered in the trial as well. Simply accepting the fact that Dahmer had a mental disease and letting him spend time in a mental health facility before he could be judged free to go would not satisfy justice, as far as the victims were concerned, especially since Dahmer had already admitted to committing the homicides.

In the wake of the nationally televised Rodney King beating by LAPD officers in Los Angeles, a Los Angeles judge's sentencing of the convicted killer of a young black woman to probation without any jail time, the uproar created by charges of racism and frame-up in the scheduled Mike Tyson rape trial in nearby Indiana, and the not guilty verdict in the nationally televised William Smith rape trial in Florida just months earlier, the atmosphere in Milwaukee was supercharged with emotion as Jeffrey Dahmer was led into the courtroom for the opening of his trial. Rarely had a serial killer case been laden with such national implications for the way justice was perceived to be carried out. Maybe all of it was a product of the times, but it didn't help the people of Milwaukee as they wrestled with the moral issues of the case. Everybody hoped the trial would settle it all. The trial had, in the six or so months between Dahmer's arrest and his appearance before a jury, transcended a straightforward debate among lawyers and doctors over a human being's medical condition. It had become a morality play broadcasted live on national television. It was also a political drama, a demonstration to the world that the good citizens of Milwaukee could give such a heinous criminal as Jeffrey Dahmer a fair trial. America had not seen anything like this since the trial of convicted Lindbergh baby kidnapper Bruno Hauptmann in Flemington, New Jersey, almost sixty years earlier.

"Jeffrey Dahmer has a mental disease," defense attorney Gerald Boyle began his case. "And that mental disease is necrophilia. Jeffrey Dahmer wants a body. A body, that's his fantasy. A body." He told the story of what happened when Jeffrey Dahmer was fifteen and became obsessed with killing and having sex with a jogger who would run by the house every day, Boyle said. Then one day he actually acted on those fantasies and sawed off a baseball bat and rode to find the jogger. But he never saw the man again. Boyle contended that that might well have been the beginning of Dahmer's obsession with killing and having sex. It was all part of his mental disease.

Milwaukee County District Attorney E. Michael Mc-Cann argued that although the confessions of Jeffrey Dahmer were grotesque and even ghoulish, his murders, dismemberments, and sex with corpses were not evidence of a mental disease because Dahmer knew what he was doing at all times and by his own admission understood right from wrong. McCann pointed to Dahmer's own confessions that were read into the record by Milwaukee police detective Dennis Murphy. He said that Dahmer not only understood right from wrong, he went to great expense and took pains to conceal what he was doing because he knew he was in the wrong. "Dahmer stated that he was fully [aware] that the acts he was committing were wrong and that he feels horrified that he was able to carry out such an offense," Detective Murphy testified. "He stated it was obvious he realized they were wrong because he went to great time and expense to try to cover up his crimes. He stated that he used quite a bit of fortune setting up alarm systems in his apartment."

Dahmer's admissions that he understood the distinction between right and wrong would form one of the centerpieces of McCann's attack on the defense's arguments that Dahmer had a mental disease. McCann pointed to his array of expert witnesses including celebrated psychiatrist and FBI consultant Park Dietz and psychiatrist Frederick Fosdal, both of whom described Dahmer as calculating in his plans for murder. McCann argued that Dahmer was very selective in his choice of victims, picking on those who couldn't drive or who didn't have a car at their disposal. He also pointed to Dahmer's statements that he had prepared his sedative powders in advance of his going out into the night to look for victims to prove that Dahmer's murders were premeditated. He cited Dahmer's statements to Dr. Fosdal that the defendant had become so desensitized to murder that "the killing got routine."

"He didn't ask them who they were so he would not get to know them so they were objects," Fosdal testified. And ultimately, the killings were not the most satisfying parts of his crimes because "killing was a means to an end." Dahmer also told Fosdal he didn't like it. "He didn't like that part. That's why he sometimes had bodies backed up and sometimes had more than one." Finally, Dahmer said to Park Dietz that when he killed his victims, "he appreciated it was wrong."

Boyle sharply contrasted his view of the evidence with the prosecution's, arguing that everything Dahmer did was an indication of his sickness. Unlike McCann who said that Dahmer liked having live sex partners instead of dead ones, "preferred the person to be alive," and "liked to hear the heart," Boyle argued that Dahmer derived erotic pleasure from dead bodies. "He did not want to stop what now had become his fantasy, his obsession, his compulsion." He wanted to create "zombies," Boyle said, "people who would be there for him."

The opening clashes between McCann and Boyle also demonstrated how the insanity defense is supposed to work. The entire case is subordinated to the precise legal definitions of insanity which sometimes don't make sense in the real world. Insanity within the legal framework means that the person pleading insane must show that he or she was incapable of understanding right from wrong. The person must demonstrate that some medical condition absolutely removed from him or her the choice of conforming his or her behavior to the law. These are specifics. No one debated whether it was a healthy act on

Dahmer's part to cut off a person's skin. No one disagreed that it was psychologically disturbed. However, the prosecution argued throughout the trial that Dahmer not only knew it was wrong to peel away a victim's skin from his skull, but that he could have prevented himself from committing that act if he had wanted to. That he was in control all the time, the prosecution experts argued, and that he understood what he was doing meant that he was not suffering from a mental disease that prevented him from conforming his actions to the law.

The defense took the same evidence to show that one might be aware that what one is doing is wrong; indeed, that's what Dahmer himself said to Detective Murphy, but that Dahmer, because he was suffering from a sexual disease, was unable to conform his actions to what he knew was right. He had been so traumatized as a child by his fears and was suffering from a mental disease known as necrophilia that rendered him incapable of making any decisions regarding his behavior. Therefore, he was controlled by a disease that prevented him from conforming his actions to the law, he should be found insane and sent to a mental hospital until he was cured.

That is how, under most circumstances, the insanity trial is supposed to be argued. The defendant is the best piece of evidence and experts on both sides try to interpret what the defendant says in order to bolster their arguments. These are usually tough cases for a defense to win, most trial experts suggest, because unless the defendant is totally catatonic or in the midst of epileptic seizures or raving in a delusional state that he works as an intelligence agent for President Grover Cleveland, juries find it hard to interpret the subtleties of sophisticated medical arguments. What is clear, however, is that insanity trials are not necessarily intended to reveal what caused the killer to kill in the first place. The causes of serial crime are many times not at issue. It is the symptoms of the disease as defined by the defendant's actions that dominate the arguments before the jury.

The opening arguments and array of experts also set out a very definable cast of characters which represented the governing class of Milwaukee as well as the Milwaukee version of justice. Judge Laurence C. Gram, Jr., for example, came across as a folksy almost grandfatherly interpreter of the law. Much to his credit, he was concerned that the jury understood at all times what was happening. Judge Gram seemed to appreciate the difficulties a jury of lay people might have in interpreting the very difficult shades of meaning the different experts would cast on the same evidence available to both sides and in hearing the very lurid details in Jeffrey Dahmer's confessions without jumping to immediate conclusions. This was not a case about guilt or innocence; it was a hearing about a confessed killer's medical conditions against the backdrop of an audience of grieving victims whose legitimate rage was spilling out into the courtroom every day. It was no easy task being a juror in the Jeffrey Dahmer trial, and Judge Gram appeared sensitive to that fact.

Michael McCann was extremely adept in his attacks on what was a formidable defense put forth by Gerald Boyle, one of Milwaukee's most articulate attorneys. Both lawyers were fierce competitors in a political arena that was a dry tinderbox of fury and emotion. The entire nation witnessed what happened just a few months after the Dahmer verdict when groups of people who felt disenfranchised and powerless erupted with anger after an all-white jury in Simi Valley handed back not guilty verdicts in the beating of Rodney King trial in Los Angeles.

The attorneys and judge knew that feelings in Milwaukee were running very high over Jeffrey Dahmer as well and had to make it clear that justice was being served.

Perhaps because the trial was being televised and Milwaukee was on display for the entire world to see, the trial was as genteel and as polite as any criminal trial could possibly have been. It seemed as though all of the parties were taking special pains to present lurid and gory details with as much dignity as possible and with as much respect to the victims and their families as possible. It appeared to many independent observers that the court sought to honor the memories of the victims while showing Jeffrey Dahmer an inordinate amount of respect. If that seems odd, it should not be. An atmosphere of respect in the courtroom goes a long way to dignify the entire proceedings, including the dead victims who could not be there.

There was a sincere attempt on the part of the court to accommodate the extraordinarily high levels of shock, post-traumatic stress, anguish, and rageful grief. These are all dangerous emotions, again as the City of Los Angeles found out, because they are explosive. People who have lost a loved one through a crime, a completely unforeseen accident, suicide, the negligence of someone else, or even after a long illness, go through an immediate period of rageful grief in which they have to accept the loss and relegate it to an appropriate place in their lives. Maybe there's a period of denial at first, but ultimately the grief will have to be dealt with. In the case of the Dahmer victims, there was very little time for grief to be expressed and released before the victims' families were brought into the proceedings to provide details to the police concerning the whereabouts of their loved ones.

There was anger over the police's role in not being able to stop Dahmer as well as anger directed at the department of probation for not protecting the community from Jeffrey Dahmer. All of this vengeful grief could have exploded all over the city, no matter what the verdict; had not the court wisely and appropriately decided to allow representatives of each of the victims' families the opportunity to address the court and Jeffrey Dahmer directly. These were dramatic confrontations and some television viewers might have been shocked at the level of pure rage that was expressed, but it was a rage that was entirely appropriate and its expression was necessary for the healing processes to start.

The prosecution and the defense set the ground rules for the mental illness debate almost immediately because of the limitations of Wisconsin's insanity defense procedures. The two sides had to agree on areas of showdown so that they were debating the same things. The two sides fought over the issue of necrophilia and whether that qualified Dahmer as a person with a mental disease. However some medical experts believed that the definition of necrophilia as a sexual disorder in which the person is sexually stimulated only by corpses was far too narrow an issue to be debated because Dahmer had had forms of sexual relations with living people and performed oral sex on some of his victims before he killed them. Therefore the debate over whether or not Dahmer was a necrophiliac virtually guaranteed a verdict of sanity because Dahmer was clearly stimulated by people who were alive.

A far better area to have debated the issue of sanity

would have been over whether or not Dahmer was paraphilic. That is, according to the *Diagnostic and Statistical Manual of Mental Disorders IV,* whether or not Dahmer was aroused in response to sexual objects or situations that were not part of the normal patterns. People so aroused are generally not involved in many reciprocally satisfying relationships because of the emotionally masturbatory nature of a paraphilia. This characterized Dahmer perfectly, but it couldn't really be debated as part of Dahmer's insanity defense because the DSM does not characterize paraphilias as mental diseases. Thus, even if Dahmer had been judged paraphilic which, I believe he most surely was, it would not classify him as being mentally ill. Thus, once the ground rules had been set over necrophilia, the outcome of the trail, in my opinion, was virtually assured. Dahmer would be judged sane.

Where the defense and prosecution differed was on the issue of control. Gerald Boyle argued that control wasn't the critical issue in Dahmer's case, rather it was Dahmer's substantial inability to conform his conduct to the requirements of the law. When left to his own devices, which I would add includes having a private lair in which to bring back his victims, Dahmer reverts to a creature who may know what he's doing, may be able to control it within a very limited capacity, but ultimately will not be able to conform his behavior to the requirements of the law. Therefore, on that definition of mental illness, the defense argued, Dahmer should have been judged insane.

The prosecution avoided that issue but instead hit hard on the issue of control. For a lay jury, that made a world of sense because self-control is something anybody can understand. The prosecution argument was as simple as it was hard to defeat: if you can control your actions, then you are in control and not out of control. If you are in control, then you do not have a mental illness and are sane. The jury bought that line of reasoning perhaps from the first cross-examination of the defense witness, Dr. Frank Berlin, the psychiatrist from Johns Hopkins.

Dr. Frank Berlin of Johns Hopkins was one of the defense's star witnesses. Berlin is an expert on sexual disorders and has been one of the principal figures in sex offender programs that offer treatment. Dr. Berlin testified that Dahmer suffered from necrophilia, a sexual attraction to dead bodies. Remember, he couldn't say paraphilia because paraphilia is not classified as a disease, only as a disorder. Dr. Berlin tried to get across to the jury that because Dahmer was a necrophiliac, he had powerful killing urges. In order to have sex, he had to have sex with the corpse of the sex partner. Therefore he was so strongly compelled to kill him, he was unable to conform his actions to the requirements of the law even though he understood that killing was wrong. His urges specifically came upon him at times when he had the privacy and the ability to have sex, in other words when he was alone. At these times, Berlin testified, "when he's left to his own resources, he is, as a result of his own mental disease, lacking substantial capacity and therefore has not been able to simply walk away on his own."

Gerald Boyle is as skilled a defense attorney as any in the State of Wisconsin. He knew that the district attorney would be all over Berlin on the issue of control like a dog on a bone. Therefore, like any good defense counsel protecting his witness from a devastating cross-examination, Boyle himself raised the issue of control in a way that he might have done if he were the district attorney.

"If a policeman were at his side," Boyle asked his own expert witness, "might you expect Mr. Dahmer to control his conduct?"

"I would think that if a policeman were standing there, watching," Dr. Berlin answered, "he would be able to control his behavior."

Thus, Gerald Boyle tried to make the distinction between Dahmer's ability to conform his actions to the requirements of the law in situations where he was left to his own devices and the issue of self-control. It was a game strategy against tall odds. But McCann, conceding the pawn in the opening gambit, did an end run around Boyle and went right after Berlin's credentials, getting him to admit that he had never before testified on the issue of criminal responsibility in a murder case anywhere in the country. With that McCann also set up his own prosecution expert, Dr. Park Dietz who, as an FBI consultant, has testified in some of the most important high-profile murder trials in the country.

McCann went after Frank Berlin's sexual offender program as well while he had him on the stand, suggesting that even at best the program was controversial and its success questionable. During Berlin's first day of testimony, he and McCann almost got into shouting matches about the distinctions Berlin tried to draw between when Dahmer could conform his sexual urges to the law and those times when he was unable to kill because he could not find anybody. If anything, McCann's commonsense approach to the issue of control and mental disease may have been simplistic, but it was designed to be so, so that the jury could understand it.

In truth, the kinds of syndromes which Dahmer suffers from are far more complex than even most experts understand. The entire nature of episodic crime defies traditional standards in the sanity defense because, I would argue, the ability to camouflage one's emotions and conform to the act of killing and not killing so as to keep on killing is part of the obsessive nature of the insane, obsessive, serial killer. In other words — and this is a tough one for a jury to swallow even though it's true — by not killing when it's not safe, the obsessive serial killer protects his ability to kill again. The hypervigilant premeditation is actually an integral part of the insanity.

Gerald Boyle's other star defense witness was Dr. Judith Becker, a clinical psychologist and Professor of Psychology and Psychiatry at the University of Arizona. She agreed with Frank Berlin that although Jeffrey Dahmer could appreciate the difference between right and wrong, he was so "obsessed" with necrophilia that he "did not have substantial capacity to conform his conduct to the requirements of the law." Dr. Becker was also able to get Dahmer to admit again to have performed a "sex act" over Steven Hicks's body in Ohio, something he admitted to the police, then denied in subsequent confessions, and finally admitted again to Dr. Becker. It was obviously something that Dahmer was so ashamed of he changed his story to protect his feelings of shame. Further, Dahmer told Dr. Becker, he performed similar sex acts over the bodies of every one of his victims. This, too, was a major change in the story he told the police.

Jeffrey Dahmer also admitted to Judith Becker that he had tried to perform crude lobotomies on his victims the way some of the Aztecs may have tried. He said that by doing so, he hoped to make them into zombies who would simply stay with him in his apartment and not leave. He became so obsessed with this idea that he had actually drilled holes into the heads of his living victims while they were unconscious. Two of his victims came to after the holes had been drilled, the *Milwaukee Journal* reported Dahmer having told Dr. Becker, but they had severe headaches. One person actually lived for a whole day but was dead when Dahmer came back the following morning from working the night shift. If what Dahmer told Dr. Becker was true, his apartment must have indeed been a chamber of horrors for his victims.

In particular, Dahmer described two homicides that were particularly gruesome, but which helped to explain why Konerak Sinthasomphone was unable to communicate with the police. First, Dahmer told Becker, he was indeed eating portions of Errol Lindsey by taking portions of him out of the freezer and cooking them. While he ate, Dahmer said, he would become sexually excited. He also said that he used a hand-held drill and bored a hole into Lindsey's skull straight through to the brain. He then injected a large syringe full of acid into the frontal lobe so that the victim, Dahmer believed, would be able to follow simple commands and not resist. Dahmer said that Lindsey awoke after the first injection and had a headache so Dahmer gave him more sleeping pills. In describing Konerak's particularly sorrowful death, Dahmer said that he drilled holes in the boy's skull and filled them with acid. *Then* the child got up and wandered through the streets. He was completely "lobotomized" when the police arrived and sat there on the couch in pain and so brain damaged that he was incoherent. After the police left, Dahmer gave Konerak another injection through his lobe and that was fatal. It was one of the first times Dahmer described these deaths (the other being to

279

Dr. Frederick Fosdal) and showed that he had lied to the police in his earlier confessions.

Dr. Becker also described Jeffrey's fantasies about building a kind of "temple" or altar in his apartment from the body parts, skeletons, and skulls of his victims. He even drew her a crude diagram of this temple from which he hoped to receive special powers that would help him financially and spiritually. Not especially demonic or cult-oriented, the temple probably represented Dahmer's externalization of certain forces that he believed were out of his control. Because Dahmer had absolutely no sense of self, he gradually became a devotee of a kind of magical thinking that would imbue him with special powers. This is a very crude and primitive strategy of people who believe they are absolutely powerless in a world that completely mystifies them. Dahmer was experiencing a straightforward stimulation/arousal reaction which he had engineered into a structure that he drafted for his psychologist. This structure would imbue him with powers because Dahmer had already become sexually stimulated from the totems that he had taken from his dead victims. Because he was experiencing a form of sexual pleasure, he believed it would give him the power he didn't ordinarily possess in his own life.

A third defense expert, Dr. Carl Wahlstrom, also agreed with Becker that the magical temple Dahmer wanted to construct was proof that he was insane, but he was disposed of very quickly by the District Attorney who attacked his credibility and credentials. McCann brought out in court that Dr. Wahlstrom had not yet passed his board certification and that this was his first defense case. While all irrelevant in his diagnosis of

Dahmer, of course, Wahlstrom's admission had an effect on the jury, which it was intended to do. McCann appeared skilled at unraveling what should have been devastating defense testimony by attacking the witnesses themselves. It was a courtroom strategy that proved successful.

District Attorney McCann's prosecution witnesses were power hitters in their own right, and they testified very forcefully for Dahmer's ability to control himself. Dietz, who is probably one of the most experienced experts in interviewing and testifying about the criminally insane argued that although Dahmer exhibited some profound symptoms of mental disorders, his ability to control and premeditate, to camouflage himself and to conceal what he did were all examples of sane, cunning behavior. The mere fact that Dahmer disposed of his bodies efficiently, planned different methods of disposal, was able to control his murderous urges for years between crimes, was able to fool his probation officer and policemen on different occasions proved that the man knew exactly what he was doing. This was devastating testimony that was backed up by court-appointed experts Dr. George Palermo and Dr. Samuel Friedman. Both Palermo and Friedman interviewed Dahmer and agreed that the defendant might have been a bundle of different psychological disorders but that he was sane under the Wisconsin law. This was also strong testimony because it told the jury exactly what it needed to hear in relation to the law.

Juries need to know exactly what the law is and what they have to decide. By addressing the law directly, McCann scored points with the jury which eventually agreed with McCann and found that Dahmer was not suffering from a mental illness. By unanimously agreeing that Dahmer was not suffering from any mental illness, the jury obviated the second question they had to address which concerned Dahmer's ability to conform his behavior according to the requirements of the law. Once he was judged not to have a mental illness, the verdict was in. Dahmer was judged sane.

There were many reasons why the defense and prosecution chose to argue over necrophilia as opposed to other forms of mental illness. Necrophilia is relatively "clean" from an argumentative point of view. It's straightforward and easy to understand. It's a very conservative diagnosis which is not difficult for a jury to understand. Necrophilia also has the advantage of being diagnosed without the expense of brain scans, ultrasound, or other high-tech devices. Moreover, necrophilia doesn't require a degree in psychology to understand.

There were experts who were disappointed in the trial because so much of Dahmer's motivation to kill was never brought out. Nor, other experts said, was there much discussion of racism and homophobia. Gerald Boyle made a point of saying during the trial that Dahmer wasn't a racist, he wasn't a homophobe, and he didn't hate anyone. That, of course, wasn't true. Dahmer hated himself more than words could explain, but getting the jury to buy that would have been tough indeed. Also, there was not much discussion of the prototypical serial killer and the ways Dahmer deviated from the model of serial killers that the FBI always runs around talking about. Dahmer knew his victims. Dahmer was seen in his victims' company. Dahmer's name turned up in Tony Hughes's address book, and Dahmer was a readily identifiable figure, who was known to be a troublemaker, in the Milwaukee gay nightclub scene. Dahmer's motivations were not the typical motivations of a serial killer, and that's what might have made him so difficult to identify and to explain during the trial.

Dahmer's story will be the subject of college debates and criminology discussions for years to come. The trial actually posed more questions than it answered, even though it got the verdict that satisfied the community of Milwaukee without resolving the mystery of Jeffrey Dahmer.

Chapter Seventeen

Dahmer's Signs, Symptoms, and Predisposition Factors

Dahmer's symptoms and aspects of his story bear looking into, not because they mediate his crimes or make them any less horrible. It is the almost inadvertent nature of Dahmer's stumbling into a life of serial murder that makes him so tragic; at the same time, it makes him so horrifying. He's like a chapter out of a Stephen King novel where it is the everyday things that made him into a killer, the same kinds of things that many people experience. However, in Dahmer's case, there were so many things that they reached a critical combination, and that's when the organic muddle that was his brain became fixated on death.

It is likely that no one will ever be able to say with absolute certainty "this is why Jeffrey Dahmer killed." It will probably always remain a subject for speculation. Not even Jeffrey knows what exactly made him kill; except that certain things about his crimes made him feel very good, other things made him feel very bad, and certain things made him feel very ashamed. Most serial killers kill because of a combination of something that fills them with terror or hate and something that gives them enormous pleasure in the middle of that terror. In Dahmer's case, he was in constant terror over being abandoned. In the middle of that terror was a pathological need to control the thing or person that was set to abandon him. In the act of controlling that person, he was controlling that terror of being alone. But because control meant murdering that person, his sense of control was fleeting and achieved again only by thinking about the dead person or fondling the dead person's remains. It was a fleeting sense of control at best, and that's why he had to go out and kill again.

From an object/relations point of view, Dahmer was so emotionally starved he was unable to interrelate socially with another person. He was emotionally starved, his thoughts obsessed over ways to achieve human contact without humiliation, annihilation, or pain. His actions were designed toward survival, and so he was able to practice some sense of deferred gratification. But in his case it was extreme because he could go for long periods without it, and then preserve what gratification he had from the murders of his victims that also provided him with pleasurable feelings. One result of this learned response to preserve gratification was that he was also so devoid of pleasurable feelings and emotions in his childhood that he became addicted to the sensation of pleasure in his own anatomy. Most serial killers become addicted to a little spot of pleasure in an otherwise emotionally dead world, and that addiction is as powerful as alcoholism or drug addiction. It is what motivates the killer from crime to crime.

Like other adults, Jeffrey Dahmer learned to sexualize his drive for intimacy. But he behaved as if he were so starved that actual physical touch was not enough. He heightened touch with orgasm and was left much more empty. As an adult he had to deal with others wanting to sodomize him in exchange for touch and that might have been intolerable so he began to overdose his companions which freed him from feelings of social inadequacy as well.

Dahmer's favorite way to have sex was to have a nice-looking young man lie with him so that Jeffrey could hold, hug, kiss, and have light sex without the threat of his leaving. This is what he indicated to Dr. Judith Becker who had interviewed him for the defense. In his desire to preserve them for as long as possible, Dahmer drugged his victims, lobotomized them by drilling into their brains and filling the holes with acid, and tried to turn them into zombies. But he preferred them alive, he said. Dr. Park Dietz said that Dahmer liked to have them unconscious, at best, so he could listen to the blood and organ sounds of their bodies. But they couldn't remain unconscious forever and they couldn't be lobotomized so he killed them and preserved their body parts for later forms of emotional gratification. What we are looking at is the primitive "wanting" brain of a child who believes itself to be pathologically deprived, but stuck in the body of a powerfully built man. This is a deadly combination.

Dahmer became so fixated on incorporating the person who was leaving into himself that he actually opened up the body to bond with the person's viscera. What should have become a repugnant act made necessary by a fear of discovery actually became pleasurable. That was why Jeffrey preserved the skulls and many of the body parts of his victims as his killing spree became more and more intense in its latter stages. He had "imprinted" as well by images of his father and him filleting fish together or preserving the remains of animals together with various chemicals from his set. These were intense moments of bonding for him, and his later attempts to preserve bodies and fillet humans could also have called up from deep in his subconscious the feelings of being together with his father. This was how Jeffrey was able to call up feelings of pleasure from deep in his childhood and attach them to the most gruesome situations in his adult life of murder.

Jeffrey Dahmer's obsessive drive to steal a life to lie beside was an act of emotional survival. He was dying inside from emotional starvation. He was losing his spiritual breath as he gradually withered into emptiness the older he got. He always perceived himself to be on the verge of extinction which was why all of his thoughts were permeated with ideations of suicide and self-destruction. However he turned those fantasies outward toward his victims and then used them to conjure up feelings of pleasure from his childhood. That's what made him such a relentless killer. Ultimately, the only parts of him left alive and vital were the most primitive portions of his neural system and the pleasure-pain centers located in his temporal lobe area. The emptiness he was feeling everyday created psychotic thought which he could only manage by completing semi-social acts like going to work or finding human flesh to hold, to fondle, and ultimately to strip from the bones in an act of butchery.

As his peak experiences faded from his memory between murders, Jeffrey Dahmer faced decay and he had to invent ways to save his contacts. He bought a freezer. He planned to preserve life by drilling into the frontal lobes of his victims. He learned to bleach and to boil and to spray paint to objectify the human objects he had removed from his victims through dismemberment. He never learned to let go because letting go, for him, would have meant his own extinction. Ultimately, his sense of mechanical existence had developed into an animal or primitive existence as he devised ways to medicate himself from killing to killing.

None of this, of course, exonerates Jeffrey Dahmer or makes anything he did less cruel or inhuman. However, it's important if serial murder is to be understood that we look at the primitive drives that govern the serial killer. It is those drives that make the killer so relentless and so bold in his act, like telling the "big lie," that the police believe the most outrageous of stories. At the same time the serial killer is telling himself the "big lie" and he believes it to be true as well. As a result, the truth is hidden somewhere amidst deliberate lies and survival-generated fantasies and ideations. It must be sifted out like panning for gold in order to find explanations for the killer's actions. If this means that psychologists have to indulge themselves in the killer's fantasies, then that is what they have to do to find the grains of truth.

Dahmer's life was also marked by a series of trauma that "imprinted" certain feelings upon him and also might have resulted in levels of neural damage that impaired him in later life. For example, according to a story that came out during his interviews, at age sixteen, Dahmer was hit on the back of his head and knocked unconscious by some older boys. After this, he began the fantasy of stalking a jogger that he had seen in the vicinity of his house and hitting him on the back of the head so he could lie beside him and cuddle. He actually went so far, his lawyer said, as to prepare a bat for this jogger for the next time he passed the house. If true, it was an activation of this gratification mechanism that would have resulted in Dahmer's first victim if he could have found the man.

When Dahmer was at the correctional center, according to former prison guards, he was attacked and probably raped by other inmates. That is a not uncommon punishment for pedophiles by other prisoners. Shari Dahmer told the Akron newspapers that Jeffrey changed dramatically after his incarceration.

The violent story that Jeffrey told about being abducted by a strange forty-year-old man after he had passed out on Thanksgiving Day in 1989 while on a twelve-hour release from the CCC was also a traumatic event. He had left his family in West Allis and wound up being a victim of sexual abuse himself in a bizarre turnaround of his own crimes. If true, this experience would have "imprinted" upon him and made him an even more relentless hunter. It was probably after that Thanksgiving that Dahmer experimented more with the lobotomies he detailed to Dr. Becker and Dr. Fosdal.

Jeffrey's grandmother discovered a male mannequin in the basement of her house that Jeffrey had stolen from a store to have light sex with. His grandmother found it and he got rid of it. This was a form of paraphilia that fits into a larger pattern of other paraphilias that Dahmer had. The overwhelming number of paraphilic reactions that Dahmer was experiencing over the course of his young adult life might well have qualified as a form of insanity or at least diminished capacity in many states other than Wisconsin.

Jeffrey Dahmer, Serial Killer:
A Short List of Characteristics

History of bizarre, out of control behavior since childhood. Stories from friends tell of Jeffrey's fascination with dead animals, viscera, and the processing of the remains of road kills or fish that he'd caught. Other stories describe Jeffrey as the abductor of animals which he later killed and eviscerated.

Influence of prescription drugs on Joyce Flint's pregnancy. If the story that Shari and Lionel Dahmer told on "Inside Edition" about Joyce's taking prescription drugs during her first trimester of her pregnancy with Jeffrey are true, this could have produced a variety of problems, learning disabilities, organic problems, nonresiliency, and a condition similar to Fetal Alcohol Syndrome.

Unwanted, unplanned child. Eldest and least favored. These were Jeffrey's perceptions about himself and he acted on those perceptions.

Parental neglect. Jeffrey perceived that he had been abandoned by his family.

Dysfunctional family. Jeffrey was affected by the turbulent marriage and bitter divorce of his parents.

Outsider in family. Jeffrey said that he felt like an outsider in his own family.

Love/Hate. A child needs to perceive he is loved by his biological parents. That need is hard to kill, but can be perverted into love/hate. Denial is natural. Dahmer is still protecting his family even though he told his psychiatrists and his parole officer that he had negative feelings about his family.

Outsider in community. Socially isolated. Stories of Dahmer's being a loner and an outcast followed him throughout school.

Rich fantasy life of violence. Ideations of violence were a part of his life from the time he was a child, and he acted on those ideations throughout his life.

Fascination with death. Jeffrey's interest in dead animals and dead bodies was an unhealthy fixation on once animate objects that became inanimate.

Fascination with viscera. His fascination with death also included an unhealthy fascination with the internal organs and bones of the creatures he dissected, dissolved in liquids, or preserved.

Chronic alcoholism since early teens. This is one of his most chronic diagnosable diseases. His need to medicate himself with alcohol contributed to his lack of control.

Personality changes after drinking. This is a warning sign of danger and potential violence that was never adequately addressed in Jeffrey's life.

Cruelty to animals, or irreverence for life. Another warning sign of danger when seen in early childhood. Almost all serial killers display this warning sign.

Chameleon-like; mercurial nature. Another facet of a serial killer's personality that indicates an unstable personality and self-perception. The earlier this turns up in a person, the more likely it is that it will result in a psychotically violent personality later in life.

Paraphilic behaviors. Pedophilia, exhibitionism, partialism, and necrophilia were among the sexual patterns he followed.

Hypersexuality. Several former sex partners claimed that Dahmer had three or four orgasms per encounter.

Profound confusion about sex. Jeffrey told Brother John Paul Ranieri, E.O.C., that he was trying to date girls at the very time that he was having necrophilic sex with other men.

Homophobia. Dahmer said that he hated homosexuals and that they deserved to be destroyed.

Hyperreligiousness. He was an active Christian, and performed or had ideations about Satanic rituals.

Obsessive-compulsive behavior. Cruising, totems, photos, body parts, skulls, excessive ritual involving powderizing and pulverizing sleeping pills and preparing exact dosages in bags before each kill display his neurotic fixations regarding his murder victims.

Delusional-marginal thinking. The murders and preservation of victims' bones would bring him love.

Mask of sanity. Jeffrey appeared to be in control most of the time, according to many people who knew him.

Sociopathic thinking patterns. Dahmer never showed respect or acknowledgement for the boundaries of other people.

Chronic underachiever. He always held menial jobs and was usually in some kind of financial difficulty.

Escalating patterns of violence. His murders display progressive degrees of severe brutality, dismemberment, and cannibalism.

A known face in the community of his victims. Dahmer, like all long-term serial killers, lived in and cruised among the community of his victims. The killer is so obvious, no one knows who he is.

Contacted the families of his victims. Dahmer called the families as well and engaged in exciting byplay with them to keep alive the fiction that the victims were still alive.

Ritualistic pattern to murder. Dahmer went through a trolling, wooing, entrapment, murder, mutilation, and totemic phase as well as a follow-up phase in which he entered the victims' lives by talking to their families.

Known to police. Dahmer had a number of arrests, was currently on probation, and had been questioned by the police in connection with missing or assaulted victims on more than one occasion.

Compulsive confession. Like most killers, each time he was caught, he confessed compulsively to the crimes then began to change his story once the process of denial started.

WALK ALONG THE BRINK OF FURY:

THE EDGE SERIES

Westerns By GEORGE G. GILMAN

HE'S THE LAST MAN YOU'D EVER
WANT TO MEET IN A DARK ALLEY . . .

THE EXECUTIONER

By DON PENDLETON

Available wherever paperbacks are sold, or order direct from the Publisher. Send cover price plus 50¢ per copy for mailing and handling to Pinnacle Books, Dept. 661, 475 Park Avenue South, New York, N.Y. 10016. Residents of New York and Tennessee must include sales tax. DO NOT SEND CASH. For a free Zebra/ Pinnacle catalog please write to the above address.